Paths to Post-Nationalism

OXFORD STUDIES IN SOCIOLINGUISTICS

General Editors:
Nikolas Coupland
Adam Jaworski
Cardiff University

Recently Published in the Series:

Paths to Post-Nationalism

A Critical Ethnography of Language and Identity

Monica Heller

OXFORD
UNIVERSITY PRESS

2011

OXFORD
UNIVERSITY PRESS

Oxford University Press, Inc., publishes works that further
Oxford University's objective of excellence
in research, scholarship, and education.

Oxford   New York
Auckland   Cape Town   Dar es Salaam   Hong Kong   Karachi
Kuala Lumpur   Madrid   Melbourne   Mexico City   Nairobi
New Delhi   Shanghai   Taipei   Toronto

With offices in
Argentina   Austria   Brazil   Chile   Czech Republic   France   Greece
Guatemala   Hungary   Italy   Japan   Poland   Portugal   Singapore
South Korea   Switzerland   Thailand   Turkey   Ukraine   Vietnam

Copyright © 2011 by Oxford University Press, Inc.

Published by Oxford University Press, Inc.
198 Madison Avenue, New York, New York 10016

www.oup.com

Oxford is a registered trademark of Oxford University Press.

Library of Congress Cataloging-in-Publication Data
Heller, Monica.
Paths to post-nationalism : a critical ethnography of language and identity / Monica Heller.
p.   cm. — (Oxford studies in sociolinguistics)
Includes bibliographical references and index.
ISBN 978-0-19-974686-6; 978-0-19-974685-9 (pbk.)
1. French language—Political aspects—Canada. 2. French language—Social aspects—Ontario.
3. French-Canadians—Language. 4. Nationalism. 5. Globalization. I. Title.
PC3609H45   2011
306.44'90971—dc22   2010007439

Printed in the United States of America
on acid-free paper

Acknowledgments

I am deeply grateful to Nik Coupland and Adam Jaworski, for inciting me to write this book and for their support and guidance.

The research I draw on here was supported by the following agencies: the Social Sciences and Humanities Research Council of Canada, the Transcoop Fund of the Alexander von Humboldt-Stiftung (Germany), the Ontario Ministry of Education, the Multiculturalism Directorate, Secretary of State (Canada), le Conseil international d'études canadiennes and l'Office de la langue française, Gouvernement du Québec.

The research would not have been possible without the involvement of my colleagues and our students (and students who became colleagues): Jean-Paul Bartholomot, Maurice Beaudin, Lindsay Bell, Annette Boudreau, Gabriele Budach, Mark Campbell, Phyllis Dalley, Michelle Daveluy, Gabriella Djerrahian, Lise Dubois, Alexandre Duchêne, Jürgen Erfurt, Stéphane Guitard, Philippe Hambye, Emmanuel Kahn, Normand Labrie, Patricia Lamarre, Stéphanie Lamarre, Matthieu LeBlanc, Mélanie Le Blanc, Darryl Leroux, Florian Levesque, Laurette Lévy, Josée Makropoulos, Sonya Malaborza, Mireille McLaughlin, Deirdre Meintel, Claudine Moïse, Hubert Noël, Luc Ostiguy, Donna Patrick, Joan Pujolar, Carsten Quell, Mary Richards, Sylvie Roy, Emanuel da Silva, Chantal White, Maia Yarymowich, and Natalie Zur Nedden.

The book has benefited greatly from the close reading, information gathering, connection making, and intellectual exploration provided by Mireille McLaughlin, Kyoko Motobayashi, and Jeremy Paltiel, who accompanied me at every step of the writing project and read every word (often more than once), and if they got tired of talking about the questions the book raised, they never let on. Patricia Lamarre, Matthieu LeBlanc, Candida Paltiel, and Joan Pujolar provided keys at crucial moments. Thanks to Meaghan Hoyle and Natalie Kaiser for the maps. Two anonymous reviewers provided thought-provoking, helpful comments.

I am most indebted to the people who taught me what I learned in thirty years of conversations across francophone Canada and beyond. They may not all agree with the story I tell here, but they have always been willing to talk.

Contents

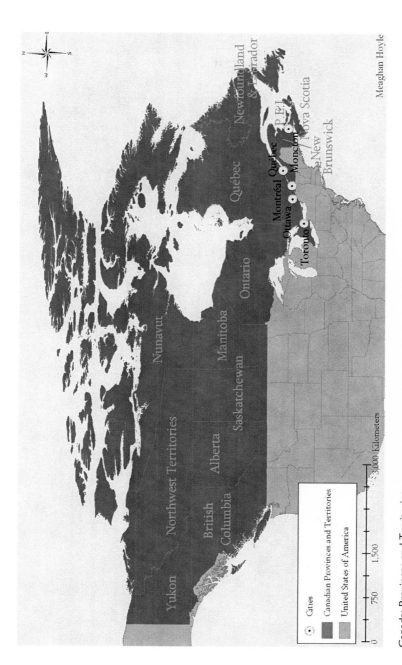

Canada: Provinces and Territories
Courtesy Meaghan Hoyle and Natalie Kaiser

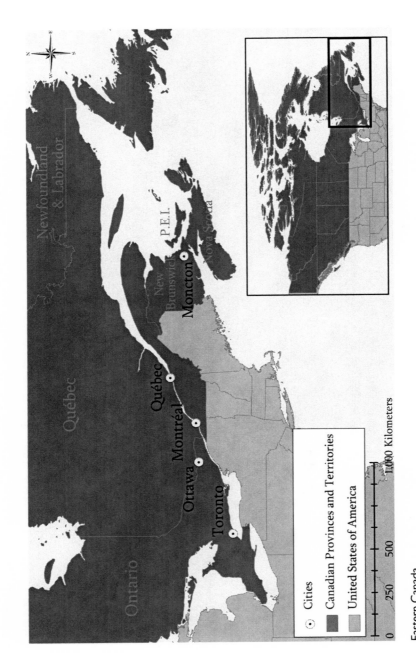

Eastern Canada
Courtesy Meaghan Hoyle and Natalie Kaiser

Paths to Post-Nationalism

1

Sociolinguistics as Social Practice

1.1 A STORY FOR OUR TIMES

A number of years ago, I got a phone call from a friend and colleague in France. She wanted some advice on how to handle what appeared to her (and to me) to be a rather unusual request. The day before, someone from the police station in a nearby city had called her, asking her to act as a consultant on a case. They had a tape from a wiretap on a suspected drug dealer, but they were having a hard time understanding what was said. The reason, they said, was that the suspect, a man originally from Senegal now living in France, was speaking Canadian French to his contacts, who, at the time of the recorded conversation, were apparently somewhere in northern Ontario. The police decided they needed a linguist with knowledge of Canadian French, contacted the nearest university, and somehow found my friend.

A number of things about this story are important for any reflection about sociolinguistics and sociolinguists today. The first has to do with the apparent facts of the case. Our discipline has been based on ideas about language and society that take as a baseline a stable connection between speakers, places, times, and social position, and then tries to get a handle on how variability is built around that. Here we have a number of things that are out of place and out of time. How do police in France end up having to figure out what a person from Senegal speaking Canadian French is saying?

The answer seems to rest with the ways the gray- and black-economy dimensions of the globalized economy work (Castells 2000). The illegal drug market requires managing a worldwide flow of resources distributed through complex and widely distributed networks; as resources move around, so do the people involved (Appadurai 1996). But managing that flow, and dealing with the many problems of state surveillance that come with the territory (so to speak) of working in cross-border illicit activity requires an ability to mobilize communicative resources and to turn in communicative performances that allow the flow to go on uninterrupted. So an African meets up with Canadians in Central America (or so the police claimed) and, for reasons and in ways we will never be able to fully describe or explain, is able to appropriate their linguistic resources and use them in ways which, we know minimally, at least confound some agents of state surveillance. Certainly people have been moving around, crossing boundaries, and learning languages for a long time, but sociolinguistics is only now confronting what it means to put this phenomenon at the center of its concerns. So the first thing I explore in this book is what it means to take seriously the possibility that maybe the baseline is not a baseline at all, but rather mobility (Sheller and Urry 2006) and multiplicity.

The second has to do with what my friend was doing in this situation. She learned her Canadian French as a doctoral candidate in linguistics, doing what in many ways is a classic thing for a sociolinguist to do. She got on a plane, and then a bus, and got off in northern Ontario. What is a nice girl from southern France doing in Sudbury? It turns out she was not particularly interested in describing the features of the French spoken there (although many other people have been), but rather in what this language meant to its speakers, a relevant question to ask in a place where people are always talking about language and judging other people on the basis of it. Nonetheless, this was not what the police were interested in, not in the least. They wanted an expert, someone who could be constructed as having irrefutable claims to knowing what the suspect and his interlocutors were saying. The place to find a language expert, of course (of course?), is a university. Hence my friend's call to me: she knew she was being constructed as a holder of objective truths, while she understands herself as a producer of situated knowledge—an interpreter, not a transmitter.

The final element of the story (no, I have no idea what happened to the suspect, or to the alleged drugs, for that matter) is what she did. She went, listened, and found the sound quality too poor to be able to make out much of anything. My point is simply that she chose to be in the conversation, knowing that whatever she did she would be making a choice about her actions in a situation complicated by issues having to do with globalization, post-colonialism, migration, and state regulation of goods and people; she also knew that she had limited control over how others would construct her, her knowledge and her actions.

While this story struck both me and my friend as intriguing at the time, it stayed with me as a precursor of things that seem to pop up more and more since then, with such regularity that it is hard to know where to store all the examples. Our ideas about how linguistic resources are brought into play in the construction of social difference are challenged on a daily basis, with people regularly doing things with language they are not supposed to do, or failing to do what we expect of them linguistically, or fighting over who should do what.

This even plays out on television. Admittedly, Canada may be one of the few places on the planet to be able to produce a situation comedy about language and identity (although I can think of plenty of places that should), and is probably the most likely to provide one that is essentially an extended lesson in dealing with diversity. In *Pure laine*,[1] we follow the fortunes of a small family living in Montreal, each one a "misplaced" person in his or her own way. He is a high school teacher, originally from Haiti; she is from the Îles-de-la-Madeleine, a region of Quebec that has more in common geographically, historically, culturally, socially, and linguistically with the Atlantic provinces than with Quebec; and their adopted daughter is from China. In each episode we deal with some situation in which at least one of them has to handle the complexity of the ways they do not fit nicely into the prevailing expectations of a putatively homogenous society, and which allow the family to explore their own ambivalences and paradoxes, but ultimately to have the last laugh over narrow-minded "Québécois pure laine." The not-so-subtle argument is that diversity is here to stay, and we had better start accepting white Québécoises who sound different from some putative Quebec norm, and black and Asian Québécoises who sound just like everyone else. The link between language, place, and identity is broken, and people must constitute links that work for them. (The possibility that they might not constitute links of any kind is not yet on the radar.)

These are the elements that I want to develop: how to shift our gaze from stability to mobility; why it is important to do so now; and what it means for our practice as sociolinguists. I lay out my own attempts to practice a sociolinguistics which places social difference and social inequality at the center of its concerns, and in which I understand myself as a participant in the conversation about how those processes work and about what kinds of consequences they have and for whom.

This means that I take a position contrary to general expectations of the role we should play in public debate, or more generally with respect to the concerns of civil society—the kinds of expectations that my friend in France came up against, and that have frequently featured in other forms of what is referred to as forensic linguistics (Olsson 2004; Coulthard and Johnson 2007), or that figure time and time again in public debates over immigration, refugee policy, public signage, language in education, and more. Sociolinguists have long struggled over the status of our knowledge versus other forms of knowledge on the same subjects, and over the roles we could or should play. Some have argued that sociolinguistic knowledge is incommensurate with other kinds and that, consequently, entry into debates is perilous; some have been dismayed at the lack of legitimacy accorded to sociolinguistic knowledge by other stakeholders; some have argued for the importance of interchanges with stakeholders different from academic ones. We have also argued over the relevance of public debate in driving research agendas. (See, for example, the literature surrounding the American debate that started in the 1970s over the educational implications of varieties of English associated with the African American population, e.g., Labov 1972, 1982; Rickford 1999; Baugh 2000; or dialogues in the *Journal of Sociolinguistics* over a wide variety of issues pertaining to the general problem of sociolinguistics in the public sphere; see Heller et al. 1999; S. Johnson 2001.)

These discussions echo concerns that emerged across the social sciences as the discursive turn which emerged in full force in the 1980s argued for turning away from the positivist model, which dominates the public view of social science research (and which of course explains why we call them social *sciences*), and for moving toward an interpretive, socially situated, and practice-oriented understanding of what we do (see, for example, Bourdieu 1972, Rabinow and Sullivan 1979, and Clifford and Marcus 1986, just to cite some texts that had a particular impact in our field). Without recapitulating that history here, I will simply point to two dimensions of the argument that I find particularly relevant for my own work. The first is the recognition of the role of the social sciences in establishing what Foucault (1984) called "regimes of truth," that is, naturalized ways of understanding the world that help legitimate relations of power and that of course marginalize, erase, and otherwise devalue other ways of doing and being in the world which would serve other interests. The second is the application to our own work of the sociolinguistic insight that social categories and relations of power are constructed in interaction. If that is true for the people we study, it must also be true for our own action.

As a result, I argue for a sociolinguistics that is not a form of expert knowledge, but rather an informed and situated social practice, one which can account for what we see, but which also knows why we see what we do, and what it means to tell the story. In other words, I want to move away from a position that claims objective, neutral, unconstrained, disinterested knowledge production which can, if called upon to do so, guide social and political action, and toward one that understands knowledge production to be socially situated, but no less useful for that (indeed, perhaps more so). I also want to confront the question of interests served, that is, how the kinds of knowledge we are interested in producing, and do produce, are embedded in complicated relations of power, not all of which may be readily apparent to us, and not all of which allow for reliable prediction of the consequences of our work.

The kinds of sociolinguistics we have inherited emerge from the links between the structure and functioning of the academy and the growth of the modern nation-state. The development of the tertiary sector, of niche markets, of intensified globalized exchange and communication networks, of shifts in regulatory relations between the public, private, and not-for-profit sectors: these are all conditions of late modernity that reinforce the discursive turn away from universalizing scientific frames. But we also need to attend to the ways in which those conditions shift our gaze away from looking at stability and homogeneity as normal, with diversity and mobility thereby constructed as problems requiring analytic activity. They encourage us to turn this relationship around, that is, to take diversity and mobility as normal. This requires us to reformulate our questions and our modes of inquiry. I want to develop a sociolinguistics for our times, one that understands our work, as well as the object of our discussion, as social practice positioned on an uneven and shifting playing field and that foregrounds complexity and mobility as key means of grasping how and why we construct relations of social difference and social inequality the way we do.

1.2 A BRIEF CONSIDERATION OF SOCIOLINGUISTICS AND THE NATION-STATE

In so many ways the sociolinguistics we have inherited was shaped through modernist nationalism. Our long-standing preoccupation with community and identity is clearly tied to the role of both linguistics and anthropology in constructing the boundaries of the nation-state. Many authors have documented the importance, in the legitimization of the nation-state, of the construction of standardized languages coterminous with state boundaries and linked to uniformized cultures understood to be the distinctive property of nations (cf., e.g., Anderson 1983; Grillo 1989; Hobsbawm 1990; Billig 1995; Crowley 1996; Bauman and Briggs 2003).

Hobsbawm, in particular, has argued that the rise of the bourgeoisie is tied to the construction of national markets that allowed the bourgeois privileged control over the production and circulation of resources, both within and between states. Their control was legitimized through the ideology of the nation, which was meant to cross-cut class, religion, ethnicity, and gender, and also served as a basis for the uniformization necessary to the integration of the market. This particular discursive legitimization therefore made possible the democratic mobilization of, and eventually control over, populations counted as "citizens," engaged in the construction of national markets, in a particular development strategy of bourgeois capitalism.

This discursive strategy helps explain the development of a number of forms of knowledge construction, especially as they emerged in the nineteenth century, which we have inherited. They include the production of knowledge about continuous occupation and cultural practice in a given territory through activities in domains such as folklore, anthropology, archaeology, and linguistics, used to justify claims to nationhood and to bounded territories (Bauman and Briggs 2003; Said 2003 [1978]). For example, scholars demonstrated the continuous occupation of a territory by showing cultural continuity archeologically, by using historical linguistic methods to show the time depth and spatial range of linguistic forms, or by using folklore to do the same for material and oral culture. Typically, these approaches focused on what could be understood as the most "conservative" linguistic and cultural forms, that is, the ones least contaminated by modernity and contact.

Such approaches also include the development of the means of producing the knowledge required to manage populations, for example through demography (Maroney 1992; Urla 1993; Gal 1995). The development of the census allowed for the measurement of populations and their variation and movement in order to facilitate policies aimed at the uniformization and eradication or containment of unwanted linguistic or cultural practices and the people who practiced them, or, on the contrary, the development of desired practices in populations. Psychology (for example, in the form of standardized testing or theories of child-rearing) and the health sciences are other domains where such forms of knowledge production prevailed (see Hegarty 2007 for a critical discussion of the role of psychology).

Certainly the issue of what counts as mastery of a language, and therefore how to measure linguistic competence, should be understood in these terms. Tabouret-Keller (1988), for example, documents how ideas about language socialization have long been tied to ideas about the dangers of bilingualism for the cognitive and moral development of children. A well-developed line of work in applied linguistics discusses the links among language teaching, the evaluation of linguistic competence, and social inequality (Cummins 2000). A related set of inquiries examines national interests regarding the regulation of labor migration and of participation in neocolonialist global expansion of capital, in particular the ways in which the teaching of English both constitutes a major labor market on its own and contributes to the ability of English-speakers to profit from markets in other goods and services (Phillipson 1992; Pennycook 1994).

The links between the social sciences and the development of the nation-state provide the backdrop for a preoccupation with community (and therefore with boundaries) and identity (who belongs and who doesn't) across disciplines and in the public sphere. It helps explain a concentration of work oriented toward establishing the objective existence of languages, cultures, and nations and managing the fuzziness both of the boundaries among them and of the diversity "within." It also helps explain a consistent tension between attempts to construct expert knowledge as an authoritative—because disinterested—basis for legitimizing discourses and the political interests that have driven the questions we ask.

Boas famously encountered the problem of the use of Darwinian ideas about biological evolution applied as neutral and objective scientific inquiry to the idea of social evolution, in particular to the hypothesis that some languages, cultures, and races might be more developed, more evolved, or simply fitter for current conditions than others (see discussion in Briggs 2005). The colonial project allowed for the collection of data in this area—data that not coincidentally was used for the construction of hierarchies which legitimized colonialism, the colonizers justifying their activity on the grounds that they were engaged in a *mission civilisatrice*, bringing superior languages and cultures to less-developed people (Fabian 1986; Irvine and Gal 2000; Irvine 2001; Makoni and Pennycook 2005;

Errington 2008). These ideas also contributed to fascist theories about language and race (Hutton 1999, 2005).

Much twentieth-century linguistics and linguistic anthropology has been devoted to developing universalizing theories designed to refute the legitimizing discourses of colonialism and fascism, although usually not explicitly. That is, in the wake of World War II, the exploration of essential differences appeared to be a dangerous project, to be countered by humanistic ideas emphasizing the importance of what we all universally share as humans, not what makes us different from each other. The postwar rise of structuralism can be seen in this light, as can the focus of cognitive anthropology on the relationship between linguistic relativism and linguistic universals (Gumperz and Levinson 1996).

This shift, however, contained its own contradictions. Among them is the vexed question of accounting for difference. In the postwar shift to generative linguistics, scholars have dealt with that problem by removing it from consideration altogether. For other linguists, it has been a central preoccupation. From dialectology to variationist sociolinguistics, from linguistic anthropology to applied linguistics, we have been struggling with the problem of diversity and inequality implicitly or explicitly for a number of years. This issue has been front and center precisely because it represents a counterexample to the most ideologically salient values of liberal democratic nation-states.

Today the focus has shifted. While diversity, inequality, mobility, and change remain major preoccupations, they are no longer understood as important because they run counter to the norm of stability and homogeneity. Rather, we have come to understand them as not only typical, but probably crucial and constitutive elements of emerging forms of social organization. Indeed, as Rampton and his collaborators have pointed out, much of late-twentieth-century sociolinguistics has been devoted to the problem of the construction of the (marginalized) Other, not simply as an investigation of counterexamples to idealized homogeneous communities, but as embedded in concerns about social justice (Rampton 2006; Rampton et al. 2007). This has required new ways of thinking about them, describing them, and addressing the issues our descriptions raise, as we attempt to hold in tension a certain degree of reflexivity with accounts of processes going on in the world, and to link the workings of communication in everyday life to processes of institutionalization and to political economic conditions.

1.3 TOWARD A CRITICAL ETHNOGRAPHIC SOCIOLINGUISTICS

Against this backdrop, we need to turn our attention to how current social changes, particularly those related to the specific forms of expansion and transformation of capitalism that we usually talk about in terms of the *globalized new economy*, require us to rethink how to explore social change through the examination of linguistic form and practice. In the second chapter, I argue for an ethnographic approach to sociolinguistics as a form of critical practice, informed by political economy. The argument for ethnography is its ability to discover how language works as situated social practice, and how it is tied to social organization. The argument for political economy is the importance of understanding the material basis of social organization, and how material conditions constrain how we make sense of things. Put in other terms, it is an approach that allows for the discovery of how social action is tied to social structuration (Giddens 1984; Heller 2001a), by understanding both action and structuration to be social processes unfolding over time and across space, rather than conceptually and empirically distinct realms of micro- and macro-social phenomena. Here I will argue for the usefulness of the concepts of *resource, discursive space*, and *trajectory* as means of organizing empirical inquiry.

I aim to account for (1) the ways in which the production and distribution of resources are regulated, as well as how value and meaning are attributed to *resources*; (2) following Bourdieu (1982), how symbolic (including linguistic) and material resources are exchangeable, given the conditions of the market, and what allows for stability and change in those conditions; and (3) how social structuration positions social actors in ways that constrain their access to resources and hence their ability to mobilize them, and mobilize them convincingly, in specific moments. I am concerned, then, about understanding how the *trajectories* of *resources* and *actors* intersect (or not), in the *spaces* where the consequential work of combining meaning-making with resource distribution takes place, with further structuring consequences in terms of how constraints are reproduced or changed, and hence in terms of the obstacles and opportunities social actors encounter. What happens in the here and now is not, in my view, a distinct entity from patterns of *social categorization* (which is what I understand the construction of social difference to be), or from how categorization is used to reproduce or challenge *social stratification* (or social inequality; understood as patterned inequality in resource distribution). Rather, the power of an ethnographic sociolinguistics is precisely its ability to follow social processes across time and space, and to see how agency and structure engage each other under specific political economic conditions.

As many anthropologists have argued in recent years, following the trajectories of resources and actors and finding the links among discursive spaces requires working in terms other than the traditional "field site." Using ideas such as *transnationalism* (Basch et al. 1994; Hannerz 1996, 2003; Pries 2001; Vertovec 2001); *cosmopolitanism* (Beck and Sznaider 2006); and *multi-site* or *multi-sited ethnography* (Marcus 1995; Burawoy et al. 2000) for understanding globalization and globalist discourse (Englund 2002; Inda and Rosaldo 2002), anthropologists have sought to focus on linkages among moments or activities understood in some way as "local," that is, as here-and-now, understanding that what is constructed and oriented toward as "here" or "there" and as "now" or "then" is shifting and shiftable (Kearney 2004). This is an endeavor I think sociolinguistics is particularly well equipped to contribute to, given its ability to capture the processes of construction of category and subjectivity as they unfold and to identify the interactional means by which inequality happens. At the same time, it requires looking beyond the local. This has led me to try to understand discourse as developing over time and across space in ways that are empirically observable, by following the trajectories of conversations and of conversational participation. *Discursive spaces* are assemblages of interconnected sites, some more easily observable than others (for example, it was easier for our research team members to show up at a series of executive board meetings than to record the telephone conversations occurring between members between meetings), traversed by the *trajectories* of participants and of *resources* regulated there. They ask us to think in terms of linkages and trajectories, of webs, rather than in terms of, say, rooted or fixed objects or even of levels.

This concern for what social process means for social difference and social inequality is at the heart of what I mean by a *critical* approach. I do not take the position that this is the only question sociolinguistics should ask, only that it is one that it can ask, and one that has in fact been an important influence in the field. Nor do I assume that the picture we get will always be a simple one; indeed, in my own work, I am consistently impressed by how complex the picture turns out to be. It generally appears that doing things in certain ways (using a minority language as a language of instruction, for example, or attending to gendered distribution of turns at speaking in the classroom) turns out to work well for some people and not so well for others; or to have some desirable and some undesirable consequences for the same people. In that sense I am less focused on "speaking truth to power" or on "giving voice" than I am on the complexities of how power works. That is, I take some distance from the idea that my work should be first and foremost aimed at showing the powerful what the consequences of their exercise of power is, or at providing access to power for those who typically have none, so doing by shaping the research around a preexisting idea of who occupies what position in a system of relations of inequality.

Instead, I take the position that my job is first to describe and to explain, and only then to decide how I feel about what I understand to be going on and what, if anything, I should do about it. In that sense, I understand my role as one of a noticer of important and interesting things, a producer of an account of them, and an interlocutor with other stakeholders about them. This is a process consisting of sets of social relations and different forms of conversation through which an account is produced, although in the end, the account is mine and I cannot lay the blame for it at anyone else's door. Whether or not I am understood as a legitimate knowledge producer and interlocutor is a question embedded in the enterprise.

From the ontological and epistemological position, and the theoretical and methodological framework that results from it, which I set out in chapter 2, I will devote the rest of the book to one particular account of one particular process, intended as an extended working through both of some of the questions I think are important to address now, and of how I have tried to address them.[2] The questions have to do with the particular constellations of language, community, identity, nation, and state that have informed so much of the social organization of the First World (and by extension, meant here in the most practical and concrete of ways, the rest of the world affected by it), and sociolinguistics along with it. I have looked at the development of that particular discursive formation through the lens of the linguistic minority movements that emerged in the 1960s, and particularly that of the corner of the world in which I grew up— Quebec and, later, francophone Canada—and its complicated connections with other discursive spaces.

1.4 IDEOLOGICAL SHIFTS THROUGH THE LENS OF FRANCOPHONE CANADA

Francophone Canada is a useful site for this discussion because this space, like other linguistic minority spaces, allows us to trace a genealogy of ideas about language, community, nation, and state from the nineteenth century to the present day, and to see how those ideas are tied to the political economy of European industrial expansion, colonialism, and postcolonialism. As a site, it also clearly reveals the discursive dimensions of these ideas, since the link between language, nation, territory, and state has long (by the short measuring stick of Canadian history, that is, since colonization in the early seventeenth century) been a vexed subject of debate and ideological struggle, today as much as in the past. Nothing about what francophone Canada is or might be is normalized; nothing is taken for granted. Its transformations over the past forty years or so show how difficult it has been to maintain the dominant discourse of "one language, one nation, one state," as the political economy which allowed that discourse to emerge in Quebec in the 1950s and 1960s underwent a radical transformation in the 1980s and 1990s.

The tensions between "traditionalist" and "modernist" discourses of the nation (Heller and Labrie 2003), which framed debates about the nature of francophone Canada over the past two hundred years or so, are now reaching their limits in the neoliberal globalizing new economy. I will brutally summarize here the ways in which ideologies of language, identity, nation, and state have shifted in relation to changing political economies, in order to set the frame for the story I tell in greater detail and at greater leisure over the course of the book.

The story of francophone Canada begins with New France and with European expansion in the sixteenth to eighteenth centuries (Wolf 1982). Britain and France struggled for domination over North America, a key link in the triangular trade that fueled European capitalist expansion. North Atlantic cod sustained the slave economies of the Caribbean; furs clothed the wealthy; wood built the ships that carried the goods.

Settlement had both economic and political aims, although the French invested considerably less in their Canadian colonies than the British did in their American ones. French settlements were begun in Acadie, the Annapolis Valley of what is now Nova Scotia, in 1604, and in the St. Lawrence River valley in 1608. Trade routes, however, spread west along waterways, giving rise to the first iconic symbols of the French Canadian, the *voyageur* and the *coureur des bois* (literally, runner of the woods). Both of these masculine icons (indexed by the *ceinture fléchée*, a woven belt, and a red *tuque*, or wool hat) embody the freedom of the endless spaces of the North American continent, proximity to the indigenous population and to nature, fearless domination of a harsh climate and of the unknown. The American colonies, in contrast, were more settled, more populous, wealthier, and more mercantile.

The decisive turning point for Britain and France in North America came in the eighteenth century. The Treaty of Utrecht in 1713 gave Acadie to the British. By 1755, the Acadian presence was making the British nervous and preventing them from occupying the fertile lands of the Annapolis Valley. When the Acadians, in an effort to remain neutral (and hence undisturbed), refused to swear an oath of allegiance to the British crown, they were deported to the United States and to Europe, in an event that was to become the founding myth and trauma of Acadian nationalism. The final conquest of New France came with the capture of Quebec in the Seven Years' War, in 1759.

The departing French colonial elite left under British rule about sixty-five thousand peasants, merchants, *voyageurs*, and *coureurs des bois*, along with members of Catholic religious orders responsible for education and health care. There was much debate among the new colonial rulers about what to do about this population, but the upshot was their absorption into a colonial political economy in which ethnonational difference (at that time understood principally in terms of race and religion) became constitutive of social stratification. This economy was initially built on extraction of primary resources, initially furs, lumber, and fish. This was the source of the last masculine icon of French Canada, the *bûcheron* (lumberjack), indexed by a red-and-black-checked shirt and the same *tuque* as the *voyageurs*. French Canadians combined extractive labor in one or more of these areas with subsistence agriculture. The smartest among them were recruited by the Catholic Church for higher education and trained as priests (or nuns), doctors (or nurses), lawyers, notaries, journalists or, later, lay educators.

Francophone Canada lived on the margins of power, articulated with but dependent on the wealth base of Canadian society. For the British, this guaranteed access to cheap labor and a bulwark against revolutionary America. For the religious and Catholic-trained lay elite, it allowed for some degree of power in the articulation of the organization of the labor pool with British political and economic structures. What formed over the course of the late eighteenth century was an alliance of counterrevolutionary elites: ultramontane Catholics opposed to the ideas of Revolutionary France, on one side, and British loyalists fleeing the American War of Independence, on the other (Lipset 1970).

For francophone Canada, the legitimizing ideology of this arrangement took the form of what we think of as "traditionalist" nationalism. This discourse, which borrowed heavily from Romanticism, was to remain the dominant discourse of francophone Canada through the middle of the twentieth century, through and beyond the creation of the Canadian state in 1867. In it, the French Canadian nation was responsible for the maintenance in North America of conservative values of religion, language, and "race" (*la foi, la race, la langue*), values understood to have been abandoned in France after the Revolution. These values were tied to the occupation of an exclusive social (but not necessarily geographical) space, and to the land understood as nature rather than as political territory (which was under British and, later, Anglo-Canadian control). This "traditionalist" discourse placed the concept of national tradition and organic community at the center of its legitimizing arguments, but located nationality not in a territorialized nation-state, but rather in the organic body of the collective and its individual constituent members. In this, it took up certain Romantic nationalist ideas about the nation as embodiment of collective spirit. The following extracts from a text written by a prominent nationalist journalist in 1881 provide an example:

> The French-Canadian people, however small it may be, has without a doubt a mission to fulfill in America, a mission analogous to that which the French long fulfilled in Europe, and which it would fulfill to this day if it had not lost itself in the inextricable labyrinth of impiety.
>
> The Anglo-Saxon and Germanic races are destined to predominate on this continent by force of numbers: that is a fact which it is necessary to recognize. But the French element has a role to play there.
>
> For centuries, Catholic France was a source of light, a fertile source of generous ideas, an inspiration for great works. Only Rome surpassed her.
>
> Is it not permitted to believe that the French of Canada have the mission of spreading ideas among the inhabitants of a new world who are too inclined towards materialism, too attached to worldly goods? Who can doubt it?
>
> But for the French Canadian people to be able to fulfill this glorious mission, it must remain what Providence wanted it to be: Catholic and French. It must preserve its faith and its language in all their purity. If it kept its language and lost its faith, it would become what the French people has

become: a people stripped of its former grandeur, a people without influence or prestige. If, on the other hand, it kept its faith but renounced its language, it would lose itself among the people surrounding it and would soon be absorbed by them. Individuals can leave, but the mission that Providence seems to have confided to the French-Canadians, as a distinct people, would be betrayed.

[Le peuple canadien-français, si petit qu'il soit, a indubitablement une mission à remplir en Amérique, une mission analogue à celle que le peuple français a longtemps remplie en Europe, et qu'il remplirait encore s'il ne s'était égaré dans l'inextricable dédale de l'impiété.

Les races anglo-saxonne et germanique sont destinées à prédominer sur ce continent par le nombre: c'est un fait qu'il faut admettre. Mais l'élément français y a un rôle à jouer.

Pendant des siècles, la France catholique a été un foyer de lumière, une source féconde en idées généreuses, une inspiratrice de grandes oeuvres. Rome seule l'a surpassée.

N'est-il pas permis de croire que les Français du Canada ont la mission de répandre les idées parmi les autres habitants du nouveau-monde, trop enclins au matérialisme, trop attachés aux biens purement terrestres? Qui peut en douter?

Mais pour que le peuple canadien-français puisse remplir cette glorieuse mission, il doit rester ce que la Providence a voulu qu'il fût: catholique et français. Il doit garder sa foi et sa langue dans toute leur pureté. S'il gardait sa langue et perdait sa foi, il deviendrait ce qu'est devenu le peuple français: un peuple déchu de son ancienne grandeur, un peuple sans influence et sans prestige. Si, d'un autre, il conservait sa foi, tout en renonçant à sa langue, il se confondrait avec les peuples qui l'entourent et serait bientôt absorbé par eux. Les individus pourraient toujours se sauver, mais la mission que la Providence semble avoir confiée aux canadiens-français, comme peuple distinct, serait faussée.] (From an 1881 text by a journalist named Jules-Paul Tardivel, as cited in Bouthillier and Meynaud 1972: 214–215)

The reproduction of this discourse was possible because the position of French Canadians in the economy was maintained even as the primary resource extraction economy became industrialized and other forms of industrial transformation took hold. French Canadians simply provided the labor for the factories, moving in large numbers to industrialized urban areas in Canada and the United States. Hydroelectricity, pulp and paper, steel and the automobile industry, fish-packing, textile mills: all were the property of English-speaking (and, originally, ethnically English or Scottish and usually Protestant) owners, reliant on ethnolinguistically marginal groups, of whom the French were the first, to provide labor. The racialization of labor hierarchies was, of course, typical of colonial regimes; what is interesting here is that one set of colonial settlers was incorporated into this kind of regime by another (while the indigenous population, here as elsewhere in North America, largely suffered elimination or extreme marginalization, despite some attempts to incorporate them as well).

As Porter (1965) noted many years ago, this led later, under conditions of modern industrialization, to what he termed a "vertical mosaic," in which class stratification overlapped ethnolinguistic (or ethnonational) categorization. This also allowed for the legitimization of the reproduction of this ethnoclass hierarchy through erasure of the class dimensions by foregrounding ethnolinguistic distinctions. If francophones were poor and badly educated, it was because (in the English view) their Roman Catholic religion led them to have too many children and prevented them from access to Enlightenment knowledge (or, in the French view, because their spiritual values were superior to the mercenary ones of the English). The ethnicization of the working class was also common in the United States, and equally in tension with unionization as a form of class consciousness (Foley 1990; Anctil 1991; Sennett 1998). By the 1960s, French Canadians remained overrepresented in the primary resource extraction and heavy industry sectors of the economy, and low in almost every measure of class imaginable (for example, mortality, income, level of education, and housing), despite the existence of a small merchant class and the professional elite dedicated to bettering the life conditions of their fellow French Canadians through Church-backed volunteerism and the cooperative movement.

It was these indicators that served to raise political consciousness in the 1960s. A crumbling British Empire and a postwar economic boom and expansion of markets (Clift and Arnopoulos 1979) created conditions for the elite to rethink its strategies. The emergence of a "modernist" discourse of language and the nation-state, linking land to political control and long established elsewhere (Hobsbawm 1990), broke apart the pan-Canadian (indeed, pan-American) solidarity of French Canadians in favor of the establishment of a Québécois nation-state. The expansion of markets to the west, spearheaded by the English-speaking financial elite, left room in the regional market of Quebec; an increased wealth base allowed for democratization of education and the development of an educated francophone middle class, which (in line with other emancipatory movements of the time) saw in political control of the Québec provincial governmental apparatus a greater possibility for social mobility than the pan-North American spiritual nationalism they had grown up with. The Quebec state wrested control of civil society (health care, social services, education) from the Church, and its bureaucracy provided the first labor market for its educated citizens.

The rest of francophone Canada tried, with difficulty but some success, to follow suit, through the adoption of a form of institutional territoriality: in the absence of a political territory, they opted for exclusive control over social institutions, notably schools. In this they were aided by the willing interlocutor of the Canadian federal government, desperate to prove that Quebec did not have to secede from Canada in order for francophones to have a good life in the northern part of the continent. In addition, by the 1960s, English Canada had to relinquish the power base that the postcolonial Commonwealth had once provided. The eclipse of the British Empire forced Canada to find a new basis for national legitimacy, and linguistic duality was one way to make sure that the boundaries between Canada and the United States might remain distinct.

The result was the construction, between the 1960s and today, of an important regional francophone market centered on Quebec, which saw the rise of an educated middle class taking its place first in the public sector, and then in the private sector. In Quebec, this saw the rise of what is commonly known as "Quebec Inc." (Fraser 1987), regional and mainly small- to medium-sized companies run by francophones. The institutions set up as an alternative power base for francophones across the country created a labor market in such sectors as education, the media, and health care, while outside Quebec the *milieu associatif* (network of volunteer associations) initially developed by the Church and the traditionalist elite stepped into the role of interlocutor with the federal government.

Despite increasing socioeconomic mobility and the establishment of a francophone regional market, Canada was able to sustain its primary- and secondary-sector activities up through the 1980s. As a result, francophones retained a strong presence in traditional areas, as workers in the Atlantic fishery, in lumber and related pulp and paper industries, in the mines, in heavy industry (such as the steel and automobile industry of southern Ontario or the textile industry of Quebec), in construction, or in agriculture. Historically, such activities have also long been combined (agriculture in the summer and lumber in the winter, say; or the men on the boats and the women in the fish-processing plants; see D. Johnson 1999 for an account of the changes in the economy of coastal New Brunswick).

From the end of the nineteenth century to the 1970s and 1980s, in industrialized urban areas, from Moncton to Montreal to Cornwall or Welland, francophones concentrated in the less-desirable parts of town, near the factories—indeed, usually downwind of their smokestacks. Francophone neighborhoods are almost always in the "east end," and on the flats. The brewery we will discuss in chapter 4 was in the eastern, flat part of Montreal, closer to where the workers lived than to the owners' neighborhood, which was farther west and up the "mountain," as the long-extinct volcano in the middle of the island of Montreal is usually called.

Welland, a factory town in southern Ontario, provides another good example: factory owners lived west of the Welland River and the Welland Canal, on the higher ground carved out of the bend in the river. East of the canal, working-class neighborhoods were arranged around their parish churches; Italian, French, Hungarian, Polish, and Croatian neighborhoods were clearly bordered by streets cutting that part of town into a grid, and populated by workers who had been specifically recruited to work in the factories and mills that lay on this area's northern and southern edges. (Initially, in the 1920s, the francophones had been recruited from Bellechasse County in central Quebec, through a branch of the textile mill that had just opened in Welland.) This kind of spatial arrangement apparently carried over into the factories themselves; according to a group of laid-off francophone factory workers we interviewed in 1996, workers sat in the cafeteria with members of their own ethnic group, even if they might mingle a bit and share a laugh with a buddy from another table (and hence from another ethnolinguistic group). The francophone elite, including educators, insurance salespeople, and doctors, lived slightly to the north or east of the working-class part of town, that is, right across town from the older, established anglophone elite.

In Moncton, in southeastern New Brunswick, francophones were concentrated in a neighborhood called Parkton and worked in the railway yards. In Ottawa, they lived east of the Rideau River, near the lumber mills. The examples are many, but in all cases, the arrangement depended on the heavy industry that collapsed across northeastern North America in the 1980s, throwing people out of work across the region. As we will see, this was a problem not only for the workers most directly affected, but for the entire ideological apparatus of modernist francophone nationalism on which it rested.

The more rural areas connected to primary resource extraction suffered their own major dislocations in the same period. Since these were the traditional bastions—the heartland, as it were, of francophone Canada—the ideological problem posed was all the greater. Lumber mills, pulp-and-paper mills, and mines all suffered, and many closed, in northern Ontario, in Quebec, in northern New Brunswick; these were all areas of heavy francophone concentration, either because francophones had been recruited to work there (as was the case for the railway-building, lumber, and mining industries that opened in northern Ontario in the early twentieth century), because they migrated to work there, or because they constituted a locally available labor pool. The cod fishery, which sustained a large proportion of the Acadian population, collapsed in 1992 because of overfishing.

This crisis of industrial modernity was widespread in Europe and North America. But it hit francophone Canada in a very specific way, because ethnolinguistic categorization was used to construct class relations, and in particular to make of francophones an available labor pool. The political mobilization of francophones, and their socioeconomic mobility, contested only their place in the hierarchical division of labor, not the overall structure. And indeed, while many successfully escaped the conditions of marginalization of the early twentieth century (not to mention the eighteenth and nineteenth), many were left behind in the old order of things. (This was nevertheless useful for the continued legitimization of the mobilization movement, because it highlighted continuing marginalization, while preserving the old solidarities and authenticities that gave meaning to the idea of the "nation." It provided people a place to come from, and a place to go home to.) Preserving the benefits of mobilization meant preserving the idea of the francophone community as a social category, and that required finding a solution to the collapse of the political economy that reproduced it.

These changes presented challenges to the welfare state, which was sustained by national economies and national markets and had played such an important role in developing an institutional infrastructure for francophone Canada, and hence in shaping the nature of that discursive space. Efforts to meet these challenges put in motion a major shift that began in the late 1980s and continues today, in which the state changed the rationale for linguistic duality away from a focus on rights and on maintenance of language and culture to a focus on economic development in the transition to an economy based on the tertiary sector.

These changes constitute, of course, a particular manifestation of global processes. As a wide variety of scholars have pointed out, the 1980s saw a leap in the global expansion of capital, afforded by a variety of conditions, notably the development of communications and transport technologies facilitating the transfer of primary and secondary sector activities to parts of the world where labor is cheaper and regulations looser (Castells 2000; Inda and Rosaldo 2002). This global expansion was also linked to a saturation of markets for standardized goods, resulting in a new focus on niche markets and on added value for products (Harvey 1989; Giddens 1990; Friedman 2002).

Five other processes flow from these. First, the First World economies from which these activities were transferred (and are still being transferred, for that matter) saw the growth of the tertiary sector, partly for the management of globalized networks of production and consumption, and partly for the production of symbolic added value. Second, workplaces adapted older Taylorist management techniques to the tertiary sector, albeit not always easily (Boutet 2001, 2008; Cameron 2001, 2004; Heller and Boutet 2006). These techniques were also merged (again, not always successfully) with attempts to develop "flexibility" and "horizontality" in organizational structures, in order to move labor around more easily in response to rapidly shifting market conditions and in order to retain an increasingly elusive competitive edge (Gee et al. 1996). Fourth, one increasingly important source for obtaining flexibility lay not only in the mobility of production sites but also in the mobility of workers. Finally, the state has been obliged to reexamine its role. The nation-state markets for which it was invented reached their limits, requiring the state to facilitate the kinds of transnational processes I have just described. Indeed, states across the First World have adopted what are commonly known as "neoliberal" discourses and practices, whose main characteristic has been to remove restrictions on the movement of capital (if not necessarily of workers) and to invest in the development of the kinds of flexible workers the new economy values.

Let me emphasize here that I see these interconnected processes as the heart of what I will refer to throughout the text as "globalization," "the new economy," and "neoliberalism." In the context of the ethnographic material discussed here, what is important about "globalization" is the ways in which local and regional markets are integrated into global ones via regimes of regulation based on economic cooperation rather than colonialism (or, sometimes, on the margins of regimes of regulation altogether), and in ways that, as Harvey and Castells point out, entail intensified and compressed circulation of people, goods, and information. The "neoliberalism" of the state is a way of capturing its return to a role of facilitating the construction and maintenance of privileged markets run by and for the private sector; a stepping back from welfarism, but within a commitment to the interests of citizens over noncitizens just the same. The "new economy" is probably the newest element of the terrain mapped out by these three terms, in terms of the emergence of new regimes of regulation of work (flexibility, individual responsibility); of modes of production that are increasingly mediated, whether technologically, linguistically, or culturally; of the growth of the tertiary sector; and of increased emphasis on symbolic added value, as well as of openings for local niche markets articulated in complex ways with global ones.

The cumulative result is an increased importance of the fields of language and culture, and a shift from an emphasis on political legitimacy to an emphasis on economic legitimacy. In the globalized new economy, communication is central to the functioning of the market; language, culture, and identity are tied to the emergence of niche markets and added value, in a process of localization that globalization has made possible, indeed necessary; and the role of the state has become squarely oriented to its capacity to facilitate global expansion of capital in ways that benefit its citizens. Despite the possibility that "economist" discourses of "globalization" may serve simply to mask rather traditional modes of regulating the expansion of capital (Tsing 2000), I take the view here that the discursive shift itself is worth examining. I argue that the shift from a discourse of rights to a discourse of profit, from the state as protector to the state as facilitator of the producer (Heller 2008b; Silva and Heller 2009), is linked to material changes in the regulation of state resources and has material consequences for the construction of citizenship. More specifically, we see the rise of the "language worker" (Heller and Boutet 2006) and the transformation of the *main d'oeuvre* (manual labor) into the *parole d'oeuvre* (speech labor; Duchêne 2009), that is, of the *workforce* into the *wordforce* (Heller 2010).

This state of affairs is also rife with tensions, since those who seek to profit from globalization also want the protection of their privileged status from the states of which they are citizens, and local identities actually gain meaning from being commodified on a global market (Tan and Rubdy 2008). Most important for our purposes, current conditions set up a tension between language and culture as commodified skills (hence, for example, the booming industry in machine translation or intercultural communication) or as markers of authenticity (as in the search for native speakers in the English-teaching industry, in the marketing of cultural experiences in tourism, or in the circulation of "authentic" performances and artifacts that are tied to specific sites but that circulate on global circuits of festivals and fairs).

I will tell this story through a set of interlinked ethnographies of francophone Canada, each focusing on a particular period of social, economic, and political change. Throughout, I will try to be mindful of making explicit the ways in which my choices, my questions, and my position are fully part of the conditions in which I was working, and which were the very same as those of the people I was able to work with over the years, and in both rural and urban areas across Canada and in other parts of the francophone world.

1.5 FROM TRADITIONALIST TO MODERNIZING TO POST-NATIONALIST DISCOURSE OF THE FRANCOPHONE NATION

I will begin my account in chapter 3 with the revealing case of the Ordre de Jacques Cartier (OJC), a secret, male-only society of the French Canadian secular elite that worked with the Catholic Church and existed from 1926 to 1965. The OJC, or "la Patente," as it was often called ("the whatsit," a euphemism designed to protect its identity), was a major source of production of traditionalist nationalist discourse. Internal debates and tensions (as revealed in archived documents and correspondence among members and in interviews with former members) allow us to see some of the reasons why the very traditionalist formations (conflation of religion, race, language, and nation; patriarchal hierarchization; the key role of religious institutions in civil society; valorization of sacrifice, cooperation, community, and subsistence over profit and individual entrepreneurship) that had allowed for the emergence of a lay elite no longer served the interests of the bourgeoisie in Quebec, which lost interest in remaining on the margins of the industrial economy. Since those structures proved unable to transform themselves, a painful crisis led to the dissolution of the order, the adoption of modernist political and economic strategies, and the emergence of the state and its agencies and institutions as the prime spaces for the production of discourse on what language, identity, community, and nation might mean.

Essentially, this process was typical of linguistic minority movements and may have a more general lesson to teach us about resistance to the exercise of power. In many ways, the traditionalist ideology of the French Canadian nation was a counterdiscourse, both to Britain's idea of empire and to emerging post-Revolutionary nineteenth-century ideas of the nation-state. Yet it was based on the Romantic idea of nation that had been mobilized elsewhere, and thus remained available to be mobilized, in arguments for legitimacy of claims to political power. The modernist discourse thus turned to that potential and, rather than contesting the very notion of the nation-state as a legitimate form of regulation, argued for privileged access to it.

In that sense, although it was undertaken in the name of the political and economic liberation of a marginalized group, it contained the elements of conservatism that bourgeois nationalism is known for (Hobsbawm 1990): its objective was the creation of a regional market to be controlled by francophones, in order to increase their chances of social mobility, as francophones (Fraser 1987). As had happened in Europe, the new and mainly urban bourgeoisie constructed its legitimacy through an appeal to a timeless past, tightly connected to the prior marginalization that modernist mobilization had set out to break free of, and to rural bastions of healthy life. This set up the urban-rural dynamic so well documented by Raymond Williams (1973), in which the city is about modernity and progress, but also about contamination and corruption, while the country is about health and purity, while also indexing backwardness and stupidity.

The next two chapters trace the rise and fall of modernist nationalist discourse in francophone Canada through ethnographic accounts of key discursive spaces. They examine the interactional basis of the establishment of monolingual sites of resource production: the workplace in Quebec in the late 1970s, and the school in Ontario in the 1980s and 1990s. Both these sites represented bases of power for the new elites, although they used different strategies in areas where francophones were a majority (Quebec) or a minority (the other provinces and territories).

Chapter 4 is based on an ethnography I conducted in 1978–1979 of a large manufacturing company in Montreal (Heller 1985, 1989, 2002), chapter 5 on a series of ethnographies of French-language minority schools in the Toronto area conducted between 1983 and 1996 (Heller 1994a, 2006). These chapters chronicle the successful use of nationalist discourses to mobilize important segments of the population and establish control over sectors of the market in which speaking French and being (ethnonationally) francophone were keys to entry. These sectors were important enough to ensure the value of *la francité*, at least for the bourgeoisie, and help explain the sudden enthusiasm emerging at that time for bilingualism among middle-class anglophones who had formerly learned to dominate through their own monolingualism. (This enthusiasm was institutionalized mainly through French immersion programs in elementary and, later, secondary schools, a form of language teaching that became widely popular across the globe and may be one of Canada's most successful exports.)

These market sectors became poles of attraction on their own terms, paradoxically attracting the very Others that francophone mobilization had sought to protect itself from. They also became platforms for entry into the increasingly globalized economy, one in which, as luck would have it, English was the lingua franca. Out of this situation flows the contradiction of nationalism: using homogeneous spaces as a base to increase access to valuable resources currently circulating globally, and with success attracting others to the resources you control, and increasing your own need for access to those others and their spaces.

The political and economic changes beginning in the 1980s made the modernist discourse difficult to sustain. In the economic realm, Canada experienced a major shift in the conditions that had sustained the reproduction of ethnolinguistic relations. The traditional bastions of francophone (and indeed aboriginal) identity went through major crises, caused by structural shifts in the primary resource economy and its related secondary sector. Much activity in both the primary and secondary sectors shifted to parts of the world where labor was cheaper, so mines, mills, plants, and factories closed down. Where they remained open or were renewed, they involved new forms of old resources, connected to new markets, and organized in new ways involving greater dependence on digital technology and more "flexible" (and less unionized) work structures. For example, the family-owned gold and zinc mines of the Northwest Territories closed down, to be replaced some years later by diamond mines owned by major international cartels.

All of these changes were part of a general crisis of primary resource extraction and manufacturing industries in North America and Europe in the 1980s and 1990s. A specific example concerns the cod fishery of the Atlantic coast, a central element of Acadian identity, which was closed completely in 1992 due to overfishing. Employment insurance and welfare subsidies from the federal government, designed to protect seasonal workers, were withdrawn a few years later.

This led to (1) large-scale out-migration from the region (both intermittent, for time-limited work in the primary resource boom economies of the North and West, involving oil and natural gas, as well as the aforementioned diamonds, and permanent, usually to urban areas; Beaudin and Savoie 1992; Beaudin 2005, 2006); (2) regional economy retooling, involving investment in tourism, arts, and culture; and (3) reorientation of fishing to a more capital-intensive crab fishery and development of niche products (like sea urchins) via aquaculture, both tightly connected to Japanese investment and consumption.

At the same time, the urban tertiary-sector economy boomed, in Canada as elsewhere. This communication-intensive sector contains proportionately more feminized jobs, thus destabilizing gender relations; in Canada it also privileges French-English bilingualism (and, in some cases, multilingualism), long the hallmark of francophone minority domination by English-speakers, and now suddenly a potential advantage in a competitive labor market. It also shifted demographic and symbolic weight to the very cities that have long been seen as dens of assimilation. Finally, it attracted migrants and immigrants into communities that up until recently had been able to sustain an image of homogeneity, that is, to reproduce the modernist discourse, albeit with increasing difficulty. The arrival of bilingual anglophones and of various kinds of migrants and immigrants calls the nature of the ethnolinguistic category into question, especially given the vociferous refusal of many of these people to silently accept exclusion or treatment as second-class group members.

A final thread in the saga of change concerns the changing role of the state. Canada took up the issue of a segmented population within the broad parameters of the welfare state, as it emerged after World War II. This was a crucial dimension for the legitimacy of the Canadian state at this time. Prior to World War II, the legitimacy of the Canadian state was framed within the discourse of the transformations of the British Empire, a kind of an attempt at reconciling independent states with the vestiges of colonialism. (The Queen of England remains Canada's head of state, and her image is still displayed on stamps, coins, and other quotidian accoutrements of the state.) The rise of modernist Quebec nationalism can be understood in the framework of the anticolonialist movements of the 1960s, with the Canadian state understood as representing the (now crumbling) British Empire.

The result was a reformulation of the legitimacy of the Canadian state toward a more modernist and nationalist form (hence the invention, in the early to mid-1960s, of the Canadian flag and national anthem; R. Breton 1984). But by this time it was too late to try for the uniformizing ideologies of nineteenth-century nationalism; francophones had gotten there first and had to somehow be kept within the new frame. (A dual state was never an option, partly due to the resistance of large minorities in each zone, and probably due in particular to that of the powerful English-speaking minority in Quebec.) The result was the Official Languages Act of 1968 (made law in 1969), the recognition of both French and English as languages of the Canadian state, and a commitment on the part of that state to facilitate life in each language across the territories under its jurisdiction and to facilitate individuals' access to French-English bilingualism.

One form this support took was the provision of funds to linguistic minority community groups (usually social and cultural voluntary associations, linked to—and sometimes coterminous with—political lobby groups) for activities aimed at the maintenance of their language, culture, and identity (remember, this is the logic of the welfare state). The francophone minorities in particular (poorer, less powerful than anglophones in Quebec) organized themselves at the community level to participate in this system (Farmer 1996). In the 1990s, however, the state's logic shifted, as did some of the communities' centers of concern, throwing the system out of balance. In the wake of systemic changes introduced in Britain and the United States, Canada also reoriented itself from a welfare state to a neoliberal regime, privatizing state-owned companies (which had been subject to regulations on use of French and English as official languages as long as they were government corporations); outsourcing social services to charitable organizations, which, like private companies, are not subject to official language regulations; cutting the welfare programs that had allowed for the sustainability of the seasonal labor in which many francophones were involved; and shifting support from cultural maintenance to profit-making.

The lobbying organizations of the institutionalized francophone community could not fail to notice the impact of radical economic change on the traditional bastions and of neoliberal government's refusal to continue to provide the subsidies that would have helped reduce the impact of the crisis across those regions generally (and specifically the impact on the possibilities for francophone community reproduction). Neoliberal policies focused on individual re-skilling initiatives (rather than, for example, welfare subsidies for areas dependent on seasonal activities, such as fishing) that did not take collective interests into account (indeed, they were specifically designed in ways that inherently removed collective concerns from consideration). They thus ran up against not only the institutionalized minority community's interest in its own survival, but also the state's interests in preserving the ideology of linguistic duality for its own legitimacy (as well as the interest in survival of the state's agencies for the implementation of its language policies). During the 1990s, this clash between neoliberal ideologies and practices, focusing on individuals' labor market skills and on welfarist collective identity politics, played itself out.

The upshot was something of a compromise: the state and institutionalized francophone community worked together to shift community interest toward a discourse of economic development as the major path to community self-determination, and the state agreed to sponsor structures that, rather than focusing on the employability of individuals, would target "community economic development." By 2003, the agencies and their funding base were solidly in place, and the discourse of "community economic development" had gained ascendancy over "survival" or "rights" or even "self-governance." The "community" in question, though, was the community constructed in the old political economy, and there is little room left to imagine new communities emerging out of the old one, or what the old one might look like under new conditions (let alone nothing like a "community" at all).

Chapter 6 will explore this process in some detail through an examination of the changing discourse and practices of the state, and their effect. Those effects will be brought out through one specific ethnographic case study. We did fieldwork off and on from 1997 to 2004 in a semi-rural area in central Ontario, one of the traditional bastions, and indeed an area frequently evoked in the construction of the idea of Franco-Ontarian identity. I will call it Lelac. (Most of the time I have given the actual names of places; I have avoided doing so when the place has such a small population. The data I use is so specific that I prefer to do what I can to ensure the anonymity of the participants.) The area, part of which was developed in the mid-1800s by farmers displaced in the population exodus from Quebec, encapsulates the discursive history and political economy of francophone Canada as I have rehearsed it here. At the time we arrived, the institutionalized forms of community were struggling with the changes in political and economic infrastructure I discussed above. After describing the local manifestations of the broader changes I have already described, I will take a closer look at how these struggles unfolded in the reorganization of the local community cultural center, in tandem with a recasting of its legitimizing discourse. We will see how the director, a full-time employee committed to a modernist view that was successful in the era of the welfare state, clashed with board members who believed that the future of the community lay in embracing the new neoliberal discourses of economic development. Through a careful analysis of practices and events over the course of a year or so, we will see how the interactional practices of such volunteer boards were mobilized to achieve a discursive shift, and with it, of course, institutional reorganization and a certain small but crucial change in personnel.

We will then take a look at how this change played out in the development of an activity representative of the discursive compromise between modernist and post-nationalist discourses: a community festival (which I will call Le Festival du Village). The community center had long organized festivals as part of its range of identity-maintenance activities, activities that had been eligible for funding under the old welfarist federal policies (under programs that of course no longer existed via agencies whose mandate had changed). It was not willing to give up the idea of such activities, and indeed was encouraged to rethink it by an emerging boom in such local festivals across the province, as part of the general expansion of activities in the tourism sector. In other words, such community festivals were being recast as profit-making tourist activities, and the commodity at the center of them was the very identity of the community. Community identity was reframed. Once thought of as an essential defining characteristic of a local manifestation of a nation (the traditionalist French Canadian nation was composed of a string of Lelacs across the country, and each Lelac constructed itself as a small part of a greater whole), it became a commodity in the national and, hopefully, international tourist industry, and a supposed trigger of local economic development. So: what does it mean to sell your identity?

We followed the meetings of the organizing committee for the year between the first edition of the festival in 2002 and its second edition in 2003, as well as attending the festival itself in 2002, 2003, and 2004, and following its representation in the local media. We also interviewed all the committee members, many of whom we already knew from our earlier fieldwork (this continuity of personnel is of course significant for understanding the reproduction of local elites in times of economic and political change). Again, the chapter will chart the discursive and interactional means through which the committee struggled to find a frame that would reconcile modernist and post-national discourses and to construct political and economic conditions that would allow their emerging discourse to take hold and crystallize institutionally, that is, to prove itself temporally and spatially durable.

This last piece of the story brings us to the post-national present. We see the ways in which the hegemonic discourse of the nation, whether in its traditionalist or modernist guise, is challenged by the globalized new economy. The image of the nation as a stable, homogeneous category is simultaneously fractured and destabilized. We are left with questions about how to reimagine ourselves, who will do the reimagining, and where that reimagining might happen.

The Festival du Village was of course only one example of the ways in which many Lelacs in traditional bastions across the country were attempting to enter the globalized new economy, and only one example of the ways in which that economy was reshaping the meaning of franco-phone identity, culture, and language practices in the traditional bastions as well as in some new spaces for the discursive construction of *la francité*, notably multilingual, multiethnic, cosmopolitan urban ones.

The kinds of performers who showed up at the festival, over the years we followed it, became more and more diverse, drawn from a larger and larger pool of potentially legitimate participants; notably, there was a major increase in the presence of indigenous communities (both the ones who currently live nearby and the descendants of those who used to but were displaced by colonial-era conflict) and of francophone immigrant groups from across the world, currently living in the Toronto area (which is about two hours away by car). So we see more complicated networks and farther-flung connections showing up in circumscribed local sites.

Chapter 7 will take up some of the ways in which the new focus on community economic development and the entry into the globalized tertiary sector have played out, through tensions between ethnonationally legiti-mated privileged markets and the reorganization of those markets in ways that commodify language and identity and diversify resources and networks. The chapter will look at the role of language in maintaining privileged access to regional markets in the new economy; the circulation of performers and artifacts, largely through the tourist industry; and the commodification of language skills in what has become known as the "language industry."

France (and other parts of francophone Europe) have emerged as an important consumer market for francophone Canadian identity com-modities, both those that are exported to France and those that involve French tourism (sometimes resulting in immigration) to Canada. This market was already developed for Quebec beginning in the 1970s, and while Quebec still dominates it, there is more and more interest in the novelty of other parts of francophone Canada, as the niche value of Que-bec becomes saturated. One dimension of new developments, then, is the commodification of identity and its circulation in globalized networks, focusing on the role of culture in the expanding tourist industry but also on the market for authentic cultural goods and performances. Language plays an important role in the authentication process, of course; for example, one of the ways you know you are buying an authentic artifact is that the person you buy from turns in a performance recognizable as culturally specific, and part of this performance is usually linguistic. This raises all kinds of questions about why some products (and performances) and not others are considered valuable-because-authentic, and about who decides what counts as cultural and linguistic authenticity (in particular, is it the consumer or the producer?).

Similar questions arise in the other emerging area, the language industry, which commodifies language as a product, not just as a mode of production. Call centers and translation are two areas of expanding activity, and they tend to draw on labor from the urban areas where bilingualism is highest. This raises a variety of contentious issues, since both sectors tend to have a normative idea of linguistic proficiency but prefer to draw from labor pools prepared to accept relatively poor working conditions. (Indeed, it is not coincidental that much of the labor is female and/or immigrant.) In addition, in the francophone Canadian context, most bilingualism is required for the Quebec market and is provided by francophones outside Quebec. This occasions struggles over who defines the linguistic market for French. Finally, much of the private sector at least tries to apply to communication the kinds of Taylorist management practices it used in the old economy, but language is difficult to manage in that way (Boutet 2001; Cameron 2001; Heller and Boutet 2006). What counts as linguistic proficiency, and how to measure it, thus becomes a site of tacit struggle.

While the knowledge economy and culture are receiving a great deal of attention from economic development planners, and traverse the transformations of francophone Canada in important ways, to study them requires some imagination. The usual focus on communities and institutions will only take us so far. This chapter will therefore also consider some of the ways in which we were obliged to follow the trajectories of actors and of goods. In particular, I will focus on the circulation between francophone Europe and Canada in the context of music festivals, Christmas markets, and commercial fairs in a variety of locales across France, Switzerland, and Belgium, involving goods and actors usually based in Quebec, Ontario, and New Brunswick. This case will draw our attention to the challenges of doing a post-national sociolinguistics.

Chapter 8 presents some of the ways in which these tensions are resolved, through various kinds of contestation or send-ups of the political militancy of the generation of the 1970s and 1980s, through forms of cultural production laced with irony and celebrating the ordinary, the obvious, and the workaday linguistic and cultural practices left out in the cold when militants struggle for high-valued resources. These new discourses will also allow me to reflect on what it means to do sociolinguistics in this kind of discursive space, when we are no longer asked to provide expert discourse but more often find ourselves in the center of tensions between post-national irony and the anxiety provoked by globalization.

The story of francophone Canada, like most stories of contemporary linguistic minorities, allows us some purchase on the reasons why we need to think about how to approach questions of language, identity, nation, and state, or questions of language and political economy, in ways that allow us to put front and center the kinds of social changes we are currently experiencing. More broadly, it allows us to think about what ethnography brings to classic social theory approaches to social categorization and social stratification, or, in other words, the ways in which social difference and social inequality are linked in ways shaped by historically contingent conditions. Finally, it allows for an understanding of how discursive shifts actually happen.

Table 1. Population by ethnic origin, Canada, 1901–1991

Year	British		French		Other		Total
	Number	%	Number	%	Number	%	
1901	3,063,195	57.0	1,649,371	30.0	658,749	12.3	5,371,315
1911	3,999,081	55.5	2,061,719	28.6	1,145,843	15.9	7,206,643
1921	4,868,738	55.4	2,452,743	27.9	1,466,468	16.7	8,787,949
1931	5,381,071	51.9	2,927,990	28.2	2,067,725	19.9	10,376,786
1941	5,715,904	49.7	3,483,038	30.3	2,307,713	20.0	11,506,655
1951	6,371,905	46.7	4,309,326	31.6	2,966,782	21.7	13,648,013
1961	7,996,669	43.8	5,540,346	30.4	4,701,232	25.8	18,238,247
1971	9,624,115	44.6	6,180,120	28.6	5,764,075	26.7	21,568,310
1981	9,674,250	39.7	6,984,215	28.7	7,684,725	31.6	24,343,190
1991	7,595,170	27.8	6,985,945	25.6	12,715,745	46.6	27,296,860

Sources: Statistics Canada; Lachapelle and Henripin 1980. Comparisons are difficult after 1971, and almost impossible after 2001, since multiple responses, different methods of calculating their distribution, and new categories (such as "Canadian," "Québecois," and "Acadian") appear. Numbers do not always add up because of methods of distribution of multiple responses and rounding.

Table 2. Population by mother tongue, Canada, 1931–2006

Year	English		French		Other		Total
	Number	%	Number	%	Number	%	
1931	5,914,402	57.0	2,832,298	27.3	1,630,086	15.7	10,376,786
1941	6,488,190	56.4	3,354,753	29.1	1,663,712	14.4	11,506,655
1951	7,923,481	58.0	4,066,529	29.8	1,658,003	12.1	13,648,013
1961	10,660,534	58.5	5,123,151	28.1	2,454,562	13.5	18, 238,247
1971	12,973,810	60.1	5,793,650	26.9	2,800,850	13.0	21,568,310
1981	14,962,785	61.4	6,249,100	25.7	2,900,205	12.0	24,343,190
1991	16,516,180	60.5	6,505,565	23.8	4,275,110	15.6	27,296,860
2001	17,521,880	59.1	6,782,320	22.9	5,334,845	18.0	29,639,035
2006	18,055,685	57.8	6,892,230	22.1	6,293,110	20.1	31,241,030

Sources: Statistics Canada; Lachapelle and Henripin 1980; Dallaire and Lachapelle 1990. Numbers do not always add up because of methods of distribution of multiple responses and rounding.

2

Critical Ethnographic Sociolinguistics

2.1 LABELING EXPERIENCE

The title of this chapter is rather grandiose, but the origins of the ideas in it are mundane. I just have happened to be in the right place at the right time: on the margins during a period of social conflict and social change. A lot has been said about marginal people as particularly useful sources of information about communities for social scientists; I suppose my peculiarity is having turned my position into my own work as a social scientist (my son claims it is just a flimsy excuse for my curiosity, but here I will try to make the case that it is more interesting and productive than that).

The city I grew up in, Montreal, is well-known for its ethnolinguistic fragmentation. The fault line between French (Catholic) and English (Protestant) is foundational to the organization of Canadian society, used as it is to legitimize social stratification, and nowhere is the policing of that boundary more evident than in the city that was long the financial center of Canada, where the stakes were high and social practices consequential. It has also long been one of the major places where the boundary is lived, that is, where constructing or contesting it was a matter of the social and linguistic practices of many people in the course of their daily lives.

Various accounts of life in Montreal at the end of the nineteenth century and through the first half of the twentieth reveal the daily work involved in maintaining the economic and social dominance of the anglophone demographic minority. Ethnolinguistic class stratification manifested itself in a number of ways: the francophone servants imported into anglophone houses, the English-speaking bourgeoisie developing (francophone-serviced) tourism in the francophone hinterland, the francophone industrial workers in factories owned and operated by anglophones.[1] For the most part, anglophones used monolingualism as a mode of domination; even if they actually spoke some version of French at some times, it was clear that to do so was not an obligation. For anglophones, monolingualism was normal; for francophones, it was a deficit.

Newcomers from outside this dichotomy, this oppositional quasi-moiety arrangement, needed to be fit in somehow. The Irish working class had both class and religion in common with the French, language in common with the English; the stories of the Irish show the complicated ways in which these ties and boundaries could be mobilized in different ways. While English Catholic institutions emerged, and with them a certain self-sufficiency of the Irish-Catholic population, it is also not difficult to find various kinds of boundary crossing, either linguistic or religious. Such boundary crossing is certainly evident in a long history of mixed marriages (French-English Catholic and Protestant-Catholic anglophone), although the complexities of how they were lived are less well-known. I did know one family that had both: two Irish Catholic sisters, one of whom married an anglophone Protestant and one of whom married a francophone Catholic. In the first family, the children were all raised as Catholic (and one at least in turn married a francophone); in the second, the francophone father, in ways consistent with prevailing notions of masculinity, gave his children French names but spoke very little in the predominantly English-speaking life of his home.

Jews like us were, and still are, more complicated (of course—that's why we're Jews, or, alternatively, that's what Jews are for), and paved the way for the precedent of using (always English-speaking) Protestant institutions (notably schools) as means of integration for all non-Catholics. However, frequenting such institutions entailed neither religious conversion nor ethnolinguistic assimilation; to this day, immigrants in Montreal tend to retain their language of origin to a greater extent than immigrant groups elsewhere in Canada (Lamarre and Dagenais 2003), a testimony to their construction of ethnic community solidarities and their exclusion from the anglophone and francophone groups whose struggle still dominates social life in the city.

Not marginal enough by its Jewishness, my own family was even marginal to the Jewish community and had a scattered post-Holocaust network of speakers of all kinds of languages, both French and English among them. It also had a (to my mind, healthy) post-Holocaust critique of discourses of identity and belonging, and an appreciation of how everyday life is tied to major forms of social change—we had plenty of stories of life in Berlin in the 1930s to drive that point home. Finally, we had little in the way of vested interest in either the anglophone or the francophone side of the story—after all, these were not our stories, as people never hesitated to remind us. We knew that in many ways both sides of a story could be deeply felt as true; my mother's family had long experienced the world as Germans, until they were excluded from that category and forced to look at the world as Jews. We nonetheless had a vested interest in paying close attention to what the stories were and to how things played out, since what happened would almost certainly be consequential for our own life conditions and life chances.

So when speaking English in the department store, as we had always done, didn't produce the normality it had used to, I was ready to understand the small moments of resistance to anglophone domination as linked in some important, albeit still mysterious, ways to the slogans of political parties working for better conditions for francophones, and to

the demonstrations, mailbox bombs, and other forms of public confrontation through which Montreal lived its own version of the 1960s. Language
choice was quite literally a weapon in the guerrilla war over who controlled public space and public institutions; its very deniability ("I was just
asking for gloves") was its strength—it was centrally about controlling
what counted as normal, about which relations of power would become
hegemonic, through being naturalized and rendered everyday, routine,
and inaccessible to consciousness.

Indeed, through the 1960s and 1970s, there was a tension between this
everyday street warfare and big-time capital-P Politics. Popular wisdom
had it that in order to make social change, the state had to act, and its
provisions would eventually trickle down to everyday life. But in the here
and now of taking buses and buying snacks, something else was going on,
something that sometimes seemed to anticipate public discourse, and at
other times seemed orthogonal to it; while we were taught to attend to
the evening news and the newspaper headlines as the reflections of reality,
reality seemed to be happening in direct experience.

In my own experience, this feeling was most present in the summer job
I had in the mid-1970s as a clerk in an outpatient clinic of a downtown
Montreal hospital.[2] In the francophone Catholic-anglophone Protestant
world of Montreal institutions, this one came down on the anglophone
Protestant side, although unlike its much more ethnolinguistically homogeneous sister institution less than a kilometer away, this one was of the
variety that immigrants oriented to; it also counted many francophones
both on staff and among its patients, for reasons having partly to do with
location, and partly to do with the prevailing ethnolinguistic hierarchy in
which by definition anglophone medicine was understood to be better
(more modern, more technologically up-to-date, better connected to the
global circulation of ideas) than francophone medicine (which, however,
might have been held superior in its ability to understand the patient and
his or her context).

The default language of the hospital had long been English, but by the
time I got there in the summer of 1974, it was no longer so clear what to
speak to whom. I quickly learned the techniques: smile at the person at
the counter and wait for them to choose a language; look at the name on
the hospital card, and guess; greet people in both languages, one after the
other (bonjour, hello?). Live with it when you guess wrong and the patient
gets angry. Those anxiety-filled (and yet somehow exhilarating) interactional moments taught me, though, that normality is constructed and
depends entirely on people accepting what Gumperz was already decon-
structing as context—a shared frame of reference in which people agree
on what will count for the purposes of the interaction as relevant and true
(Gumperz 1982). What I was witnessing was one key dimension of that
process of constructing context: the struggle over who was going to get to
define it. Awkward moments were about whose interests would prevail,
in a situation in which the playing field was never level.

Those awkward moments (the nonverbal communication, the close mutual inspection, the silence, the endless code-switching) were also crystallizations of the deeply political nature of everyday interaction. In those moments I came to learn—indeed, to live—the ways in which, on the one hand, relations of power don't happen unless we make them happen, and, on the other, nothing happens at all unless relations of power are sorted out.

For this reason, when I started learning the language of social science, the distinction between macro and micro made no sense to me. The distinction seemed to imply that there were two separate realms of existence—connected, to be sure, but nonetheless to be approached with different methods and understood on different terms. The empirical challenge was to figure out how they were connected. But for me, they were in some way the same thing; the challenge became to figure out how it came to pass that normalities came undone and got built up again, and how the multiple heres and nows of our existence were shaped by, and shaped in turn, more durable arrangements, some of which ended up codified in laws or built out of rock (and drywall) in a particular spot on a particular hillside.

The three dimensions of my chapter title—the critical, the ethnographic, and the sociolinguistic—are simply an attempt to label experience, albeit experience I turn into tools for describing, understanding, and explaining the role of language in constructing the relations of social difference and social inequality that shape our world. This chapter is devoted to the argument that sociolinguistics brings something important to the ability to describe and explain social change in general, and the movement toward the globalized new economy we are currently experiencing in particular, through its appreciation of the complex role of language in constructing the social organization of production and distribution of the various forms of symbolic and material resources essential to our lives and to our ability to make sense of the world around us.

2.2 CRITIQUE AND ONTOLOGY

The last phrase—describing, understanding, and explaining the relations of social difference and social inequality that shape our world—is what I understand critique to be. The question remains, however, of the ontological nature of what I think I am describing and explaining. Intimately connected to that question is one about who gets to ask what questions: that is, what is the nature of the knowledge we produce? Let me begin to address this through yet another story.

Several years ago, I taught a graduate seminar on qualitative methods, using a 2002 textbook written by Jennifer Mason. For me (and, for that matter, for Mason), it is not possible to discuss methods without reference to a specific research question. As a result, I encouraged discussion of what kinds of questions the students in the seminar were thinking of ask-ing in their research. One student, white and North American–born, began talking about questions raised for her when she taught English for two years at a high school in Japan. She wanted to understand better what she thought might be gendered patterns of educational streaming and success. A student from Africa suggested that to do so was inappropriate; first, how did she know that what she saw was gender inequality? Perhaps, the African student said, the Japanese understand it differently. Second, who was she to ask such questions of another society?—surely, if she was concerned about gender equity, she should begin at home. A few minutes later, a Native student, a member of the First Nations of Canada, raised his hand. Native communities, he said, are angry about how whites used their anthropological and linguistic research in First Nations communities to build their own careers on the basis of knowledge that served to legiti-mate the exploitation of First Nations peoples.

This experience was for me an instantiation of Foucault's idea that power and knowledge are the same thing (Foucault 1975). No knowledge can be constructed outside of the relations of power, which render certain kinds of people more likely to be defining the questions and doing the asking than others; the questions they ask will make sense to them because of their position in the world and the interests they have with respect to that world, and the knowledge they produce will serve to reinscribe those relations of power in ways of understanding which normalize them—that is, which render them invisible and hence less susceptible to critique and contestation. What does it mean, then, for me to ask the questions I ask, in terms of the power connected to the knowledge that I produce, given how I am positioned and position myself in the particular field I find compelling and important?

This can of course be a completely paralyzing question, one which, just to make matters worse, also forces us to essentialize ourselves and others, so we only ask questions that have someone else's stamp of approval, that no one finds threatening in any way, and that reinscribe accepted notions of social categories and existing dominant modes of inclusion and exclusion. I don't think a white North American woman can't ask ques-tions about gender relations in Japan; I do think she has to ask herself what it means that she should be able to do so, and should want to. I also think she has to use her position to find out what categories are relevant to the enterprise, and why that should be the case. If knowledge is power, does that mean we must renounce trying to understand things? My pref-erence lies in reflexive knowing, in constructing knowledge understand-ing fully that I am simultaneously—indeed, through the very act of doing that knowledge construction—engaging in relations of power, some dimensions of which I may be aware of, some of which I may discover as I go along, and some of which will forever escape me.

The idea of critique, then, requires me to think in terms of the pro-cesses that underlie the ways in which social difference is bound up in relations of inequality, or, to put it differently, in terms of what social categorization has to do with social stratification. It requires me to make some sense of what I think categorization and stratification are, as domains of inquiry.

My experience in Montreal led me to understand ethnolinguistic categories not as natural objects (although people treated them, and still treat them, that way), but as ideas that people struggle over, sometimes working hard to make them real (in the sense of having concrete and observable effects on people's lives, from influencing what food you eat and whom you can marry, to your morals and your beliefs about yourself and the world), and sometimes trying to redefine or even destroy them. The question, then, becomes one of trying to understand why certain categories are meaningful to people and in what ways, of how people work at reproducing or challenging them, and with what consequences, for whom. In Barth's terms, it means paying attention to boundary processes (Barth 1969). But it also means paying attention to the relationship between boundaries and the moral and semiotic orders that give them legitimacy.

In the same way, I understand inequality, or stratification, as a process rather than a fixed structure somehow outside of everyday life, but a process based on some fundamental material conditions for getting the resources necessary to survive and prosper. Why did people, do people still, invest so much energy in constructing categories or struggling against them? Why does it matter so much to be able to buy bus tickets in French, or to stick a Lost Cat sign up in English in a store window?

Here Bourdieu's ideas about markets are helpful (Bourdieu 1982): we can think of language as a form of capital which is unequally distributed and elements of which have different value in a market in which people participate. Indeed, they have to, because that is where the resources they need circulate. Stratification is about struggles over who controls the production and distribution of those resources, who controls the value attributed to them, and how those relations of power are legitimized. But any such market system is based on concrete bases of resource production and circulation: that is, on the nature and availability of those resources. In Canada, the resources of greatest value historically have been primary resources: furs and fish in the first instance, then lumber, wheat, and minerals, now also oil and gas. Extracting them, and in many instances processing and manufacturing them, became important in the twentieth century.

But even such resources are not simply about food and shelter. Beaver pelts were valuable because they were used to make gentlemen's hats; the houses and furniture made out of the lumber are not all identical, but imbued with all kinds of symbolic value meant to provide their owners with what Bourdieu (1979) calls a capital "of distinction," that is, a means to use symbolic capital to conduct struggles over prestige and status. As Gramsci (1971) also pointed out, sometimes the power of coercion is weaker than the power of consensus; in other words, while people certainly fought physical battles over the furs, fish, rocks, and trees, they were also, from the beginning of colonialism, interested in using symbolic power to build a consensus around arguments that justified why some groups deserved better to exercise that control, and why the others were better placed doing their bidding. The symbolic resource market was important both at the production and at the consumption end. And the categories of "French," "English," and "indigenous," which still inform the process of stratification in Canada today (although the exact labels used over time have changed in significant ways, I will use these for the purposes of this discussion), clearly date from the political economy of the colonial period, as the expanding capital of European monarchies led to the search for new sources of goods (especially of prestige goods: furs, jewels, precious metals, silk, spices) and for the labor to extract them, as well as to competition among them for those goods.

Language is involved in this process of organizing unequal relations of production and consumption in several ways. It is, as we have seen, central to the processes of categorization that are mobilized to organize and legitimize inequality: without the right kinds of linguistic capital, you simply do not get access to the spaces where other important resources are produced and circulated, and you do not get to have anything to say about what is valuable and what is not. Since linguistic socialization is deep, like other dimensions of socialization, linguistic performance is not always easily subject to conscious manipulation. This is, I think, what Bourdieu (1972) means when he talks about "habitus." He refers to permanent orientations toward how to interpret and act in the world that have key linguistic or, more broadly, communicative forms. While I am not so sure they are necessarily permanent, their usual normalization and embodiment makes them hard to undo and reshape, especially since most such performances are simultaneously imbued with substantive ideas about how a member of a particular category should act, in order to uphold the moral order. (For example, try as I might, I find it really difficult to sit on the subway with my knees spread apart, letting my body flow over past the metal strips in the bench which indicate where it should be contained; many of the men on the train sit just like that, and it doesn't seem hard for them at all.)

Acquiring the right ("legitimate," in Bourdieu's terms) kind of linguistic capital is hard on two counts: first you have to work your way into the spaces where that socialization can happen, and second you have to let yourself, and be allowed to, be resocialized in ways that allow for demonstrations of profound mastery. This is risky; you may never be accepted as a legitimate speaker, those who control the linguistic resource can always change the rules again, and those you leave behind may punish you for betraying them: Goldstein (1997) tells the story of a Portuguese-speaking factory worker in Toronto who learned enough English to be appointed supervisor, only to find it unbearable to give orders to her Portuguese-speaking former "sisters," still working on the assembly line.

Second, since language plays such an important role in boundary making and boundary maintenance, it becomes an important resource in and of itself. It is used as a basis for exchange against other resources, both material and symbolic (such as trust and confidence, which can lead to a job, and a paycheck, and food; or to friendship and someone to take care of your children when you are stuck on the highway in a traffic jam). It is also used as a basis for making distinctions, between those who master valued forms (again, Bourdieu's "legitimate language") and those who do not, either because they are simply removed from the source, or, more often, because their exclusion leads to active rejection or opposition and the embracing of contestatory forms; Bourdieu (1977) gives the example of how the French middle class, in tension because of its constant ambition to gain what the upper class has, speaks with a mouth that is closed and tight, while the working class mocks them by speaking slack-jawed, from the throat.

Third, using language to operate processes of inclusion and exclusion also legitimates those processes, or, more precisely, masks their real source by offering a morally legitimate reason for why they happen the way they do. However difficult it may be to switch the way we talk and write, our ideology of language still maintains that it is something we learn, not something we are born with. In a democratic society, we are not supposed to select people (for good grades in school, jobs, housing, and so on) on the basis of social categories (gender, race, ethnicity, religion, class, sexual orientation, disability, or anything else). We can select on the basis of talent and achievement, and learning language supposedly falls into that category. So we have invented the idea that some forms of language are good and some are not, and some of us are better at them and some are worse. The fact that some people master good forms of language and others do not can be understood as a problem of individual merit (talent, effort) rather than a problem of social inequality.

Language standardization and language teaching in schools and other educational institutions are central institutionalizations of this process (Bourdieu and Passeron 1977); they set up as objective and neutral facts what ought to count as valuable linguistic resources, and place the school in the center of access to that resource, while, as Bourdieu and Passeron argue, expecting students to come to school with the linguistic proficiencies the school claims to teach. Without those proficiencies, students are placed in lower streams, or, in some cases, other schools altogether, where what they learn leads them farther and farther away from what they would need in the higher, more prestigious streams (Heller and Martin-Jones 2001). For example, they are left learning how to fill out job applications, while their peers are learning how to critique high literature (Heller 2006). I explore in greater detail how this has played out in francophone Canada in chapter 5.

Finally, to return to the issue of stratification as process, language is involved in the varied ways in which categorization, selection, and legitimization occur. It is involved in those spaces where legitimizing ideologies are constructed (the very idea that language is a neutral object, outside of social construction, and that it can be pure or corrupted; that selection needs to be made on transparent, bureaucratic meritocratic bases; that some categories of people are "naturally" better at some kinds of things than others; and so on). It is involved in those moments of encounter when evaluation and selection happen ("key situations," in Gumperz's terms—that is, situations where something is clearly and fairly immediately at stake; Gumperz 1982). But it is also involved in encounters where seemingly nothing specific is at stake (no one's job, no admission to university, no visa, no refugee status) but parties are nonetheless, in their everyday lives, producing, reproducing, or challenging the social order which has them positioned in ways that result in their particular access to those particular material and symbolic resources. Why should I care if my client asked for her gloves in English? Because her English is better than mine for reasons that have to do not with the specificities of who we are as individuals, but because of how we are each positioned socially in a market that allows her to stay monolingual in English and for me to have to try, in vain, to speak it as well as she does.

Doing critique means discovering how those processes work in the specific sites and specific moments we attend to. It means getting underneath why people get excited about things in order to figure out what is at stake for them, and why (whether or not they are aware of it themselves). It means identifying what resources are circulating, what resources people are competing for, as well as the conditions that make them available and valuable; it means figuring out how their distribution is organized and how it works, and how people position themselves with respect to them; and it means figuring out what the consequences of these processes are, for whom, in terms of who gets to control access to resources and who gets to assign their value.

How we feel about what we find is a different matter. In my own experience, I usually find that things are complicated: that things work out pretty well for these people in some ways, but not so well in other ways, while other groups may have a different constellation of advantages and disadvantages. Or that some groups may be excluded, but that dealing with that exclusion is not a simple matter, as the case of the Toronto factory worker shows. There are always risks, and always things to be lost, and I believe we are better off taking those complexities into account before suggesting courses of action. So once I have described and explained, and figured out what a situation does or does not do for whom, the position I take on whether or not to do anything about it, and, if so, what, has to be informed by an appreciation of the conditions and complexities that are a necessary part of critique.

2.3 ETHNOGRAPHY

My goal of critique, and the reason I think of it as an important part of my own sociolinguistic work, requires getting a pretty good handle on how processes of categorization and stratification unfold in real time and in real life, while accepting that I can never be everywhere all the time, and that I necessarily have my own vantage point and my own set of questions to answer. I have been drawn to ethnography as a way to accomplish this.

My first training was actually in interactionist sociolinguistics, an experience that gave me a deep appreciation for the indeterminacy of social processes and the crucial role of agency. At the same time, several decades of close examination of social interaction have taught us that people draw on communicative resources in patterned ways, and their interactions often have predictable outcomes, but for reasons that may have less to do with the nature of the interactions themselves than with an understanding by participants that engaging in them might have positive outcomes. That is, in order to explain why interlocutors get the floor or not, whether their contributions are taken up by others or not, may have less to do with the nature of interaction than with the ways interaction simply structures engagement among participants who can variably mobilize resources or who are variably considered legitimate participants in the first place. That kind of explanation requires a broader field of inquiry.

At the same time, the kind of *longue durée* history practiced by Braudel (1958) is necessarily comprised of moments lived by individuals, without being simply the sum of those moments' parts. The challenge, then, is to capture both the ways in which things unfold in real time, and the ways in which they sediment into constraints that go far beyond the time and place of specific interactions. Giddens (1984), as mentioned in chapter 1, proposed thinking about this problem in terms of a process of *structuration*, in which the consequences of interactions link up to and shape other interactions across time and space, going beyond the control or knowledge of specific interlocutors. In his view, there is no such thing as a dichotomy between "macro" and "micro"; rather, there are observable processes that tie local forms of social action into durable, institutionalized frames that constrain what can happen along chains or flows of interactions: they constrain the distribution of resources, the mobility of social actors, the shape activities can take, and where and when they can unfold.

I try to operationalize this idea by thinking in terms of chasing down intersecting trajectories of goods, people, and discourses, through spaces where resources are produced and distributed and out of which the consequences of interactions can potentially be tracked. Most of this book is devoted to showing how I have tried to do this, in ways that are necessarily partial, since in any case I have had to give up any notion of completeness, whether of my own gaze or of the process I am trying to describe and explain from within the process itself. I have tended to privilege moments of social change, that is, moments when the routine is made strange and daily life reimagined, since those are moments when processes are most exposed and things made most explicit.

My starting point has also tended to be spaces where major resources are at stake: the private-sector work world in Quebec in the 1970s; schooling in francophone Ontario in the 1980s; francophone community associations and new-economy work sites in the 1990s and 2000s. In many ways each has led to the next in an organic way, so I have been able to trace processes over time in a way that is relatively new for our field. And each point of entry has led me from the local processes of categorization and stratification to the trajectories of actors, of the goods involved, and of the other spaces directly or indirectly involved, most notably the government agencies responsible for matters touching on francophone Canada as they work through major shifts from welfare to neoliberal modes of governance.

Ethnography with this orientation is obviously no longer the ethnography focused on specific institutions or communities that has been the hallmark of linguistic anthropology for many years. In recent years, anthropologists have tried to meet the challenge of capturing mobilities in order to be able to describe new phenomena we place under the general heading of "globalization," by which is generally meant an acceleration and expansion of the mobility of goods and people in the (globalized) new economy (Harvey 1989; Appadurai 1996; Burawoy et al. 2000; Castells 2000; Inda and Rosaldo 2002). Multisite ethnography is one proposal that attempts to capture how examining mobilities and linkages can help us get at the nature of contemporary social, economic and political processes (Marcus 1995), whether by tracking tuna from its source off the coast of Massachusetts to the sushi tables of Japan (Bestor 2001), or by following journalists on the international beat (Hannerz 2003). Critical Discourse Analysis has tried to follow the circulation of political and media discourses over time (Blackledge 2005; Fairclough 2006). And greater attention is being paid to the practices of supranational agencies and transnational NGOs (Gal 2007; Muehlmann and Duchêne 2007; Duchêne 2008). All of these seem like reasonable attempts to find a window into processes of concern to us, in ways that also allow us to concretely identify where to go when, whom to talk to, what to ask, and what all this has to do with the agencies that pay salaries or fund activities, with the institutions that train the actors, with how consumers learned to value the object of consumption, and with who gets what in the larger scheme of things.

Ethnography that focuses on processes and practices has to justify its points of entry, which from my perspective could be the trajectories of resources, of actors, or of discursive spaces where legitimizing ideologies are developed, contested, or reproduced in connection with the production and circulation of resources and of the regulation of access to them. It also needs to attend to the conditions that allow us to understand where those resources come from and why they have value. Finally, it needs to attend to how things unfold over time, which in some cases may mean tracing processes historically, and in others projecting them forward. In this book I have done parts of all of these forms of data organization (identification, collection, analysis), and each chapter discusses a slightly different kind of point of entry, and the modes of tracking of mobilities and consequences that it was possible and useful to attempt in each case, given the material and social constraints of being who I am, with the resources available to me, and asking the questions I ask in the ways that I ask them.

Since the stance I take always assumes that reality is socially constructed, my point of departure is that there is no "true" reality somewhere that we need to gain access to by somehow effacing ourselves. No matter what, by virtue of the questions we ask and how we ask them, we are there; we are better off trying to understand how people make sense of us and our activities than trying to pretend we can disappear.[3] We also need to build a relationship of trust. This certainly means, in my view, telling people what we are doing (and any North American ethical review board will insist on this). It also requires, and permits, the discovery of what the stakes are, and for whom, in the issues we are looking at. Finally, it allows us to understand the limits and possibilities related to our own social positions, which already illuminates what categories are meaningful to people and why.

While these considerations are vital points of departure, they are also part of an ongoing negotiation of relationships and understandings that will unfold throughout the ethnography and continue well beyond it. It is important, therefore, to be prepared to make mistakes and have to repair them, and to have to make difficult choices and understand their consequences. So if you want to enter a conversation, you need to find out where it is happening and who can take part, and you have to learn the rules of turn-taking and politeness that operate there.

At the same time, at its heart, ethnography is most focused on what happens; hence the notion many people have that it is primarily about description. As a first step, that is certainly true: the first ethnographic commitment is to discover what is going on (without assuming beforehand that we know). But it is important not to stop there; the second key dimension of data collection has to do with what will help us explain why things happen the way they do, in the circumstances in which they occur. Such an explanation then allows us to make predictions (about what might happen next, or what would happen in similar circumstances), and if we feel we need to, it would also allow us to figure out where and how to intervene to change things.

Explanatory data come in two varieties: the first concerns the (observable) context in which things happen, the ways in which social (including linguistic) practices are tied to particular conditions, particular resources, particular interests; the second connects practices to people's accounts of why they do what they do (recognizing that all accounts are just that: not transparent windows into the workings of intentionality but, rather, narratives that help us see how actors make sense of their world). Any ethnographic project needs to include data-gathering techniques that allow for an adequate description of the phenomena of interest, in the circumstances in which they occur, as well as for an adequate explanation of why they occur where they do, when they do. These techniques should also allow for the discovery of consequences: what difference does it make, and to whom, that things happen the way they do?

These ethnographic techniques can, and indeed should, be multiple: the more ways you have into apprehending and understanding something, the better off you are. Nonetheless, sometimes choices have to be made, and some techniques might make more sense than others under certain circumstances. For example, one research project I was involved in concerned the language practices and ideologies of francophone Canadian women married to anglophone men (Heller and Lévy 1994). The research budget was small, and it is difficult to find comfortable ways to spend time sharing the intimate lives of couples. As a result, we opted for an interview study, with questions inspired by the kinds of ethnographic concerns we might have liked to have been able to investigate more directly. The consequence, however, is that we had to treat our data as accounts, as discursive performances, with no way of verifying whether or not the practices reported bore any connection to practices we might have observed. The interest of the study ended up lying at least as much in how such women portrayed their bilingual lives as in how they may have lived them.

Further, some research techniques are more amenable than others to helping us interpret the data they generate. Questionnaires, for example, may help generate data for a large population, but it is generally difficult to be present when participants fill them out. As a result, we have little way of knowing how our participants interpret either the communicative act of filling out a questionnaire (for many people it is reminiscent of complying with state bureaucratic procedures of social control, and may be more or less welcome as a result; other people may have no frame for understanding it at all) or the questions themselves (for example, does "What language do you speak with your children?" mean what that language would be called if it were the standard version? or what I call it? Do you mean my biological children or the ones I take care of? and so on; see Foddy 1996 and Mason 2002 for related commentary). In addition, in order to be usable, questionnaires usually have to ask questions in ways that are more context-free and more closed than bilingual practices and ideologies usually are. They may not, therefore, be the best ways of getting at the complexity of the processes of categorization and stratification that interest us here.

Much ethnographic research on language, identity, and power uses a combination of observation (usually accompanied by audio- or videotape recording) and interviews, since so much of this work is devoted to spoken language. Some studies also pay attention to other forms of expression, whether in the form of written manifestations of social practices or in the form of artifacts (written or otherwise) relevant to contextualizing spoken and written language.

I have already made the point that interviews (and other forms of elicitation) provide you with accounts, accounts that are situated performances in and of themselves (see also Lafont 1977; Briggs 1986; Cicourel 1988). They are what a certain kind of person tells another certain kind of person, in certain ways, under certain conditions. In the mixed marriages study I referred to above, it was clear from a variety of traces (explicit comments, hesitations about using English, flagging of various kinds) that participants oriented to my colleague and to me as speakers of normed varieties of French, as well as to public discourses about the importance of the quality of French and about maintaining French as a minority language in Canada; we had to take all that into account in understanding what they had to say about things like the choices they made regarding languages of instruction for their children, or how they managed bilingualism at family gatherings. In the study I did in a French-language minority high school in the early 1990s (discussed in chapter 5), it was clear from the use of polite address forms ("Madame"), and of fully formed but rather short and hard-to-elicit sentences, that adolescent boys did not feel fully comfortable with me; interviews with them would produce impoverished accounts intended for the eyes of authority, so a male graduate student did them instead.

These are not arguments against using interviews; they are simply arguments that interviews need to be understood for what they are and analyzed accordingly, and that they will generate the most useful data when it is possible to understand what they mean to participants. This can mean that it makes more sense to do them once relationships have been established and once the researcher has a sense of what things mean to participants. This is particularly important in the kinds of research I discuss here, since it is so often the case that people are oriented toward norms which value certain kinds of language practices and linguistic forms over others; people may not want to display their linguistic resources, or even own up to possessing them, in what they perceive to be a communicative situation governed by dominant discourses on language that favor very specific performances and forms, usually monolingual standard-variety ones. Alternatively, they may be inclined to claim greater mastery of practices and forms than their behavior might actually warrant. When language is a particularly charged topic, traversed by all kinds of ideologies and values, these will emerge in any communicative situation one way or another, whether connected explicitly to research or not.

Having said that, interviews are indeed one very useful way to elicit people's accounts in two major areas. They are important for getting a sense of participants' life trajectories and social positioning, data that can help explain the interests they have in doing things certain ways (like buying gloves in French), or supporting or opposing certain things (such as bilingual education). They are also important sources of accounts, which allow glimpses into the beliefs and values and ideologies that inform what people do and why they do it. These can also then be juxtaposed to data about practices, or to other kinds of accounts, as ways of discovering coherences and contradictions and how people strategize around them.

Practices and accounts are usually approached through observation, the hallmark technique of ethnographic research. As I mentioned earlier, many people spend a lot of time worrying about how to be a fly on the wall, so as not to unduly influence people's behavior. My own view is that this is impossible, and not even desirable; we are present by virtue of the questions we ask and what we attend to, and we are best off taking our participation fully into account, and constructing our ethnographies as the stories we tell about things we want to argue are interesting and important. And we *can* take our participation into account: the data are always full of traces of how we are taken up, oriented to, and understood, information that in and of itself provides indexes of the norms, frames of reference, ideologies, positionings, and interests that are such important dimensions of sociolinguistic research.

Observation, then, is centrally a question of discovering where it is that things relevant to our concerns occur, and under what circumstances. It is about mapping out the landscape, and then investigating the interesting bits in greater detail. Some things can be recorded manually, in writing, by memory; some things require recording and more careful transcription, bearing in mind that like any other research technique, recording can be more or less familiar or more or less comfortable for different kinds of participants and is therefore probably best begun once participants know you and have a sense of what you are doing. Many participants, school-age children in particular, like to satisfy their curiosity about how the research process, and the machine, works; they need to appropriate it for themselves in order to be at ease.

There is some debate as to whether to ask participants to record themselves or whether to be present, and whether to audio- or video-record. I doubt there is a hard and fast rule to follow; rather, as usual, it will be a question of trade-offs and feasibility. Recorders do tend to get taken up as mechanical incarnations of the researcher; participants send you little messages whether or not you are there, some of which can be extremely interesting (Rampton 1995; Heller 2006). But sometimes the recorder will be invited into situations that your body may be excluded from. Not being there, though, does deprive you of contextual information, which can be so crucial to understanding language practices.

There are also trade-offs to ponder regarding audio and video recording. Both can be done with relatively small and mobile machines. Video recordings provide information about nonverbal communication, a dimension of interaction to which sociolinguistic research could surely attend to more usefully than it has in the past. At the same time, they do frame observation in rather constricted ways. They are easiest to use in institutionalized settings like classrooms or offices, or for regular meetings, where people do not move around much. But uninstitutionalized practices can be vitally important, and there field notes are usually the best means of recording them.

If one does use recordings, they should not be relied on alone. At a minimum, field notes help contextualize them, providing the information needed to make sense of interactions and to build up the basis for comparison or developmental analysis that allows us to link interactions to institutional and social processes and structures (Heller 2001a,b). They can also tie what is recorded to other kinds of material that may be physically co-present or linked in looser ways to the interactions being recorded (for example, texts used in the classroom, posters on the wall, flyers lying around the office, or the policy document being discussed at a meeting). And of course, much written material deserves analysis as a source of information in its own right; one can learn a great deal, for example, about the Canadian federal government's ideology of "linguistic duality" simply by inspecting the ways it displays that duality in the documents it produces.

Because ethnographic analysis relies heavily on the discovery of patterns of co-occurrences across time and space, it matters greatly what happens where and when, and with whose involvement. The different kinds of data generated by the techniques I have discussed are best used by linking them together, by discovering not only the various dimensions of what is happening, but also how these phenomena are produced and unfold over time, how they are linked across space, and, perhaps most importantly, what difference they make to whom. We can compare what people do (practices) to what they say (accounts); explain them in terms of the resources different kinds of people are able to mobilize; look at their consequences; and see what difference it makes to whom that things go the way they go.

Another dimension of ethnography that requires discussion is representation: how we tell the story we think the analysis of the data warrants. This is an issue of ideology of language and discourse, and a question of voice. Clearly, how we represent the linguistic resources and practices we wish to discuss says a lot about how we think of them; do we consider them to be elements of distinct and separate linguistic systems, are we most concerned with how speakers orient to them, do we want to portray them as varied elements of speakers' repertoires? Are we most concerned with form, or do we want to attach our representation to what we understand to be the discursive position adopted by speakers? What about how we represent written or nonverbal material? How do we represent the elements of context (spatial or temporal organization, for example) that we consider important to the analysis? Finally, how do we make it clear that, while we do want to make claims about how we understand speakers to orient themselves and to construct accounts, this is, in the end, a story we tell, one for which we must find our own voice and for which we must take our own responsibility? Our own accounts, our representations, are major turns at talk in an extended conversation. We have to think about them in terms of what we want to say and to whom, in terms of how what we say is likely to be understood, and in terms of what the potential consequences may be of the claims we want to make.

In this book, I have made a number of choices about representation which I need to make explicit here. The first, and most obvious, one is that I have chosen a textual narrative form. I do this partly for reasons of my own habitus, and partly because of the political economy of knowledge dissemination in contemporary academia (for example, which forms a publisher will accept as a product, and which forms are recognizable in the criteria the university uses to evaluate my work). I do it also partly for ontological reasons: the knowledge production I see myself to be doing is something I understand as a story I have to tell, a story that needs to take a form I think my audience will share with me sufficiently for a conversation to be possible, bearing in mind all the while that this is my voice, my idea of what is happening, and nobody else is to blame. I have also adjusted the storytelling to an audience that I imagine knows little about Canada in general, and less about the corners of it I will be discussing here.

I have had to make choices as well about when to present some transcription of data (whether of written text or oral action) and when to gloss, and how to present those bits of data I do choose to present (Bucholtz 2007), either because they are good examples of what I am trying to show, or they were key moments in the unfolding story, or they tell that story better than I could. Almost all of the data is in French, requiring difficult choices of both translation and representation. In many of the original transcriptions, our team made a series of choices that I have tried to respect here (Heller and Labrie 2003). These mainly involve balancing user-friendliness (for the most part, I will be interested in content and fairly untechnical aspects of form that can be easily represented with the technology available) with respect for the orality of much of the data (readers do tend to expect written representation to look like, well, writing). I also want readers to be able to retrieve aspects of speaker stance (signaled, for example, through repetition or hesitation or lengthy pauses, or laughter) that help interpret how speakers position themselves with respect to their interlocutors and to what they are saying, and I want also to be able to show co-construction of accounts or actions (with researchers or with each other). So I am aiming at transcriptions that are uncluttered but retain many elements of what was actually written or said.

This has resulted in the following choices:

1. I have usually presented my English translation first, with the original French transcription following, or side-by-side.

2. Both English and French quotations are in roman type, though isolated French words or phrases may be italicized. Where English was used in the original French text, it is italicized in the English translation.

3. I have tried to translate fairly closely to the text, where possible (fortunately the syntax of English is not wildly distinct from that of French), making lexical choices that reflect, to the best of my ability, my understanding of tone and style.

4. I have mainly transcribed in standard orthography, making exceptions when the nonstandard variant used is somehow relevant to the example (the most frequent one is *yes* versus *yeah* to translate *oui* versus *ouais*, since the contrast can signal agreement with propositional content versus communicative channel maintenance, as well as class or distance stance).

5. I have maintained back-channel cues (mhm, mmm) and hesitations or turn-holders (uh, um).

6. Where length is relevant, I signal it with a colon (a:nd).

7. Pauses and laughter are signaled in parentheses, as are any other comments on form or content.

8. Rather than punctuation, I use a single slash (/) to indicate a minor tone boundary and a double slash (//) to indicate a major boundary (what might be represented by a comma and a period in standard orthography).

9. I indicate brief (one- or two-syllable length) unintelligible stretches with (x), longer ones with (xx) or (xxx).

10. At times I have removed sections of a transcript or text for readability; this is signaled through an ellipsis within square brackets: [. . .]. If it is within one text paragraph or turn at talk, it is embedded in the transcription of the turn (xxxx [. . .] xxxxx). If it is between turns or paragraphs, it is interlinear:
     A: xxxxxxxx
     [. . .]
     B: xxxxxxxx

For all these concerns are connected to ethical issues. Doing research on the role of language on social categorization, and about the construction or contestation of boundaries that serve to regulate relations of power, is to participate in that process. Ethnography is one specific form of social action understood as research, but one that more obviously leads us to understanding that we are part of the picture. As researchers we enter and engage with that social world (differently if we are already part of it); but we also produce knowledge about those processes that has its own value in the discursive space we participate in. We therefore need to think about how to manage those relations of power and how we fit into them, so as to retain some control over how that knowledge is used, and to whose benefit or cost.

2.4 SOCIOLINGUISTICS

The kind of approach I am describing here opens sociolinguistics up to social questions, and more broadly to social theory, since the questions at its heart are fundamentally social questions: What is social difference? What is power? How do they work? However, sociology and sociocultural anthropology tend not to problematize language when they ask similar questions. Part of my point is to show that language is not a transparent window into social processes but, rather, a constitutive element of them, both in the ways that it forms part of the social practices that construct social reality, and in the ways it serves as a terrain for working out struggles that are fundamentally about other things. Language and culture typically serve to legitimize the ways in which the construction of social difference is embedded in, or rather mobilized for, the construction of relations of inequality. I learned that in the (usually) genteel street wars of 1960s Montreal, people were not exercised about language itself; they were worried about their jobs, their futures, and control over their own lives. Why the displacement? Because naturalizing ideologies of language and culture help naturalize relations of power, and make struggle safer.

In this view of language, it is necessary to pay attention to what people do with language, what they say about it, and what they believe its nature to be. Most of the story that will unfold over the next chapters is based on the fact that most Canadians believe language is a natural object and an autonomous system that needs to be respected. Without those beliefs, none of what people do makes much sense. Indeed, they tend to be so important in the struggle that people are prepared to do a fair amount of work to reproduce them, not only sending their children to learn a second or third language, but correcting themselves and each other in ordinary conversation, and reading the language columns of both French- and English-language media. They also usually believe that ethnolinguistic categories are based on immutable cultural differences among groups, although that idea is losing strength, especially in the extremely diverse urban areas. Still, most people accept the obviousness of categorical differences; they remain real, in the social sense of the word.

This leads to a rather Bakhtinian view of sociolinguistics (Bakhtin 1981; Pujolar 2001; Tsitsipis 2007), which privileges what actors do with linguistic resources that circulate through social spaces and social networks, both in terms of how mobilizing linguistic resources is part of other forms of social action, and in terms of how that contributes to the construction of linguistic ideologies (Schieffelin et al. 1998). Such a view allows for an emphasis on process and practice; to the extent to which some of the traditional areas of interest of the field, notably communities and identities, remain salient, we can see them as sedimented structures that are built, and can remain stable under the right conditions, with the right kind of daily interactional work put in to make them function. They emerge out of the analysis, rather than being a starting point. In that sense, sociolinguistics is resolutely a social science with a specific contribution to make, one that allows agency and structuration to be linked empirically.

2.5. CRITICAL ETHNOGRAPHIC SOCIOLINGUISTICS AND THE GLOBALIZED NEW ECONOMY: FROM WORKFORCE TO WORDFORCE

The approach I have outlined above is particularly helpful, I think, in this early-twenty-first-century period. The expansion of capital, and what Harvey (1989) refers to as "time-space compression" (that is, things happen faster over greater distances than they used to), have had an important effect on the place of language in economic activities. First, postwar economic expansion and the subsequent relocation of the primary and secondary sectors out of the First World has left space for the growth of the tertiary sector, based on services and information (Castells 2000). Unlike the primary and secondary sectors, where verbal communication is usually difficult and often highly regulated because it is seen to interfere with production, the tertiary sector is all about communication, to the point where language has become central not only as a work *process*, but also as a work *product* (Boutet 2008).

In 1978, when I was doing fieldwork in a factory, looking at language on the factory floor made no sense: the noise from the machines was so loud that most of the workers wore earplugs. At most, they used a small set of gestures to signal important things, like a backup on one part of the assembly line. If necessary, they went on a break to the glassed-in foreman's office, where they spoke in the only language they knew: French. These were typical working conditions for the francophone urban male working class at that time. About thirty years later, I was on a new kind of factory floor: a call center employing a hundred or so bilingual Acadian women. There, the noise of work was the hum of a hundred voices, speaking English and French, and the tapping of a hundred keyboards, again in both languages. What labor sells now is not its physical strength but, rather, its communicative capacity.

As the call center examples also illustrate, language has become central in an additional way: time-space compression, the growing importance of niche markets and the emergence of new consumer markets, the service economy, and global expansion of production also mean dealing with more linguistic variety than was necessary earlier. Earlier emphases on standardization that made sense in the days of national markets for industrial goods make less sense in the days of flexible work conditions, flexible employees, and localization, although much work on call centers shows that companies still try to use Taylorist (standardized and step-by-step) management practices, albeit with a greater amount of difficulty (Cameron 2001; Mirchandani 2004; Golati 2005; Sonntag 2006). This applies not only to the by now infamous use of scripts, but also to what is called "location masking," that is, attempts on the part of call center representatives to act like members of the same community as those they are calling, or else to be located in the local or regional branch office of a business being called, rather than its call center thousands of kilometers, and sometimes many time zones, away. This requires a complex linguistic repertoire, both in terms of what is usually thought of as "multilingualism" and in terms of what is frequently thought of as regional accents or varieties.

All of these developments challenge some of the ideas on which sociolinguistics was founded, notably that linguistic variability could be mapped in fairly predictable ways onto social position (age, gender, class, race) or community. Instead, we need to use it to shed light on the changing terrain of identity, nation, state, and capital in the contemporary period.

To get there, however, we need to step back a bit. The rest of this book looks at how ideologies of language, identity, nation, and state were set up in francophone Canada after the Second World War and how discourses of *la francité* were constructed, contested, and modified through the changes in the political economy of the late twentieth and early twenty-first centuries. We cannot understand what discursive and communicative resources are available to the social actors of today without an apprehension of why they circulate the way they do, and of who has an interest in fighting for them or against them. Today's concerns come out of a long history of francophone marginalization in Canadian political economy. But the story is not a straightforward one pitting oppressors against oppressed. Instead, it involves actors positioning themselves in complicated and often contradictory ways, and doing things that have had unforeseeable, and sometimes perverse, consequences.

In the next chapter, I will begin the story of the transformation of francophone Canada through a secret society that was an important space of production of traditionalist francophone nationalist discourse in the middle part of the twentieth century. Against the backdrop of its struggles with modernization, and its eventual demise, we will be able to chart the rise of modernist territorial state nationalism and, in turn, the challenges it has been meeting from the end of the twentieth century to today.

3

La foi, la race, la langue

Catholic Ethnonationalism in Francophone Canada
(1926–1965, with an Interjection from 2000)

3.1 DISCURSIVE AND INSTITUTIONAL CHANGE

In the spring of 1998, I went with several members of our team to do fieldwork in Welland. We were trying to understand the development of francophone institutions there, in the context of the community's working-class history. One evening, two members of the team, Normand Labrie and Carsten Quell, left a message for the rest of us, saying that they had been invited by someone they had interviewed that day to attend the monthly dinner for a francophone, men-only charitable and social club. They came back later that evening with secret handshakes and a story about L'Ordre de Jacques Cartier (hereafter OJC; also known as La Patente).

It is not surprising that it had not occurred to us to think about the order before; it was a male Catholic nationalist secret society that had disbanded in 1965. We were all too young, most of us too female, and many of us not French Canadian enough for it to have impinged on our consciousness in our own life experiences. Those of us who grew up in Canada had been taught the thesis of the radical rupture of the 1960s, when the so-called Quiet Revolution supposedly broke Quebec off from its conservative Catholic past and from the rest of francophone Canada. We had not expected to run into the conservative Catholic past in Welland, especially not in conjunction with contemporary institutions.

The door Carsten and Normand opened for us (and it had to be them; they were the only pair of men on the team working together that day) led to an exploration of the ways in which the institutions producing the traditionalist discourse of francophone Canada in fact laid the groundwork for the modernization that followed. That modernization was connected to a discursive shift (to the modernist nationalism we had grown up with) now becoming destabilized by the kinds of massive layoffs Welland's francophone industrial workers were then experiencing.

In this chapter I describe the OJC as a key space of production of traditionalist French Canadian nationalist discourse, drawing on secondary sources, archival work, and interviews with surviving members in Ontario and New Brunswick.[1] The changing political economy of the 1950s and 1960s made it difficult for the OJC to maintain the conservative, patriarchal, Catholic view of the nation, and the hierarchical, patriarchal, and secret mode of operation that accompanied and indeed incarnated that view. By educating and mobilizing a broad network of social actors and constructing discursive spaces for reinventing the nation, the OJC produced social actors with the resources necessary to take advantage of the new opportunities created by the postwar economic boom and the growth of the welfare state. Since the order's structure was too rigid to adapt, it was overtaken by new, public, state-oriented forms of mobilization, often organized by OJC members frustrated by their society's inability to seize the moment.

Hierarchy and rigidity, an asset in the prewar period, became a liability later on. Nonetheless, it laid the groundwork for the work of modernization undertaken by many of its own former members. That work produced new institutional structures and processes, legitimized by a new discourse, in ways that changed the life chances of French Canadians and produced a new middle class. The discursive shift with which we were familiar turned out to have been prepared by social processes and institutions we had consigned to the past. The discourse of reinvention of francophone Canada that many of us grew up with in the 1960s and 1970s turned out possibly to be less about the sudden emergence of social change and more about the re-entextualization of discursive formations (Silverstein and Urban 1996) and the restructuring of institutional forms. To begin my story, then, I start with the organization arguably most responsible for laying the foundations for the modernization of francophone Canada and the emergence of the discourse of the modern nation-state.

3.2 L'ORDRE DE JACQUES CARTIER

The OJC was a francophone male Catholic secret society founded in Ottawa in 1926. It disintegrated rapidly in the early years of the 1960s, finally closing down officially in 1965. It was named after the French explorer who claimed what is now Canada for the French king in 1534. The order used the name of his boat, L'Émérillon, as the title of its internal publication.

The OJC had been founded at the instigation of the parish priest in a town since incorporated into the city of Ottawa, in what was then one of the typical eastside working-class neighborhoods I described in chapter 1, and an important space for the development of francophone political consciousness in the twentieth century. The priest collaborated with parishioners who were frustrated civil servants angry at the ways their anglophone colleagues used their own secret societies (the Orange Order and the Freemasons) to block the career advancement of francophones like them. They represented a lay conservative nationalist elite and quickly recruited members across Ontario and into Quebec, where they found fellow communicants reacting to the recent recruiting success of the U.S.-based Knights of Columbus, a Catholic male benevolent society, largely because they did not trust English-speaking Americans to respect the interests of French Canadians (Trépanier 2007). Indeed, the OJC understood itself explicitly as "oligarchic" and select, in contrast to the Knights' broader appeal to the masses (Trépanier 2007: 135).

In the words of Gilbert Finn:

> The Ordre de Jacques Cartier [was] a francophone and Catholic association founded in the fall of 1926 in Ottawa by federal public servants of the national capital, victims of injustices and discrimination on the part of a majority of Anglophone bosses. Meeting together at the presbytery of Msgr. F.-X. Barrette in the parish of St-Charles, 14 people had then decided to found a secret order to defend the rights of French-Canadians [. . .] the Ordre had the mandate of bringing together and training activists to meet the needs of the religion and of the country.

> [L'Ordre de Jacques Cartier [était] une association francophone et catholique fondée à l'automne 1926 à Ottawa par des fonctionnaires fédéraux de la capitale nationale, victimes d'injustices et de discrimination de la part d'une majorité de patrons anglophones. Réunies au presbytère de Mgr F.-X. Barrette dans la paroisse Saint-Charles d'Ottawa, 14 personnes avaient alors décidé de fonder un ordre secret pour défendre les droits des Canadiens français [. . .] L'Ordre avait pour mandat de réunir et de former des militants pour les besoins de la religion et du pays.] (Finn 2000: 70)

The order had a hierarchical structure, modeled on that of the Catholic Church, with a Grande Chancellerie based in Ottawa. This group came to be composed of representatives of the four main regions with OJC membership: Ontario, Quebec, the Maritimes, and the West. These regions were divided into *commanderies régionales* (CRs: regional commands), which were in turn divided into local *commanderies*.

The OJC reached its height in the late 1950s. Accounts of the numbers vary. An exposé published by a former member in a national magazine in 1963 (Dubé 1963) gives a membership of 40,000, but this might reasonably be read as the total number of people who were ever members of the order. Bertrand (1998) gives a figure of 9,822 in 1953, and Laliberté (1983) of 11,257 in 1958, although National Archives (NA) material contains a memo from one member voicing concerns that the small increase over the 1950s does not account for the 10,000 members supposedly recruited during that decade.[2] It certainly appears that there were a large number of both recruits and defections from the late 1950s to about 1963; in any case, archival documents detailing the membership in 1963, when the OJC undertook a massive self-study, show a total membership of 11,272, most of whom were between thirty and fifty years old and had joined the order since 1953.

This document also shows that the OJC was divided at that time into sixty-four CRs: five in the Maritimes, one in Saskatchewan, one in Manitoba, twelve in Ontario, and forty-four in Quebec. There were 567 numbered *commanderies*, although, as Laliberté (1983) states, only 540 were accounted for in 1963. Membership of *commanderies* varied from five to seventy-two, although most were in the range of twenty to thirty members. Of these members, 243 were in the West (Manitoba and Saskatchewan), 732 in the Maritime provinces (New Brunswick and Nova Scotia), 1,755 in Ontario, and 8,542 in Quebec. The largest concentrations of members were in Quebec City (1,669), on the island of Montreal (1,062), and in Ottawa (652).

They included traditional members of the lay elite: professionals like doctors, notaries, educators, civil servants, and lawyers, including members, such as agronomists and journalists, whose work allowed them to travel around francophone areas (and who therefore served as good recruiters, as well as acting to funnel information up and down the order's strict hierarchy).[3] However, the 1963 survey (NA) also shows large numbers of members in commerce, manufacturing, and construction, and various records also show that broader ranges of professions, from butchers to carpenters to miners, were also represented.

Given that the French-mother-tongue population of Canada in 1961 was 5,123,151 (Statistics Canada), the OJC was clearly not a mass movement. It was, however, for a significant period of time one crucial space for production of discourse on what it meant to be French Canadian (perhaps the major one outside the Catholic Church), and it recruited and trained influential leaders whose effect remains with us today. The distribution of members between urban and rural areas, and the increasing concentration of members in Quebec, foreshadow tensions to come. We will examine those tensions as they were experienced by former members in rural areas of Ontario and New Brunswick.

3.3 A SECRET SOCIETY SEEN FROM BELOW

On a sunny morning in late August 2000, I drove north out of Toronto toward a region of lakes and forests where many people have summer homes and others spend weekend days, picnicking, boating, and swimming. I was headed for Lelac, a small town that had been settled in the middle of the nineteenth century by farmers from Quebec and still retains a strong sense of local identity connected to a broader sense of belonging to a francophone space far beyond the borders of this one municipality. I was to spend the afternoon with three gentlemen, Jacques, Clément, and Robert.[4] They were the surviving members of the local cell, or *commanderie*.[5] I had already encountered Jacques and Clément many times, in other guises, in the course of several years of fieldwork in that region; I had heard about Robert, although since his retirement he was less publicly active than the other two were. I had no idea how they would react to my request to talk about the local OJC *commanderie*, but as it turned out I needn't have worried.

Robert was a retired doctor; Jacques, a retired educator now running his own contracting company and building luxurious waterside homes for owners from as far away as Russia and Germany; Clément, a retired federal civil servant who had married into a locally well-established family and who owned both a house next to the presbytery on the town's main street and a waterside lodge established in the 1920s, when tourism in the region was just beginning. Jacques had brought with him a box full of OJC documents he had been keeping at home ever since the dissolution of the order. We spent the afternoon going over how the OJC had come into their lives, how it had shaped them, and how it suddenly left them, seemingly overnight.

As Jacques, Clément, and Robert related, the OJC was devoted to advancing the "cause" of francophones in North America, understood as a Catholic, French-speaking nation that was being politically and economically oppressed by the English. The work of the OJC was to be carried out by reliable (*fiable*) men, which generally meant that those men were practicing Catholics with families and occupied those white-collar jobs open to the Church-educated francophone elite. They were recruited one by one, in secret, usually at a university or through professional networks (although Jacques said he was recruited by his doctor, probably Robert). Here is their account of how their recruitment work began when the *commanderie* was set up in 1955. Jacques begins by reading from the minutes of an early meeting:

> JACQUES: Minutes / the meeting of the core group of Lelac July 23rd 1955
> MONICA: Mhm mhm
> ROBERT: Fifty-five / that's it I thought not later than fifty-five
> MONICA: Mhm
> JACQUES: The meeting is held such-and-such / we we see that it's kind of at the beginning they're trying to make lists of the francophones of the region things like that
>
> [JACQUES: Procès verbal / la réunion du noyau de Lelac le vingt-trois juillet mille neuf cent cinquante-cinq
> MONICA: Mhm mhm
> ROBERT: Cinquante-cinq / c'est ça que j'ai pensé pas plus tard que cinquante-cinq
> MONICA: Mhm mhm
> JACQUES: La réunion se tient telle chose / on on voit que c'est le un peu le tout début là ils essaient de faire des listes des francophones de la région des choses comme ça] (Group interview, Lelac, August 2000)

Once recruited and initiated in a secret ceremony, members were admonished to reveal their membership to no one—not to their wives, their children, their friends or colleagues or families. (Apparently not everyone kept this secret, at least not from their spouses. The 1963 survey [NA] revealed that only 1,322 of 4,482 respondents had kept their membership a secret from their wives.)

Their work was aimed at facilitating the access of francophones to the modern world: at creating its own economic base and achieving positions of power in important institutional spaces such as education, law, and health. But the entry into the power bases of the modern world was clearly meant to be tied to traditional values associated with Catholicism. As Jacques insisted: "Le but premier de l'Ordre c'était / catholicité / [. . .] francisation [. . .] c'e / c'était pas l'inverse" (The main goal of the order was / Catholicism / [. . .] francization [. . .] it / it wasn't the reverse).

What this meant in practical terms was that the order's hierarchy not only mimicked that of the Catholic Church, it was actually tied to it: each *commanderie* had its *aumônier*, who linked the work of the order to that of the Church. In turn, the Church lent its parish halls and pulpits to OJC members for their meetings, rituals, and other work. Henri, in New Brunswick, recounts how the church helped out when he was sent by the order to develop parish-based credit unions (*caisses populaires*). (This was the earliest economic campaign of the order. The establishment of credit unions was meant to allow francophones access to capital, especially since English-owned banks usually refused credit to francophones, and some English employers went so far as to use scrip rather than money to pay their francophone workers.) Henri was able to conduct his campaign through collaboration with parish priests who sent the women home after Mass and handed the pulpit over to Henri so that he could persuade the men to put their money in a *caisse populaire*:

> [. . .] We went there and we gave them flamboyant speeches to convince they them that that they would become bankers / and they would control their savings / create means for themselves of / credit well / if it weren't for the parish priests / because at that time the parish priest / people had a lot of confidence in the priest / they were all practicing / and uh in certain parishes the priest invited me on Sundays / uh instead of him giving the homily / after mass he would say to the men you are going to stay / it's Henri who is going to give you a / well he called it a sermon / so I would speak about savings / of (xx) they are almost (*laughs*) (xx) more virtuous than the one who / who wastes for uh drink and all kinds of things / so I would speak to them for about fifteen minutes / and then I would say the solution / to become virtuous is to become a member of the credit union (*laughs*)

> [[. . .]On allait là pis on leur faisait des discours flamboyants pour leur les convaincre que qu'ils allaient devenir des banquiers / pis ils allaient contrôler leurs épargnes / se créer des moyens de / de crédit ben / n'eut été des curés / parce qu'ils ce temps-là le curé / les gens avaient beaucoup confiance

dans le prêtre / ils étaient tous pratiquants / et euh dans certaines paroisses
là le curé m'invitait le dimanche / euh au lieu que ce soit lui qui fasse
l'homélie / après la messe il disait aux hommes vous allez rester / c'est Henri
qui va vous / donner un là il appelait ça un sermon / alors moi je parlais de
de l'épargne / du (xx) / ils sont presque (*rires*) (xx) plus vertueux que celui
qui / qui gaspille pour euh de la boisson pis toutes sortes de choses /
alors je leur parlais une quinzaine de minutes / pis là je disais la la solution /
pour devenir vertueux c'est de devenir membre de la caisse populaire
(*rires*)] (Interview, Caraquet, 1998)

But as Henri hastened to point out, the discourse of religious virtue
was also accompanied by a discourse of nationalism:

The / credit unions uh I would say we built them on patriotism [. . .] when
we made a speech / we say [to] them / we would speak to them not only
from the economic point of view / we would say if you are able to build a
strong economic system / you will also save the Acadian parishes / which
will disappear without that

[Les / caisses populaires euh je dirais qu'on les a bâties sur le patriotisme
[. . .] quand on faisait un discours là / on leur di / on leur parlait pas seulement du point de vue économique / on leur disait si vous êtes capables de
vous bâtir un système économique fort / vous allez également sauver les
paroisses acadiennes / qui sans ça vont disparaître] (Interview, Caraquet,
1998)

In addition to the credit union, OJC cells also established public
assembly groups, ranging from local "social clubs," devoted to charitable
works and socializing, to the national Association culturelle canadienne
(Canadian Cultural Association). These associations were understood as a
strategy of *extériorisation*, that is, a means for the OJC to have both gathering spaces for the larger francophone community, and therefore a space
for ideological reproduction and construction of solidarity, and also a
public cover for its activities. In many cases, after the order dissolved
those social clubs remained, as the public overcame secrecy as the main
mode of mobilization; this was the case both in Welland, where Normand
and Carsten were invited to what had remained an exclusively male club,
and in Lelac, which long ago had decided to admit women.

The OJC did not limit itself to working within francophone networks
to establish autonomous institutional spaces whenever possible; its other
major strategy, known as *noyautage* (introducing into a hostile environment agents responsible for taking it over, or at least influencing its direction), involved organizing the placement of members in key positions in
public institutions, such as school boards, where important resources were
controlled by a majority of anglophones. As Henri described it, their
objective was: "qu'on puisse rentrer nos hommes dans tous les domaines
hein. [. . .] Dès qu'il vient un poste / tu trouves ton gars et tu le pousses
hein" (that we could get our men in, in all the domains eh [. . .] As soon
as there is a position / you find your guy and you push him eh).

This strategy served many purposes. Jacques, Clément, and Robert talked about how they used it to place members on the local school board, which was dominated by the regional anglophone majority. Their goal was to fight for the use of French as a language of instruction. Long after the order was dissolved, that fight continued (see chapters 5 and 6; Sylvestre 1980; Heller 1994a). Indeed, in the late 1970s their community became known across francophone Canada for the ferocity of its fight to establish a French-language high school. In our conversation, Jacques and Clément insisted that none of that would have happened without the prior work of the OJC:

> JACQUES: Without without the order / the French high school in Baytown [pseudonym for the larger municipality nearby] there would not have been
> CLÉMENT?: There wouldn't even have been a bilingual school
> JACQUES: There wouldn't even have been a bilingual sch / that is the bilingual schools there wouldn't even have been French schools in the area // I think that it was on that score I do not think I am exaggerating at all. [. . .]

> [JACQUES: Sans sans l'Ordre là / l'école française secondaire à Baytown il n'y en aurait pas
> CLÉMENT?: Y aurait même plus d'école bilingue
> JACQUES: Y aurait même plus d'école bil / c'est-à-dire les écoles bilingues y aurait même pas des écoles françaises dans le milieu // je pense que ça a été là-dessus je ne pense pas d'exagérer du tout (Group interview, Lelac, August 2000)

In Welland, the OJC worked to get members elected to the town council. Indeed, when we were there in the mid-1990s, one such town councillor, an insurance agent by profession, was celebrating his third decade in office. At a higher political level, both Finn in his memoirs, and Henri in the interview he gave us, argued that the election of Louis-J. Robichaud in 1960 as the first Acadian premier (the prime minister of a Canadian province) of New Brunswick was due to the activities of planted agents of the OJC. Here is Henri's account:

> HENRI: So that was our strategy / and our strategy was the same in New Brunswick / for example I think we can say that Louis Robichaud / that was thanks to the Ordre de Jacques Cartier / but largely if he was elected because we had / cells in all the Acadian corners who worked like crazy to have
> MONICA: Mhm
> HENRI: An Acadian premier

> [HENRI: Alors c'était ça notre stratégie / pis notre stratégie était la même au Nouveau-Brunswick / par exemple je crois qu'on peut dire que Louis Robichaud / ç'a été grâce à l'Ordre de Jacques Cartier / mais grandement s'il a été élu parce qu'on avait des / des cellules dans tous les coins acadiens qui travaillaient comme des forcenés pour avoir

MONICA: Mhm
HENRI: Un premier ministre acadien] (Interview, Caraquet, 1998)

Clément, Jacques, Robert, and Henri, and of course Gilbert Finn, devoted greater or lesser parts of their adult lives to the Ordre de Jacques Cartier. For Finn, the insurance agent, it was a direct path to power. He played an important role in the election of Louis-J. Robichaud, who used his position as premier to open up avenues of social mobility for Acadians; Finn was rewarded with a position in the Grande Chancellerie as well as that of lieutenant-governor of New Brunswick. Henri remained influential across New Brunswick long after the order was dissolved. Jacques, Clément, and Robert retained their status in the region, whether or not anyone knew they had been members (or even knew about the existence of *La Patente*), and had long and distinguished careers (indeed, in Jacques's case, two). They all continue to support the idea of the importance of national solidarity, and of language as its distinctive feature and mode of functioning, in defending francophones against the multiple ways in which majority anglophones actively seek to exploit and marginalize them, or, at best, passively ignore their fate.

The specific stories of the OJC as seen from below, that is, through the eyes of members from the highest to the lowest ranks of the order, show both abiding conviction in the worth of that endeavor, and recognition that its time necessarily passed. In the next sections, I will first review the core of its ideology and then, through an account of its dissolution, explore the ways in which its very success created the conditions that allowed francophones to fully take part in the movements for enfranchisement and political transparency that were the hallmark of the 1960s. The fact that this required a repudiation of the order and, in many cases, of the Catholic Church, with which it was so closely entwined, was still a source of pain for many of the former members with whom we spoke. They convinced us that their work was foundational to the modernist political movements that came later, insofar as they showed what could be done in the way of accumulating and redistributing both economic and political resources (and using both in exchanges between the two spheres) on an ethnolinguistic basis (Heller 2003). As the OJC itself recognized:

> With the O. [the use of such abbreviations is widespread in OJC texts, presumably as part of its ways of maintaining secrecy] was founded a multitude of institutions or intermediary bodies which French Canada needed. It goes without saying that this took members away from us. But the effervescence which we see today in French Canada is a direct consequence of what we sowed.

> [Avec l'O., s'est fondée une multitude d'institutions ou de corps intermédiaires dont le Canada français avait besoin. Il va sans dire que ceci nous a enlevé des membres. Mais l'effervescence que nous connaissons actuellement au Canada français est une conséquence directe de ce que nous avons semé.] (Document from OJC archives: Secretary of the Commission of

Inquiry on the O., February 8, 1964, Archives du Centre de recherche Lionel-Groulx, P16/E, 113)

However, we could also see that their strict adherence to hierarchy, secrecy, and patriarchy proved fatal to the organization, albeit not to central aspects of its cause.

3.4 THE OJC, MODERNITY, AND TRADITIONAL IDEOLOGIES OF LANGUAGE AND IDENTITY

The hierarchically organized network of educated francophone Catholic males that was the OJC worked hard to increase their power in Canadian society by mobilizing ideologies of solitary nationalism and religious morality (the "patriotism" and "virtue" of which Henri speaks). They operated in the political sphere, by influencing the selection of candidates and working for their campaigns. They operated in the social sphere through social clubs and national associations devoted to fund-raising and community support, and they operated in the economic sphere by setting up credit unions run by and for francophones.

They did this as a small elite devoted to the welfare of their fellow francophones, and as patriarchs devoted to the welfare of their wives and children. They reproduced the traditional ideology of the francophone nation, based on religion, kinship networks, and attachment to the land, with the family the source of the biological reproduction of the monolingual, ethnically homogeneous nation. Men might have to be bilingual in order to carry out their work of *noyautage*; women and children could remain safely monolingual. The Church educated the children and recruited the best and the brightest to higher education in economics, medicine, law, agronomy, or theology (sometimes with the help of OJC-raised scholarships); indeed, higher education was where at least one of our participants (Robert) was recruited to the order itself. To be francophone was to seek to live in a monolingual world, whose social order was based on the precepts of Catholicism and whose moral universe also had Catholicism as its source. It meant working hard, retaining an attachment to the land and its resources even if one were living in a city, and holding fast to the Romantic ideal of the nation as residing in an organic ideal of culture, reproduced biologically by women (Heller 2007a; McLaughlin and Heller in press).

But despite the ways in which ethnic stratification set up moral oppositions in which the French were poor but virtuous, and the English rich but corrupted by an inappropriate interest in material wealth (Heller 1999, 2005a), their goal was not autarchy; their goal was to win access to spaces in mainstream society, but as a collective, and as francophones. They wanted investment capital for fishers and farmers; they wanted factory workers to be able to own a small house; they wanted the Church and the state to allow them to live freely as citizens in French: to go to

Church in French, to go to school in French, to plead a case in French, to get health care in French.

Noyautage worked fairly well, as we have seen, to make sure that candidates for political office at all levels were fielded and elected, in any case in those areas where demographic concentration coincided with electoral circumscriptions. There were, of course, francophones who disagreed with the OJC's conservatism, so the traditionalist ideology of the OJC was scarcely hegemonic; this tension certainly manifested itself politically between those who favored a more liberal-democratic ideology and the social and cultural conservatism represented by the order. (And those tensions were to play a central role in the order's demise.)

The economic sector was more difficult, since resources were in the hands of English-speakers, both Canadian and American, and sometimes British. The following text, published (internally, of course) by the OJC in 1958, shows how the situation appeared to the order at that time:

> French Canadians do not occupy the place they should in the economy of Quebec. This lack is even more marked in industry than in commerce. We are almost completely absent from heavy industry. And that is why we hardly profit from the industrialization of our province and from the value accorded to its natural wealth.

> [Les Canadiens français n'occupent pas la place qui leur revient dans l'économie du Québec. Cette carence est encore plus marquée dans l'industrie que dans le commerce. Nous sommes presque complètement absents de la grande industrie. Et c'est pourquoi nous ne profitons que médiocrement de l'industrialisation de notre province et de la mise en valeur de ses richesses naturelles.] (From CRCCF archives)

The OJC proposed to take action on this front by forming what it called La Compagnie Nationale de Gestion Inc. (the National Management Company Inc.):

> The National Management Company Inc. aims at remedying this gap to a certain degree by resolutely involving itself in midsize industry in order to eventually gain access to heavy industry.

> [La Compagnie Nationale de Gestion Inc. veut remédier à cette carence dans une certaine mesure en s'engageant résolument dans la moyenne industrie pour accéder éventuellement à la grande industrie.] (From CRCCF archives)

In other words, the order decided that the best way to get into the market was to buy small companies and use the profit from them to make investments in larger ones. However, it only managed to buy four or five companies (the exact number is not clear). They were unable to make a profit, and at least one was involved in complicated dealings that made newspaper headlines and did the order's reputation no good. The order's lack of familiarity with the workings of capital, and its somewhat unorthodox (for the private sector) ways of making decisions about investments and management, are likely elements in the explanation for the order's complete failure to use its experience in setting up credit unions to make a foray into big business (or even medium-sized business). This had two kinds of repercussions: first, and most immediately, it depleted the hard-won resource base of the OJC, which rested almost exclusively on membership fees. Second, it undermined the credibility of the order's leadership in this crucial domain: if francophones were attuned to anything in the postwar period, it was to the ways in which the industrial boom might pass them by in any shape other than jobs on the factory floor. They attended carefully to the order's capacity to achieve this goal.

During the period between the late 1950s and the 1965 dissolution, the OJC grappled with more than economic change. In the political sphere, actors more and more frequently sought to adopt the values of democratic transparency as a basis of legitimacy. The ACRLG archives we examined, for example, show that while Jacques Parizeau, later leader of the Parti Québécois (an independentist party that emerged out of the 1960s) and premier of Quebec, accepted an invitation to address the Montreal *commanderies* in the early 1960s, at about the same time his predecessor René Lévesque refused to do so, saying that whatever he had to say to the OJC he could say in public. In 1963, a former member published an exposé in a national magazine (Dubé 1963), and the order's existence (in some quarters possibly already an open secret) became public, obviously compromising its ability to function as a secret society.

Two Liberal premiers who were elected in 1960—Jean Lesage, of Quebec, and Louis-J. Robichaud (whom we have already met), of New Brunswick—used their mandates to strengthen the role of the welfare state, weakening the role of the Church, and working to establish regional and national markets in classic nation-state moves. There is reason to think that Lesage's "Achat chez nous!" (Buy at home!) campaign to establish a national consumer market was originally thought up within the OJC. We see evidence for this in a text called *Manifeste: Éléments d'une doctrine nationale pour les temps nouveaux* (*Manifesto: Elements of a National Doctrine for New Times*), developed by dissident Quebec members of the order in 1963. (I discuss this manifesto further below.) They democratized and expanded education, creating a newly educated francophone class with ambitions for social mobility, and absorbed the first wave into the newly expanded public service, thereby also cutting off an important avenue of recruitment for the order and the church.

This period also represents the emergence into the public sphere of the long-standing tension between spiritual and state-territorial ideologies of francophone nationalism; the increased importance of the state necessitated an inquiry into the criteria of inclusion for selection of the population that state was to regulate. Ethnonational, kin-based criteria fail to work well in liberal-democratic secular states, and this tension has emerged and grown in the forty-five years since Lesage and Robichaud were elected. As I will argue in the following chapters, it goes a long way toward explaining the increasing salience of language as a criterion of inclusion, since unlike ethnicity it can be learned, and unlike religion it is compatible with the idea of the secular state. But we have seen here the roots of the equation of language with ethnicity, and that association has proved durable.

Economic growth (notably the growth of the female-friendly service sector) also had as a consequence the inscription of women into the labor force, and their alliance with other marginalized groups in an identity politics of empowerment. The OJC archives show how difficult that problem was for the order (see McLaughlin and Heller in press for a more detailed discussion of the role of gender ideologies in the OJC). In 1963, faced with numerous murmurings of disquiet, the order asked a commission to examine what the future orientation of the OJC should be. Among the questions debated was the role of women.

> "Should we accept into the O. the wives of members, as regular members?" The commission is of the opinion that it should not!
>
> "Has the hour rung for a feminine movement analogous to the O. of Jacques Cartier?" The commission does not think the moment has come or is opportune. . . .
>
> [. . .] On the admission of women, this point should be studied on the basis of the individual merit of the women. Example: professional women, women who work.

> ["Doit-on recevoir dans l'O. les épouses des membres, à titre de membres réguliers?" La commission est d'avis que non!
>
> "L'heure d'une formation féminine analogue à l'O. de Jacques-Cartier a-t-elle sonné?" La commission ne croit pas le moment venu et opportun. . . .
>
> [. . .] Sur l'admission des femmes, ce point devrait être étudié en raison du mérite individuel des femmes. Exemple: les femmes professionnelles, les femmes qui travaillent.] (From CRCCF archives: Chancellier Guy Tremblay, Report of the Commission on the Orientation of the O., November 1, 1964)

As we can see, the commission took the position that only women who were in some sense honorary males (women who work) could be recruited into the order, although the 1963 survey results seemed to show the rank-and-file firmly against admitting women (2,682 to 981). Indeed, at the assembly following the deposition of the report however, the order voted only to allow men to tell their wives about their membership, and only their membership (which, as we have seen, most of them already knew about anyway):

> It is agreed that our members should confess to their spouses, under conjugal secret, their membership in the O., without however identifying their colleagues, describing the structures or revealing secret campaign plans.

> [Il est acquis que nos membres confessent à leurs épouses, sous secret conjugal, leur appartenance à l'O., sans pour autant énumérer leurs collègues, décrire les structures ou révéler les plans de campagne encore secret.] (From CRCCF archives: C3/5/9 COJC)

McLaughlin and Heller (in press) argue that the gendered ideology of the nation on which the order was based made it impossible for the order to remain faithful to its goals and adapt to the reshaping of gender roles at work in their society. A gendered division of labor in the reproduction of the nation, and a gendered view of that nation as something to be biologically reproduced by women and ideologically reproduced by primary socialization by mothers in the home and by female educators at school, could not simply adapt in bits and pieces. Newly educated young francophones, including women in the workforce or men married to them, had no interest in the OJC as a space to advance their interests. Membership plummeted, and with it the resource base of the order, already depleted by bad investments and poor business practices.

In a similar vein, a view of the nation as spiritual and, while attached to the land, not state territorial, could not simply be adapted to the new possibilities arising in the 1960s of using the apparatus of the state to increase francophone access to symbolic (mainly educational) and material capital. These two opposing views began to manifest themselves within the order itself in the early 1960s, as Quebec members, who represented the majority of members of the order, began to complain that their interests were not accorded sufficient weight in an organization based in Ottawa and run by a Grande Chancellerie in which Quebec, Ontario, and the Maritime provinces had equal say. Their attempts to define their own interests and their own terms (published as the manifesto in 1963, at the same time that the commission on the reorientation of the OJC was completing its work) were poorly received by the Grande Chancellerie, which saw evidence of subordination both in the organization of the consultations behind the manifesto and in the unauthorized publication of the text. Attempts to discipline the leaders of the movement backfired. At the OJC Assembly held in 1965, enough Quebec members withdrew their support that the order simply could not go on.

A few days after the assembly, the OJC leadership held a press conference to announce its existence (despite the magazine article of the previous year that had already revealed it). As we will see below, although the content was simply an announcement of the order's existence, in fact, it was the moment of the order's dissolution. Two of the highest-ranking members, one of them Gilbert Finn, were asked to distribute the holdings of the order and to archive its documentation.

3.5 THE DISSOLUTION AND ITS AFTERMATH

MONICA: When the note came from Ottawa to say that it was over, how
    did you / was it a surprise?
JACQUES: Was what?
ROBERT: It was a surprise

MONICA: Yeah

ROBERT: Oh yes we were (x) surprised that

JACQUES: Yes

ROBERT: We wondered what was going on / we were far from
Ottawa but

CLÉMENT: We got no explanation at all

MONICA: Just like that

JACQUES AND CLÉMENT: Yes (xx) [. . .] telegram

MONICA: But you decided to / telegram

JACQUES: Here text of an official press release

MONICA: Press release?

ROBERT: Oh we got a telegram

JACQUES: Yes yes it's a telegram / here it's the official press release / the
Ordre de Jacques Cartier reveals its status as a secret society

(*Jacques hands me the text*)

JACQUES: Here

MONICA: Press release

JACQUES: I have two copies // the Ordre de Jacques Cartier decided
yesterday to reveal its existence and its status as a secret society / that
is to make official what the general public already knew / it said it
existed for thirty-seven years and possessed since its foundation a
public federal charter // the order ended in this way a two-day
triannual uh triennial congress which it called exceptional in the sense
that it gathered together the largest number of regional and local
groups since they started holding such congresses / during most of the
proceedings in Quebec / five commissions sat simultaneously with the
charge of studying the future of French Canada / our means of
information / our severe problems in the area of (x) / our severe
problems in the area of the economy / you see that's where

MONICA: Ah yes

JACQUES: That's where the francophone community has always been
weak / in the economy / on each of these subjects says the Ordre de
Jacques Cartier in an official press release the delegates wished to
achieve a new awareness following the many changes which have
occurred in Canadian society in the past three years / they reaffirmed
their intention to continue to collaborate with the other organizations
institutions and structures which work in this way for the advancement
of French Canada / fine / we have only published this one release / as
for the other forms of information everyone is free to imagine their
source and to look at it

CLÉMENT: But that's it they decided to go public

MONICA: But

CLÉMENT: But it wasn't the dissol /

MONICA: [. . .] (xx) must have continued to exist since they say that

CLÉMENT: [. . .] But it wasn't the dissolution

MONICA: (xx) another congress in three years

JACQUES: No but it's that in when we met we decided to stay uh / we
would do nothing for a period of time [Note: It is difficult to translate
this utterance; in the original Jacques uses the impersonal third person
pronoun *on*, which could refer to the local cell or to the order as a

whole. I have chosen to translate this as "we" because Clément picks up Jacques's comments below in ways that clearly refer to the local cell]

MONICA: Ah

JACQUES: And we never met after that we remained inactive / of that domain / like like

CLÉMENT: Like a member [members?] of the club

JACQUES: As [a] member[s]?

CLÉMENT: As a cell not a cell / but like

JACQUES: As a *commanderie*

MONICA: And you all you just / you stopped

JACQUES: Well simply / we didn't even call each other / everything had stopped there

MONICA: Wow wow / it must have been a shock no?

JACQUES: A bit / well what is / you see the [social] club already had twenty-seven twenty-eight members

MONICA: Yeah

JACQUES: And they were almost all the same members so we continued a bit to *chi* [I am not sure what Jacques intended to say here; possibly *chialer*, to make noise in complaint about something]

CLÉMENT: Yes

JACQUES: To toss around ideas in that area

CLÉMENT: Yes

JACQUES: Because uh

(*Clément and Jacques talk at the same time; unintelligible*)

CLÉMENT: More openly you see it was no longer an organization

JACQUES: Very openly yes

MONICA: Did it make a difference to no longer be a secret society?

(*pause; laughter*)

ROBERT: The difference in my opinion is that you no longer had a directing leadership / as it is everyone pulls

JACQUES: Pulls in one direction and the other like the very beginning of the organization

ROBERT: So there was no longer any coordination despite all the coordinators we [they?] (xx) there is no continuous general leadership

MONICA: Mm

ROBERT: So it's (xx) three horses which pull in three different directions

[MONICA: Quand le la note est venue d'Ottawa pour dire que c'était fini comment vous avez / est-ce que c'était une surprise?

JACQUES: Est-ce que quoi?

ROBERT: C'était une surprise

MONICA: Ouais

ROBERT: Oh oui on était (x) surpris que

JACQUES: Oui

ROBERT: On se demandait qu'est-ce qui se passait / on était loin d'Ottawa mais

CLÉMENT: On n'a pas eu d'explication du tout

MONICA: Juste comme ça

JACQUES ET CLÉMENT: Oui (xx) [. . .] télégramme

MONICA: Mais vous avez décidé de / télégramme

JACQUES: Ici texte d'un communiqué de presse officiel

MONICA: Communiqué de presse?

ROBERT: Oh nous-autres on a reçu un télégramme

JACQUES: Oui oui c'est un télégramme / ici c'est le communiqué de presse officiel là / l'Ordre de Jacques Cartier révèle son caractère de société secrète

(*Il me passe le texte*)

JACQUES: Tiens

MONICA: Communiqué de presse

JACQUES: J'en ai deux copies // l'Ordre de Jacques Cartier a décidé hier de révéler son existence et son caractère de société secrète / c'est-à-dire de rendre officiel ce que la population en général savait déjà / il a dit exister depuis trente-sept ans et posséder depuis sa fondation une charte fédérale publique // l'Ordre a terminé ainsi un congrès triannuel euh triennal de deux jours qu'il a qualifié d'exceptionnel en ce sens qu'on y voyait réunie la plus forte délégation de groupes régionaux et locaux depuis que de semblables congrès se tiennent / durant la plus grande partie des assises / à Québec / cinq commissions ont siégé simultanément avec comme sujet respectif d'étudier l'avenir du Canada français / nos moyens d'information / nos grands problèmes dans le domaine de (xx) / nos grands problèmes dans le domaine de l'économie / tu vois c'est là que

MONICA: Ah oui

JACQUES: C'est là que la francophonie est a toujours resté faible / sur l'économie / sur chacun de ces sujets dit l'Ordre de Jacques Cartier dans un communiqué officiel les délégués ont voulu atteindre une nouvelle prise de conscience à la suite des changements nombreux survenus depuis trois ans dans la société canadienne / ils ont réaffirmé leur intention de continuer à collaborer avec les autres sociétés institutions et structures qui œuvrent ainsi pour l'avancement du Canada français / bon / nous n'avons émis que ce seul communiqué / quant aux autres informations libres à chacun d'en imaginer la source et le et de le regarder

CLÉMENT: Mais ça c'est ils avaient décidé de devenir public

MONICA: Mais

CLÉMENT: Mais c'était pas la dissol /

MONICA: [. . .] (xx) ont dû continuer à exister puisqu'ils disent que

CLÉMENT: [. . .] mais c'était pas la dissolution

MONICA: (xx) un autre congrès dans trois ans

JACQUES: Non mais c'est que dans lorsqu'on s'était réuni on on avait décidé qu'on restait euh / on ne ferait rien pour un certain bout de temps /

MONICA: Ah

JACQUES: Et on ne s'est jamais rencontré après on est resté à faire rien / de ce domaine là / comme comme

CLÉMENT: Comme membre du club

JACQUES: Comme membre

CLÉMENT: Comme cellule pas cellule / mais comme

JACQUES: Comme commanderie

CLÉMENT: Commanderie

MONICA: Et vous-autres vous avez juste / vous avez arrêté de

JACQUES: Ben simplement / on s'est même pas téléphoné / tout était arrêté là

MONICA: Wow wow / ça a dû avoir été un choc non?

JACQUES: Un peu oui / ben ce qui est / tu vois déjà le Club [social] avait déjà vingt-sept vingt-huit membres

MONICA: Ouais

JACQUES: Et c'était presque tous les mêmes membres alors on a continué un peu à chi

CLÉMENT: Oui

JACQUES: À brasser des idées dans ce domaine là

CLÉMENT: Oui

JACQUES: Parce que euh

(*Clément et Jacques parlent en même temps*)

CLÉMENT: Plus ouvertement tu vois ce n'était plus une société

JACQUES: Très ouvertement oui

MONICA: Est-ce que ça a fait une différence de ne plus être une société secrète?

(*pause, rires*)

ROBERT: La différence à mon avis c'est que tu n'a plus de tête dirigeante / comme c'est là chacun tire

JACQUES: Tire d'un bord et de l'autre comme le tout début de l'organisation

ROBERT: Alors il n'y a plus de coordination en dépit de tous les coordonnateurs qu'on (xx) il n'y a pas de direction générale suivie

MONICA: Mm

ROBERT: Alors c'est (xx) trois chevaux qui tirent dans trois directions différentes] (Group interview, Lelac, August 2000)

In their small Ontario town, as Jacques points out, the local cell was far from the action, indeed, so far as to be completely unaware of it. In his film *Les invasions barbares* (2003), Denys Arcand includes a scene in which a French representative of a high-end auction house is asked by a priest in Montreal to inspect the religious art he has collected from the churches that closed all over Quebec starting in the 1960s. He explains to her that one day in 1965, everyone just got up and walked out of their churches and have never gone back.

The same sense of surprise and bewilderment in the face of social change informs the reactions of my interlocutors that summer day in 2000. Having been part of a nation-wide movement one day, they found themselves returned to the immediate and the local the next. And although they quickly found (as the commission reported above) that the public spaces put into place by the order served just as well for their purposes as the secret ones, Robert (in his last comments in the quote) shows that he still has some nostalgia for a time when it was clearer what the line of action would be and they did not have to deal with "three horses pulling in three different directions." But past and present frequently collapse in their discourse, as they switch between the present and the past tenses (for example, Robert says in one utterance that "there was no longer any coordination" and "there is no continuous leadership"), as do the local and the national (notably in Jacques's frequent use of the ambiguous *on*), pointing to the ways in which the ideas and forms of action first experienced through the order are likely only one form of institutionalization in a longer chain reaching into both past and future and attaching the local to a wider discursive space.

In any case, as far as the OJC itself was concerned, the various horses present at the congress continued to pull in a variety of directions, some away from the OJC altogether and into the public domain, and others attempting to preserve something from within. Each main region of the OJC set up a successor organization to receive the OJC's divided resources and to redefine its work on a regional basis. In Quebec, two rival successor organizations battled it out for legitimacy. However, the last of them seems to have petered out in 1970, with few members and next to no resources. However, the principle of the divisions between Quebec, Acadie, and the francophone population of each province became the foundation for the open and democratic state and community organizations that emerged out of the wreckage, forming in Quebec and New Brunswick through the 1960s and in the rest of Canada from the early 1970s on.

As is usual for such moments of social change, accounts of what happened differ. Certainly the nationalist movements of the 1960s were predicated on ideas of social change in which the new was an essential legitimizing trope; the Catholic Church and secret societies like the OJC were characterized as conservative and repressive, interested mainly in maintaining a political economy that served their interests as elite representatives of a marginalized population. Certainly the OJC's attachment to hierarchy and patriarchy shows the centrality of those values to its vision of the nation. Nonetheless, its interest in modernity needs to be acknowledged, and indeed, as Jacques and Clément claimed, many of the institutions they set up stood the test of time, even as the overarching framework that imagined them in the first place disappeared, to be replaced by liberal-democratic state structures more centrally aimed at full modernization.

The manifesto developed beginning in 1963 by dissident Quebec-based OJC members provides us with a view of how the elite's view of modernization was developing. (I draw here on a version published in March 1965 by *Présence*, a publication of the group aiming to be the successor organization of the OJC in Quebec.) The cover features an outline map of Quebec, and the slogan "Québec: État national des Canadiens français," or "Quebec: National state of the French Canadians," thereby already announcing the linkage among concepts of ethnonational belonging (French Canadians, the national state) and state formation (with the map of territorially bounded Quebec and the use of the term "state").

While the mission statement retains the strong commitment to Catholicism characteristic of the order, the rest of the document focuses on constitutional, political, economic, educational, linguistic, and cultural concerns, in a twenty-one-page framework, followed by a fourteen-page "action programme" ("for progress and for the emancipation of Quebec"), and a forty-three-page detailing of social and economic priorities. The framework (the manifesto itself) is based on the idea that

> a nation cannot flourish if it does not have at least four indispensable instruments: complete internal autonomy, management of its economy, mastery of its language and culture and a set of political, social and administrative institutions which emerge naturally from the nation and which are in perfect harmony with its ideals and its needs.

> [une nation ne peut s'épanouir, si elle ne dispose pas au moins de quatre instruments indispensables: l'autonomie interne complète, la direction de son autonomie, la maîtrise de sa langue et de sa culture et un ensemble d'institutions politiques, sociales et administratives surgies naturellement de la nation et parfaitement accordées à ses idéaux et à ses besoins.] (*Présence*, 1965, p. 6)

The manifesto goes on to say that the best way for the French Canadian nation to acquire these instruments is by investing in the role of Quebec as French Canadian state. Furthermore, that state must be sovereign, so it will be necessary to find the possibility for that sovereignty in the "constitutional order" (p. 7). The state (of Quebec) must take a leading role in the "economic emancipation" of French Canada (p. 10), develop a democratic system of secondary and postsecondary education (pp. 30–32), and exert control over immigration policy (p. 24). The political, economic, and social objectives of development of a modern nation-state in Quebec, while it must be conducted in the framework of Christian religious values, must mainly be conducted through the development of a language policy. Indeed, it is revealing how much text is devoted to linguistic concerns, as opposed to the occasional, and rather marginal, statements of commitment to Catholicism. We see here a shift from older ideas about the nation, in which religion and race predominate, to newer ones that are more consistent with modern liberal democracies and foreground language as a means to build participation in the nation-state, on the grounds that anyone can learn a language, and hence are inclusive (although most of what I am about to show in the following chapters contradicts that claim, as Bourdieu and others have long argued).

The linguistic concerns (pp. 13–15) include the declaration of French as the (only) official language of Quebec; the use of French as the sole language of instruction in schools (and the introduction of second-language education only in high school); the privileging of French as the language of the workplace, and of French or bilingual public signage and federal government services; and concrete efforts to ensure the maintenance of the "quality" of French, especially in and through the education system. We see here discursive elements already circulating elsewhere in Quebec society, for example in the platforms of political parties, in the press, and in popular culture.

By 1963, the radical leftist Front de Libération du Québec (Quebec Liberation Front) had already begun its campaign by placing bombs in armories and mailboxes in a neighborhood of Montreal associated with the anglophone elite; the first independentist political party, the Rassemblement pour l'indépendence du Québec (RIN), had already been in existence for a year; the Office de la langue française was established by the provincial government to ensure the quality of the French language and to develop French terminology for the private-sector enterprises used to doing business in English; and singer-songwriters like Félix Leclerc and Gilles Vigneault were developing repertoires that would serve as means of political consciousness-raising for the next several decades. Even the federal government was beginning to respond, by creating that year a Royal Commission on Bilingualism and Biculturalism.

Nonetheless, the manifesto shows how the discourse established by the OJC—a discourse focused on collective action, on entry into and control over modern political and economic structures, and on language as the key terrain for achieving these goals—can be understood as more linked to than disconnected from what became the public discourse of modernist francophone nationalism. Indeed, former members of the OJC were directly involved in the États généraux du Canada français (Estates-General of French Canada), which was held in 1966 and aired in public many of the debates that had been conducted within the OJC up until its dissolution (Martel 1997). Many members turned their experience directly to advantage in public politics (Bernard Landry, a former premier of Quebec and leader of the independentist Parti Québécois, is a major example), while in other cases the *noyautage* of public institutions and the networks of associations established by the OJC continue to this day to serve as a basis for political mobilization. As Trépanier (2007) points out, Laliberté (1983: 364–367) even argues that the Parti Québécois was a direct product of the dissolution of the OJC.

The hierarchical, patriarchal, collective, and secret modes of operation were poorly adapted to using the tools of the democratic state to seize the moment. Prewar flirtations with fascism were no longer options for postwar nationalists, and the postwar economic boom and Western expansion allowed for the francophone bourgeoisie so carefully recruited and trained by the OJC to begin to think in terms of more radical redistributions of resources than had been imaginable earlier, and specifically the marrying of political and economic control. But this required political mobilization across classes, the entry of women into the workforce, and the development of expertise in technical and commercial fields.

The next two chapters provide accounts of what this modernization looked like, and what consequences it had for the ideology and practice of language and identity in francophone Canada from the 1970s to the 1990s. The first focuses on Quebec and its use of the apparatus of the state to complete the work of construction of a national market in the private sector. It is directly linked to the manifesto's call for French to serve as the language of work in Quebec, a move that was not formally legislated until 1977. The chapter is based on an ethnographic study I carried out with three assistants in a large manufacturing company in Montreal in 1978–1979, just at the time when the provincial government's legal provisions for making French the language of work were going into effect. As discursive tensions in the manifesto foreshadow, the *francisation* of the private sector was tied up with its *francophonisation*; that is, making French the language of work could not be untangled from privileging access of ethnonationally categorized francophones to jobs in the private sector. This ambiguity continues to pose a problem for the legitimacy of the Québécois state as a democratic and inclusive political arrangement.

The second (chapter 5) examines French-language minority schooling in Ontario in the 1980s and 1990s, a site of institutional nationalist territorialism faced with problems of inclusion and exclusion related to diversification of the population, and with the increasing commodification of language that marks the new economy—phenomena cast as "problems" only because of the ideological heritage of insistence on "autonomous" French Canadian institutions. As we saw in the text of the manifesto, this autonomy is linked discursively both to exclusive use of the French language and to control by people understood in an ethnonational sense to be French Canadian. Neither corresponded to reality, although the first proved ideologically more defensible than the second. Nonetheless, the gap between the regime of truth, both in the workplace and in schooling, turned out to be difficult to manage, in ways that help explain the further developments of the 1990s to the present day.

The OJC aimed at sending francophones into the modern world as francophones. The state took up that banner. In the next two chapters we will see what the modernizing movement was able to construct, and what unintended consequences their actions had.

4

Brewing Trouble

Language, the State, and Modernity in Industrial
Beer Production (Montreal, 1978–1980)

4.1 INVESTIGATING MODERNIZING NATIONALISM: SOCIOLINGUISTICS IN THE BREWERY

The modernizing project of Quebec had many elements, and social sciences were involved in quite a few of them. Demographers correlated census questions about language with levels of education, revenue, and other important quality-of-life indicators. Anthropologists and historians undertook the construction of the story of Quebec's traditions. Sociologists and political scientists debated the best forms for the new social institutions (such as regional high schools and community health care centers) and political structures that were developed. Linguists got involved in two things: demonstrating, through linguistic description, the regularity of the vernacular that served as an authenticating symbol of the Quiet Revolution, and the specificity of Québécois French; and developing standards and policies for the spread of French through all domains of Québécois life.[1]

By 1978, I had already decided that social, economic, and political change in Quebec was going to be easiest to understand by looking at the relationship between language practices in everyday life and the discourse and practices of the institutions regulating ethnonational and ethnoclass organization. Since Canadian academics were not asking that question, I went to study in the United States. I reached a stage in the program in which I was required to produce an empirical study in a subfield of linguistics different from my area of specialization.

This posed a problem, since I really didn't want to do anything different, until my mother suggested I look up her former graduate school classmate Pierre-Étienne Laporte. Laporte was then head of the research services of the Office de la langue française (OLF) and might be persuaded to let me do an internship. The OLF was set up in 1961, one year after the election of the Liberal government that ushered in the Quiet Revolution (Cholette 1993). Its role was (and still is) to help the state with the development and implementation of its language policy. This work was crucial, since the hallmark of the Quiet Revolution was a move away from religion and toward language as the key criterion of belonging to the Québécois nation, both because language was understood as democratic and because the political nationalist strategy required a break with the Catholic Church.

Not one to turn down an offer of free labor, Laporte agreed, and we worked out a plan for a study in the lexical semantics of automobile terminology. This worked for the OLF, since one of their long-standing concerns was the development of standardized technical terminology in French, especially for those areas where the field was dominated (usually because it was owned) by the British, Anglo-Canadian, or (most often) U.S. corporations that had introduced industrialization into Quebec (Hughes 1943). The Canadian automobile industry, run out of Detroit, was a prime example, one that touched just about everybody in Quebec. It was also particularly rich and complicated, not only because of the large numbers of parts in any car, but also because monolingual Québécois at some remove from the industry itself (simple drivers, say) had appropriated the terminological space using their own linguistic resources, resulting in a wide variety of forms drawing on both French and English. I started my internship at the office, then, by walking the streets of Montreal with blank line drawings of cars in my bag, asking mechanics, dealers, and service station attendants to add in the names of the parts indicated on the drawings.

Besides giving me an enormous appreciation of the numbers of different ways it is possible to say "hubcap" in Montreal (albeit without any explanation for why, of all the parts of a car, this one should be so particularly variable), this experience also raised some questions for me about what kinds of knowledge the OLF wanted, why, and what it might take to acquire it. Clearly, in order to effect a change in the way people talked about cars, the OLF needed to know what they said, but an overeducated young woman may not be the best person to find out what is going on in the nation's garages, and removing the terms from their context of use was unlikely to help. Certainly, at minimum the issue required thinking about what people might make of any suggestions coming from the office at all (as we discovered a few years later when the terminology bureau was laughed out of town for suggesting that people going to McDonald's should ask for *hambourgeois*).

These questions were haunting me as I completed the other part of my internship, which mainly involved "helping" (that is, being taught by) two researchers in Laporte's department, André Martin and Denise Daoust (these are their real names, as is Laporte's). They had been assigned research aimed at facilitating what had become the major portion of the OLF's role, the implementation of La Loi 101 (Bill 101), the Charter of the French Language, which had been passed by the Quebec government the previous year. This law, which is still in effect (and still controversial), takes up many of the points developed in the manifesto developed by the dissident members of the OJC. The two that concern us here are the declaration of French as the official language of Quebec and also as the language of the workplace. This element was understood to be central to the possibility of finally gaining some power in the private sector, where the value of French as a linguistic resource was understood to lie.

The law spells out what applies to what kinds of workplaces, and, like any other law, leaves open for a certain amount of interpretation exactly what it might mean for the language of the workplace to be French. Nevertheless, companies of a certain size had to meet certain criteria in order to obtain the *certificat de francisation* they needed to have in order to do business in Quebec.

These measurement and evaluation problems were part of what Denise and André had to tackle, and they did so largely through the use of survey methods. Questionnaires were distributed to employees in the large companies considered the highest priority, surveying language choice in various domains of workplace activity and asking questions about the kinds of technical terminology issues I was trying to address with my car-part sketch (Daoust-Blais and Martin 1981). These questionnaires were largely inspired by structural-functionalist work in the sociology of language and language planning of the 1960s and 1970s.[2] It was assumed that: (1) "francization" would take the form of extending the use of French to all "domains" of life at work (in the realm of what Kloss [1969] called *status planning*, or work on the use of a language in socially significant domains); (2) that French would be standardized, including removal of traces of contact with English (in the realm of Kloss's *corpus planning*, or work on linguistic form); and (3) both processes could be measured in a straightforward way by simply asking large numbers of people to self-report and quantifying the results.[3]

This bothered me. It seemed to me that to be asked those kinds of questions by the office at the same time that companies were being evaluated for their compliance with Bill 101 would incline people to be vigilant about how they filled out such questionnaires. I was also not sure how one might interpret the answers, given that, especially in large companies, people occupied different positions and were likely to have different opinions on the social changes occurring in their milieus. I discussed this with Denise one day after I had driven out of the city with her to collect completed questionnaires from a large U.S.-owned automobile manufacturing plant situated in a predominantly francophone town.

She asked me how I might do it differently and ended up offering to help me write a grant proposal to the OLF's funding program: in addition to conducting its own research, for a number of years the OLF funded independent academic research in areas relevant to its mandate. The project proposal I developed with Denise's help focused on an in-depth ethnographic study of a single workplace, through which, I argued, I could grasp what "francization" meant to workers, what practices it was connected to, and why people did and said what they did.

When the project was funded, Denise and André helped me find a site. We wanted a workplace that was relevant both to the formal criteria of Bill 101's priorities (mainly that it had over one hundred employees) and to the spirit of its concerns (namely that its management had historically been English-speaking and that it was tied to a North American, or at least pan-Canadian, market). André narrowed the possibilities down to two: a branch of an American company that manufactured lightbulbs, and an industrial brewery. In addition to the fact that, to be honest, I found beer more interesting than lightbulbs (for no good reason other than sheer prejudice), the brewery was located on a subway line, which was important since I had no car, and in any event, they agreed. The company had been founded in late eighteenth century by a Briton whose family still owned and ran it. It had breweries across the country, and part of its head office was located in Montreal, with the other part in Toronto. The Montreal plant manufactured, bottled, and delivered beer in the Quebec market zone.

The OLF insisted that I add three people to the research team, so I recruited three graduate students, one from the Université de Montréal (Luc Ostiguy) and two from the Université d'Aix-Marseilles on an exchange program with the Université de Montréal (Laurette Lévy and Jean-Paul Bartholomot). We agreed on a six-month fieldwork period (August–December 1979; I returned in July 1980 to do some follow-up fieldwork for about a month).

Luc and Jean-Paul were easy to place; in a company with an almost exclusively masculine workforce there was lots of room for them. They ended up spending most of their time in the delivery section, working in various capacities, from loading cases of beer to riding in delivery trucks. Laurette and I were more of a problem, being women. Laurette could type, so she was placed in secretarial services, also in the delivery sector. I was placed in the quality control laboratory, where there were two female lab technicians, Hélène and Maryse.

In addition to having a place for a woman, the quality control lab presented a number of advantages. First, it allowed me to follow Hélène or Maryse, whichever of them was assigned to the daily round of collecting samples. This took us all the way through the manufacturing and bottling sectors and allowed me to get a good idea of who worked there and how they worked. Second, unlike most other workspaces in the plant, this one allowed for a fair amount of coming and going (employees were not stuck to their desks, or even to their lab benches), and it was quiet, so employees from other sectors sometimes came by to chat during their coffee breaks or lunch, or hung around for a few minutes if they had come on official business (for example, to pick up a lab result; this was an era before email). Finally, it turned out to have many of the kinds of employees whose position, I would discover, were crucial to understanding the francization of the workplace: an older anglophone lab technician (Maurice) who was actually of Acadian origin; his young anglophone Ontarian supervisor (Paul), who, married to a francophone, had requested a transfer to the Montreal office in order to allow his wife to live in French and in order to improve his own; his young francophone Québécois counterpart (Marcel), who had only recently been hired to replace the older anglophone who had retired; and three lab technicians, Hélène, Maryse, and Pierre. Two other employees were frequently around: Charles, a young Franco-Ontarian, and Emil, an older employee of Eastern European origin (one of the handful in the company who were born outside Canada), who used to work in production but was moved off the lines because of an injury.

In addition to simply observing every day, I learned what I could about the history of the company, about its current network and market, and about how it was regulated by the state. This data was made available to me mainly through internal company documents, although some published studies of the company did exist. In the latter half of my time there, I interviewed employees who, based on what I had seen and on what people told me, occupied revealing positions with respect to the francization process, and tape-recorded ongoing everyday interactions in some key sites (that is, key sites where it was possible to tape-record, given that a large proportion of the work done in the company involved extremely noisy heavy machinery). I will discuss the rationale behind my choices further below.

In the following two sections I describe the history of the brewery as it pertains to understanding francization; not just for this company, but for Quebec as a whole. I will also sketch out how this history helps us understand how certain kinds of employees ended up working there, and how their trajectories shaped their understanding of, and investment in, language practices and ideologies that shaped what the process of francization actually turned out to be: a process inextricable from the entry into the management level of francophones (as members of an ethnonational group) who had been trained in the new science and technology programs developed in the democratized education system that Quebec put into place in the course of the 1960s and 1970s.

The last part of the chapter examines more closely the patterns of language choice in daily interaction in the workplace. These patterns served to advance the interests of the new young technical francophone management cohort, while avoiding either the open conflict with anglophones that might otherwise have occurred, or the alienation of the other two groups of francophones: older francophones used to working under anglophone supervisors, and the francophone workers in whose name the francization process was being undertaken but who were unlikely ever to profit from it themselves. Much of the work of interaction was devoted to the quiet achievement of both normalization and normativization, in the service of the legitimization of francophone control over the regional market of Quebec, as anglophones turned increasingly to the broader English-dominated markets of North America.

4.2 THE ETHNOLINGUISTIC ORGANIZATION OF EXPANSION AND TECHNOLOGIZATION

I first got a hint that the history of the company was important when I was told that the quality control lab in which I was working had been founded in 1960, over 150 years after the founding of the company. Accounts of the company's development showed that this was neither a coincidence nor neutral. Indeed, until the 1950s, even through the industrial transformation of brewing (and of this brewery) a decade or so earlier, the company thought of brewing as an art. Brewers thought of themselves as artisans, and they were trained on the job by "master brewers," that is, people who had mastered that art.

In the 1950s, however, at least in Canada, the entire food-production and food-processing industry began to be reorganized on a larger scale, and understood through the lens of science rather than art. (This shift had a major impact, as we will see in chapter 6, on Lelac as a farming community; by the 1960s it was no longer able to support the family-owned mixed lumber and subsistence farm economy that had been the basis of reproduction of francophone identity there. As we will see in the next chapter, it also had an impact on large urban centers like Toronto, to which the increasingly displaced rural population headed.) In the brewery, we see this transformation in a considerable investment over the 1960s in new equipment whose use was linked to a scientific understanding of brewing, and, of course, the opening of the quality control laboratory itself. The lab's job was, and remains, the use of scientific methods to assure that the beer produced would uniformly and reliably have certain characteristics.

This shift had, of course, a major impact on hiring. First, the automatization involved in the process led to a hiring freeze in the Montreal plant from 1955 to 1970. Second, the mode of recruitment changed. Before the freeze, people were largely recruited through word of mouth, through family and neighborhood connections (the traces of this were still visible, actually, in the social networks of the men on the lowest rungs of the ladder, those who worked on the factory floor). Afterward, a human resources department was put in place, staffed largely by francophones with degrees in the field from the new francophone postsecondary institutions established in the 1960s and 1970s. They used their institutional networks to recruit employees with formal training in the natural sciences, engineering, or management. Thus the 1970s saw the arrival of a cohort of young francophones who had technical training (like Marcel, Hélène, and Maryse, as well as Albert, whom we will meet later) and whose personal histories usually revealed that they were in the first generation of their rural families to move to Montreal and to get a postsecondary education. Many of them filled management positions that older employees with more seniority would earlier have had access to when the sector head retired or was transferred.

A second important shift, occurring at around the same time, was the company's expansion across Canada and even beyond its borders (indeed, for a while, beyond brewing). This expansion, again, was not confined to this company but fits an overall pattern related to the postwar economic boom (Clift and Arnopoulos 1979). The brewery had long been based in Montreal, and served its expanding market from there until the improvement in the communications infrastructure and increased wealth made the opening of branch plants a more attractive option. Experienced managers were needed to oversee these operations; these were, of course, all anglophones based in the Montreal plant. The sector heads in the quality control lab and in technical services, for example, both had headed west before our fieldwork started. In addition, given the hiring freeze, many managers were reaching retirement age by the mid-1970s. Thus management positions were opening up through transfer and retirement at exactly the moment when the first generation of technically trained francophones were entering the labor market.

The final shift is linked to the context in which the westward expansion of the brewery was occurring: the financial center of Canada was moving from Montreal to Toronto, in a long process that began in the postwar boom and accelerated rapidly in the 1970s. Factors included the opening of a maritime transport route linking Toronto directly to the Atlantic, the development of metals industries in southern Ontario through wartime arms manufacturing, and some specific investment strategies on the part of the Toronto elite, out to wrest control away from Montreal (Clift and Arnopoulos 1979). This shift forced anglophone Montreal business to orient itself to a greater extent to Toronto and began drawing head offices there. As this opened up space in the Quebec market for francophone entrepreneurs and financiers (Fraser 1987), anglophones began to increase their withdrawal from a market in which they were at a disadvantage. The final (and apparently fairly stable) result has been the creation of a regional market run largely in French internally, by francophones, wherein an articulation with national and international markets is ensured by increasingly bilingual anglophones who invested in learning French, and by francophones who learn their English through travel or temporary transfers to English-dominant parts of North America (and this often includes a stint at the head office in Toronto or Calgary). Quebec does, after all, represent a significant portion of the Canadian market.

The brewery itself was symbolically attached to Montreal, and moving its head office out of Quebec would have done irreparable damage to its important market share there. Its solution was to divide its head office into two and send the financial sector to Toronto. However, even in Montreal, the head office remained quite distinct from the plant; they were located in separate buildings, with little traffic between them. Indeed, I had no access to that other building, although I can say that most staff members there were anglophone.

The cumulative effect of these changes was to open up space in the brewery for francophone managers, to run the Montreal plant and serve the Quebec market. By 1978, while francophones were still overwhelmingly present at the lowest levels of the hierarchy in the production, distribution, and marketing sectors, they had made significant inroads at the two highest levels in those same sectors (they also dominated the human resources sector, but were not yet as dominant in the administration sector). In the next section, we will take a closer look at what this meant for employees with different positions in the brewery, and different trajectories leading them there (or away).

4.3 POSITION AND INTEREST IN THE FRANCIZATION OF THE BREWERY

I received a quick introduction to the politics of language and ethnicity in the brewery, as well as a confirmation of my assumptions about the social significance of the OLF, a few days after I started showing up for work in the lab. I had been assigned to the quality control section of the lab, with Marcel, Hélène, Maryse, and Pierre. But we had constant contact with Maurice and Paul, whose biochemical laboratory was linked to ours by a short, wide corridor (in addition, Maurice and Paul had to pass through the quality control lab to go in and out, and they often had coffee breaks with everyone else in the little storage room off the quality control lab which was furnished with a small table and a few chairs).

One day after lunch, Maurice asked me (in English) to come down to his end of the lab for a chat. We sat in his workspace, off the main lab and separated from it by a glass wall and a door (which we left open; in any case, Paul was not around). He said that I had been the subject of discussion among the people with whom he often had lunch, mostly men around his age, most of them English-speaking. They were wondering what I was really doing there, whether perhaps my job was to secretly evaluate the extent to which the brewery was in conformity with Bill 101. They were more or less worried about whether I was a spy for the office.

I no longer recall exactly what I said, partly, I am sure, because I was concerned and upset and trying to stay calm and not make more of a mess of things; I know I told him about the fact that this work was for my PhD thesis, a public document; about my studies in the United States; about what I wanted to know; and about how the OLF figured in to the picture. We spoke in English, he understood more about my rather complicated life history, he could certainly make sense out of what it meant to be a student, and that encounter began a friendly relationship.

On the other hand, some francophones had expectations of me I was not able to fulfill, such as an active involvement in advancing efforts at francization, or direct intervention with the OLF on issues that concerned them. Exactly the things that reassured anglophones (my unclassifiable name, my studies in the United States, my ease with English) were sources of worry to them and required the same degree of demystification and personalization. I had to work hard to gain credibility with both groups and to retain ease of access to relationships with members of both groups. But that experience also taught me exactly how the boundary worked and what the categorization was all about. Being enough of a Montrealer and enough of an outsider was both a problem and a resource.

Part of my job, then, became identifying the relevant groups and their members, which I did by a combination of observing who had what relationships with whom, and asking people about their trajectories, usually informally, but sometimes, when I had to, in the context of an interview. I have alluded to many dimensions of the ethnolinguistic composition of the brewery, but I will try to provide a summary profile here.

The workers on the production lines and in delivery (mostly on the ground floor; the management offices and cafeteria were on upper floors) were almost all francophone men, with the exception of a few immigrants, mainly from Eastern Europe, who had been in Canada for about twenty years. Most of the francophones spoke only French. They paid little attention to the company's francization program, for the most part ignoring, for example, foremen's attempts to introduce new terminology into their work activities. In many ways, language had little to do with the core of the activities of the production line workers. They were also far removed from possibilities for promotion, which would have involved more than new terms in any case.

The foremen were also all francophone men. In contrast to the men working under them, they were active and invested in francization. They frequently asked for texts (such as forms they had to fill out) and terms to be translated, and sometimes worked on the translation themselves. They were as concerned about extending the ranges of use of French as they were about ensuring the "quality" of that French (in the form of finding the "right" term, for example). The younger ones among them were quite articulate about the political aspects of francization, associating it with the chances that people like them could hope for better lives. One of them told me:

> In the beginning / the guys on the floor started laughing as soon as you talked about *soutireuses* / what's that a *soutireuse*? / they've been working on a filler for twenty-five years and then you tell them / it's not a filler it's a *soutireuse* / but it goes in / even if you don't want it to it changes [. . .] young people today are more ready to change it because we're all tied to the Quebec situation / we want to francisize / we want to be more free / but for that you have to make an effort

[Au début / les gars sur le plancher partaient à rire dès que tu parlais de soutireuses / c'est quoi ça une soutireuse? / ça fait vingt-cinq ans qu'ils travaillent sur une filler pis tu leur dis / ce n'est pas une filler c'est une soutireuse / mais ça entre / même si on veut pas ça change [. . .] les jeunes d'aujourd'hui / ils sont plus prêts à le changer parce qu'on est tous reliés à la situation québécoise / on veut franciser / on veut être plus libre / mais pour ça il faut faire un effort.] (Interview with francophone foreman, 1978)

In fact, from what I could tell, none of the management positions were ever filled from the ranks of the foremen; at that level the company recruited only people who had had formal training in a technical field outside the brewery. But the prospect of "liberty" remained powerful.

Only one foreman failed to fit this profile. In our daily rounds, Hélène, Maryse, and I would run into Mike, a young anglophone who worked alone in the bowels of the plant, supervising the brewing tanks. He talked to us once about his former anglophone buddies, most of whom had retired (but Mike was too young for that) or had moved away (but Mike wanted to stay in Montreal). He had found the perfect solution for someone who does not want to, or for some reason cannot, learn French under those conditions: a position in which only the most rudimentary knowledge of French was required.

The small group of superintendents occupied, quite literally, a position of mediation between the workers and their foremen, on the one hand, and management, on the other, frequently visiting both types of spaces in the course of their work day, and having to interact with people at both levels. A small group, they were all bilingual, and most of them of Irish origin (as I mentioned earlier, francophones in Canada share both religion and class with the Irish, leading historically both to conflict and to intimacy, including learning each other's language). They tended to keep apart from other employees, possibly as a way to minimize the risks that their role could entail.

The management level, as we have already begun to see, was more complex. No sectors were exclusively or even mainly anglophone anymore, apart from the head office in the other building. The human resources department and the quality control lab were the two sectors now dominated by francophones, mostly young and including both men and women. Most of them were very actively involved in the francization of the company, scarcely surprising given that they had benefited so directly from it and that their presence was legitimated by it. In many other departments there was a mix, including older male anglophones, usually with a great deal of seniority; older male francophones used to working under anglophone sector heads; and younger (also usually male) managers who had been hired recently. Administrative assistants (then still called "secretaries") were all female, and mainly francophone. Like the superintendents, they played an important role as linguistic mediators. They standardized their supervisors' texts and made sure they conformed to norms of written language, drawing on monolingual and bilingual dictionaries and grammar books when they needed to. They translated into French work produced by the older anglophones still around who had never needed to write in French before in their careers, and helped francophones in their efforts to francisize their own work practices. (I will provide an example in the following section.)

The embedding of ethnolinguistic categories in workplace stratification, the gendered nature of the work, and the different generational perspectives on those relationships all help us understand what francization meant to differently positioned employees in terms of the capital they could mobilize, the markets they had access to, and the risks and potential benefits involved in trying to acquire new capital or invest the capital they had in different markets. As we will see further below, it was the francophones in upper management who had the highest, thinnest tightrope to walk. Anglophones had retreated to Ontario, the head office, or the basement (the basement excepted, these were not exactly hardship posts). Low-ranking workers were too far removed from the potential benefits of francization to get too excited about it, and the superintendents, most of whom had been around for a long time anyway, could draw little benefit. Foremen, especially the younger ones, had everything to gain and nothing to lose. Higher-ranking young managers had to balance the obvious benefits francization represented for them with their remaining dependence both on the older anglophones who were still around (and who, often, were in line for the jobs filled by the newly arrived francophones) and on the anglophone head office, in a national company that was still, at the end of the day, numerically dominated by English-speakers and whose finances were run out of Toronto.

In the next section, I will take a closer look at how this worked in interaction, with a focus on one specific department, technical services, which included most of the kinds of trajectories and interests we have discussed up until now. It also was the service I encountered where the issues raised by the changes going on were the most salient for its members, and from the widest set of positions.

4.4 THE INTERACTIONAL ACCOMPLISHMENT OF FRANCOPHONIZATION

Technical services included employees at a variety of levels. It included mechanics, electricians, and other tradespeople whose job was to maintain the physical infrastructure of the plant, whether on a routine or troubleshooting basis. They had dispatchers and supervisors. Upper management was involved not only in ensuring the quality of this basic function but also in longer-term planning. There was one secretary, Linda, who worked in the central office on an upper floor, with the department head, Albert, and his two assistants, Claude and Bob.

Linda was a young francophone with a strong mastery of English. Bob was an older Scot with a background in engineering who had been recruited directly from the United Kingdom twenty-five years before, precisely because of his technical training; he had chosen not to take opportunities for transfers to other provinces, saying simply that he wanted to stay in Montreal. Claude was a bilingual older francophone responsible for the maintenance work who had long been used to being the only francophone on the management team. His work, however, required him to move around the building a great deal and to interact with the francophone tradesmen and dispatchers. Albert was a young francophone formally trained in engineering at a francophone postsecondary institution; he had very recently replaced the former head of the department, who had left to supervise the opening of a new plant in one of the western provinces. He had some working knowledge of English. A fourth member of the management team, Daniel, a young francophone with very limited knowledge of English, had also recently been promoted after his anglophone predecessor retired. He occupied a position under Claude and Bob and was based on the production floor, although, along with other people in the department, he often came by the office for a variety of reasons, including, in his case, attendance at the weekly management meeting in Albert's office. Together, they represented fairly well the range of trajectories of workers in the brewery.

How did they make things work in the office? Linda, of course, played a key role. She spoke mainly English with Bob, although she used a few fixed formulas from French, which Bob in turn picked up and used when addressing her and other francophones. She was his main mediator with the world of French, translating or editing his letters and memos. She was also a key linguistic resource for francophones invested in francization. In the following extract, we see her helping Simon, a young francophone supervisor, and his colleague Marc. They have come explicitly to ask Linda for help in translating the term "shopman," a designation for a low-ranking job in their area of work. Linda takes out her dictionary and leans on the counter to carry out the discussion.

LINDA: I just looked for a dictionary oh (x)
SIMON: *Homme d'atelier* [workshop man] makes a perfect literal translation
LINDA: (x) What in English?
MARC: Shopman
SIMON: Shopman
MARC: It's a guy who works in a [work]shop / an *homme d'atelier* well no
LINDA: A *journalier* [day laborer]
MARC: A *journalier* I've seen that somewhere
SIMON: No *journalier* doesn't work for me
LINDA: No a *manutentionnaire* [handler, packer]
SIMON: A *manutentionnaire* doesn't work for me either / an *homme d'atelier* works for me

(*they laugh*)
MARC: But what does it mean?
SIMON: Well it's the it's
MARC: That's why the [pl.] (x)
SIMON: Well it's for
MARC: It's the [pl.] the [sing.] the [pl.] the guys from the factory [floor]
SIMON: It's that's going to be a mechanic who'll be employed as a "gofer" /
    "gofer this gofer that"
(*they laugh, and shortly afterward Simon and Marc go back to work*)

[LINDA: J'ai juste cherché un dictionnaire oh (x)
SIMON: Homme d'atelier fait une traduction littérale parfaite
LINDA: (x) Quoi en anglais?
MARC: *Shopman*
SIMON: *Shopman*
MARC: C'est un gars qui travaille dans un atelier / un homme d'atelier
    ben non
LINDA: Un journalier
MARC: Un journalier j'ai vu ça quelque part
SIMON: Non journalier ça fait pas mon affaire
LINDA: Non un manutentionnaire
SIMON: Un manutentionnaire ça fait pas mon affaire non plus / un
    homme d'atelier ça fait mon affaire
(*Ils rient*)
MARC: Mais qu'est-ce que ça veut dire?
SIMON: Là c'est le c'est
MARC: Ça c'est pourquoi les (x)
SIMON: Ben c'est pour
MARC: C'est les le les gars de l'usine
SIMON: C'est ça va être un mécanicien qui va être employé comme gofer /
    gofer this gofer that
(*Ils rient*)]

Simon and Marc are already well into their conversation about what constitutes a good French term for the English "shopman" (a worker in the "[work]shop") by the time they arrive at Linda's desk. Linda proceeds by hauling out her French-English dictionary and asking for the English term they are trying to translate. Neither Simon nor Marc is particularly seduced by the dictionary, however; whether it is opaque to them (Marc's "But what does it mean?"), or somehow just doesn't feel right (Simon's "It doesn't work for me"), the term is rejected, and they proceed by trying to go closer to what they understand the core meaning to be, for them ("the guys from the factory [floor]," "a mechanic who'll be employed as a gofer"—this last triggers Simon's association with a well-known play on words (go for—go fer—gopher) understood to be at the origins of the term "gofer" to designate an employee whose job is to supply materials to his superiors in a workshop or other workplace involving materials, at their orders: "go for this, go for that"). It may be an old joke, but it serves to defuse the tension around the terminological—and sociopolitical—impasse the three have found themselves in: the men are not prepared to alienate themselves entirely from the referential realities and social register they need to operate in (*homme d'atelier* works for Simon; *journalier* and *manutentionnaire* have no resonance in their repertoires, they do not actually mean the same thing, and they sound, well, they sound like they come out of the dictionary, not out of a foreman's mouth). The joke also serves as a reminder of the English work world with which Marc and Simon are familiar; they know exactly where the term "gofer" comes from, but no idea what *manutentionnaire* might mean.

Linda, her counter, and her dictionaries are important spaces for negotiation of francization among some of its interested parties—foremen and superintendents like Marc and Simon. In that conversational space, they can move back and forth between French and English, and between sanctioned linguistic authorities on the standard language and what people actually say in situated practices, in an attempt to create something sayable that is also recognizably French. Francization is thus exposed as not simply a matter of substituting the objectively constituted "francophone" way of talking about things for the existing "anglophone" way but, rather, as a complex constitution of a social voice that does not yet exist. Simon is not quite prepared to assume the authority for creating that voice (and going ahead and using *homme d'atelier*); he would rather be able to draw on the authority of sanctioned sources like the dictionary. He is caught ideologically between language as neutral and autonomous object, and language as social practice. Really, the only way out is a good laugh. This example also displays the hidden work of people like Linda.[4] Translation and corpus planning are not in her job description, but they occupied a significant portion of her time and allowed many members of her department to achieve their linguistic goals.

With her and the younger francophones, Bob used a few fixed phrases and formulas in French (usually "Bonjour, comment ça va?"—Hello, how are you?), a kind of symbolic recognition of the new place of French and francophones in the department. He did not invest much more time and energy in learning French than that, but he didn't really need to. He was soon going to retire, so there were few consequences for him if he failed to understand everything that people were saying around him. As we will see below, if his colleagues needed his expertise or his approval, they spoke to him in English.

Bob continued to speak English with Claude, as they had always done, although Claude spoke French with other francophones. For people like Claude, francization was complicated. He had built his career around being able to function in both French with those under him, and English with his colleagues and supervisor in the office (although his English had the prosody, phonology, and syntax typical of francophone Canadians speaking English fluently but identifiably as a second language, a long-standing strategy of mutual boundary maintenance developed when francophones of Claude's generation had to deal with anglophones in positions of power; it was the kind of English former Canadian Prime Minister Jean Chrétien spoke, and by the 1990s was criticized for, as his "little guy from Shawinigan" persona became less politically legitimizing than the increasingly expected guise of the sophisticated, educated, urbane francophone). In particular, this had always meant that Claude read materials and wrote his reports in English. Now that Albert was his boss, and Bill 101 was in the picture, he was expected somehow, magically, to read these texts and produce these reports in French, and the latter especially proved extremely difficult.

Daniel was the newest on the scene, a unilingual francophone (and direct beneficiary of francization, like Albert). His recent promotion put him for the first time in contact with anglophones like Bob. In those instances, Linda and Albert helped out.

Like everyone else, Albert had competing pressures to juggle. His relationship with Bob required constant facework, since in terms of seniority Bob should have been promoted to Albert's position, and everyone knew that. Albert, the newcomer, also needed to be able to rely on Bob's knowledge, not only in terms of his technical expertise, but also in terms of the knowledge built up in twenty-five years of service to the brewery. At the same time, Albert needed to construct his legitimacy in relation to the francophones under him, both as their sector head and as the representative of the processes that were opening up possibilities and changing their status in the workplace. Not surprisingly, Albert often switched between French and English, a clear index of his position on the cusp of the wave of social change flowing through the brewery.

Let me illustrate the ways in which the different positions of Bob, Claude, Daniel, and Albert played out in the workplace. Below I provide some extracts from their regular team meetings, usually held once a week in Albert's office. Most of the time, Bob spoke only when explicitly invited to by Albert, and most of the time he did so in English, with some transition routines in French like those I show below. Everyone else spoke French. The extracts below show some of the moments of confrontation of past and present, the visible seams of change in progress, that required other forms of interactional management.

The meeting usually followed the following format: Bob, Claude, and Daniel delivered an oral version of their weekly written report (a text they normally brought with them into the meeting), and any member of the team could comment on it or ask questions about it. Albert transmitted information from the higher ranks of management and ensured that his team members made the necessary decisions and achieved a consensus on any forms of action that needed to be undertaken.

At the beginning of the following extract, we pick up (that is, I start the recorder) as people are coming in and standing around. Albert is having a side conversation with Bob in English. After a pause, everyone moves to a place around the table. While I had already met everyone but Daniel, this extract is from my first visit to a department meeting. It is possible that my association with francization added pressure on Albert to establish a French framework for the meeting, but his French opening routines are followed quickly by a repetition in English of the same utterance, specifically addressed to Bob.

> ALBERT: He would have got
> BOB: He's twenty-one years of age
> ALBERT: Yeah twenty-one years of age
> (*pause*)
> ALBERT: *Bon mais vous pouvez fermer la porte c'est tout ce qu'on va avoir aujourd'hui / tout le monde connaît Monica?* (okay but you can close the door that's all we're going to have today / everyone knows Monica?) Bob, have you met Monica?

Although Albert addresses Bob in English, Bob does his best to include a little French in his response.

> ALBERT: On Monday afternoon we have a meeting with Daniel Vincent?
> BOB: What time is it?
> ALBERT: Uh
> CLAUDE: Right signs
> ALBERT: *Douze heures* [12 o'clock] signs
> BOB: *Quelle place?* [What place?]
> ALBERT: I think it's in my office

Bob continues to do his best to include French in his responses to Albert; below, his French is part of a series of strategies both Albert and Bob use to mitigate the face-threat of Albert's request, a request that would normally be issued from senior to junior.

> ALBERT: Uh it's like passing the buck to somebody but uh (*he laughs*) can you spend some time some time with Pierre (x) Monday / it could be a good thing
> BOB: *Avec plaisir* [with pleasure] [. . .] okay I'll do that uh / I charge Anne *rien* [nothing] / but *spécial pour toi* [special for you] forty-five dollars an hour

While Albert is doing the discursive work of including Bob, Bob is doing the discursive work, within the limits of his proficiency in French, of recognizing the new regime and of Albert's legitimate occupation of a position that might otherwise have been his. He could simply have stuck to English, but here and quite systematically in every conversation involving a francophone, he engages in similar practices.

In the following extract, we see how Claude copes. He has on the table in front of him the written text of his report, in English. He navigates back and forth between that text and an oral summary in French. His hesitations and pauses can be read as markers of the tension this causes in him.

> CLAUDE: *Oui* [Yes] / uh vacation staff / Roland Masse George Kovacs *cette semaine / la semaine prochaine* [this week / next week] Roland Masse George Kovacs again / uh uh temp Denis Blais he's on the

lubrication survey Léo Charrette uh working on the expense budget but he's going off for two weeks *hein? il prend deux semaines de vacances ça je l'avais donné ça y a un bout de temps* [eh? he's taking two weeks vacation that I gave him that a while ago]

The team (with the largely invisible contribution from Linda) is constructing francization in the "language of work" sense, as a process. Implicitly and consensually, they move toward a new convention of language choice, in which French is the unmarked language. Each one draws on the linguistic resources at his or her disposal, as a function of their life trajectories and their structural position in the organization of the company. Those who profit the most from the change provide scaffolding and safe zones backstage for those who do not have the capital they need. (That backstage can be a physical space, like a conversational space formed by the orientation of two bodies to each other in a corner of Albert's office, or an interactional one, carved out by lowered voices, the pragmatics of parenthetical commentary or other discursive means.) As long as people like Bob (and to a lesser extent Claude) do not resist, they are offered the means to continue to function without losing face. Albert is not cut off from their expertise and can construct his legitimacy as a trained francophone manager. Daniel is a legitimate participant, which would have been impossible earlier given his lack of English. And while Linda's salary may not take her contribution into account, she does accumulate symbolic capital, and makes herself indispensable.

The discursive strategies adopted are a way to keep the company going, avoiding open conflict or loss of employee time that might otherwise have had to go to expensive recruitment and training efforts. None of the brewery's employees has an interest in hobbling his or her employer. Their strategies allow for the peaceable introduction of francophones into new positions of power and the concomitant establishment of their language as the language of work (which legitimates their presence and their exercise of control). Francization is centrally about francophonization; and while the state uses clumsy, awkward means to push the process along, on the ground, actors draw on their resources to appropriate the process in ways that make sense to them. Notably, these are ways that allow for the company to slowly carve out the space of a regional Quebec market, and continue to make a profit while doing so.

4.5 DISCURSIVE SHIFT AND POLITICAL ECONOMIC CHANGE

The transition from traditionalist to modernizing discourses happened under particular political economic conditions. Along with growing wealth and consumption, the reorganization and expansion of markets during the postwar boom years, the ethnonational mobilization that succeeded in asserting control over the apparatus of the state (of Quebec), and the increasing importance of science and technology all help to explain what happened in this workplace and many others.

These conditions also help explain the trajectories of people like those we have met here. Life worked out very well for the Alberts and the Marcels. Other francophones, like Daniel, Hélène, and Linda, were doing things they would not otherwise have been able to do, but it is not clear just how much of a career path was really opening up for them, at least without further training. The Maurices and Claudes had made choices that made sense for them at the time, but they were overtaken by events. The Bobs and the Mikes got left behind, but their counterparts had options in other markets, or invested in learning French. As options became severely constrained, their hesitations, reformulations, jokes, silences, and meta-comments show how they had to navigate a moment of uncertainty.

In the end, the investment in unilingual spaces didn't make bilingualism less valuable; it simply reorganized it. It made bilingualism less the privileged domain of the francophone male working class, and more that of the emergent middle class involved in national and international markets, whether they belonged to the ethnonational category of "francophone" or "anglophone." It forced anglophones to choose between involvement in a wider English-speaking market outside Quebec (commonly known as "taking the 401," for the highway connecting Montreal and Toronto) or learning French to capitalize on new opportunities as bilingual brokers between the Quebec market (or "Quebec Inc.," as it became known [Fraser 1987]) and the national and increasingly globalized market dominated by English. Francophones were able to remain monolingual while profiting from the expanded opportunities of the regional market, until they bumped up against the need for English at higher corporate levels. Sooner or later they had somehow to invest in English.

At the same time, modernization was centrally about using the apparatus of the state to create the conditions for such economic mobility. Once that social mobility was created, and the ethnoclass disparities blurred, the ethnonational basis of legitimacy of the Quebec state became fragile. If the transition from traditional to modernizing nationalism had the Catholic Church as its main victim, the development of modernizing nationalism calls into question ethnicity as a basis for political legitimacy, partly because success kicks the legs out from under mobilization for emancipation, and partly because liberal democracy is legitimated on the basis of inclusion.

This had yet to become an issue in the late 1970s. Then, francophones were just beginning to get a generalized experience of modern, technologized, credentialized life. But that tension began to emerge around the contradiction between the focus on language skills (as opposed to ethnonational group membership) in official discourse (as in Bill 101), and the real-life salience of ethnicity in organizing access to advantageous positions in reshaped markets. This tension, which we follow over the next chapters, calls into question who counts as a francophone, what counts as bilingualism, what role the state should play in the reproduction of the nation, and, indeed, whether we should be talking about nations at all.

While I was never able to return to the Montreal branch of the brewery, I do drive by one of its Toronto branches regularly, and follow with one eye on the business section of the newspaper how the brewing industry of North America has seen both the growth of microbreweries (in an assertion of the local, authentic, and ecologically sound) and the global consolidation of industrial brewing, as well as, most recently, their intertwining. In some ways, the Montreal brewery was a first step toward that reshaping, serving a regional market with its own consumer trends within a global network of supply and demand. In the next chapters, we will follow some of these processes as they emerged over the following decades in other parts of Canada.

4.6 AND WHAT IS A CRITICAL ETHNOGRAPHIC SOCIOLINGUISTICS HERE?

I have showed here some of the ways in which a critical ethnographic sociolinguistic approach can be applied to what looks like a simple policy problem: is a company adopting French as the language of work? By asking how language is related to the resources at stake in the company (from information, to promotion, to jobs), and to legitimate access to them, I ask how language functions in struggles over power, and how it is embedded in the reproduction or production of various social categories.

I have tried to show that the OLF's question cannot be answered in simple, categorical terms. The question, and how to answer it, can only make sense once the political economic conditions that underlie the ideologies of language and identity we use to organize ourselves are apprehended. The question is premised on the idea that monolingualism is the normal state of affairs, and that language is an autonomous system as well as cultural property. Those beliefs make sense only if bourgeois capitalism is aligned with the politics of the nation-state.

I have also tried to show how the fictive homogeneity constructed by that framework gets both built and undone under the complex constraints of specific conditions. This has made it important to capture how things work out for different categories of social actors, and to explain why it works out well for some, maybe not so well for others, and in ways too contradictory for a law to foresee for still others. I want to account for Albert and Bob, but also for Simon and Mike and Linda. If the brewery was indeed moving more and more toward adopting French as the language of work (albeit in ways unplanned by the OLF, or even by brewery management), this depended on some change in personnel and in organizational structure that had begun to come into existence prior to, indeed one could say made possible, the legislation that was most salient in everyday consciousness.

By uncovering the sources of value of resources, how they are distributed, and how people strategize around them, it became possible to see why and how language became central as a terrain of struggle over control of the private sector. Critical ethnographic sociolinguistics allows us to uncover the contradictions and conditions that not only explains why people do what they do (why Mike hides in the basement, why Marcel cares more about how to say "stripping" than Hélène does, why Linda has dictionaries) but also foresees the zones of fragility and tension, the areas that require management.

In the following chapters, we will see how the fragility around the uneasy relationship between language and identity plays out as a consequence of the kinds of processes examined here. Modernization turned out, not surprisingly, not to have an end state of stability. Rather, modernity propelled francophone Canadians, now recast as Québécois (and others), into the world of expanding capital. Eventually, globalization engendered neoliberalism, with relocations of the old (primary resource extraction and industrial) economy, and the growth of the tertiary sector, all of which ask new questions about language, identity, and the role of the nation-state and its agencies.

5

From Identity to Commodity

Schooling, Social Selection, and Social Reproduction
(Toronto, 1983–1996)

5.1 IF THEY ARE QUÉBÉCOIS, WHO ARE WE?

The last two chapters have traced the carving out of a modern territorial
francophone space from the Romantic spiritual imagining of le Canada
français as an organic nation that was the francophone elite's initial response
to anglophone domination. Here we will return to the moment of reckon-
ing, when Quebec played the nation-state card. Rather than follow Quebec, as in chapter 4, we will follow what happened outside Quebec in the
aftermath of the shock that Jacques, Robert, and hundreds like them felt
when they received the telegram from Ottawa announcing the demise of
l'Ordre de Jacques Cartier. For many of them, the experience was one of
going to bed as a Canadien français (French Canadian) and waking up to
find that that term no longer applied, since most of the members of the
category had decided, seemingly overnight, to become Québécois.

While some members of the old elite struggled to preserve the older
framework, most were quick to follow Quebec's lead as best they could,
taking advantage of Quebec's threat to the Canadian Confederation to
press the federal government for rights and resources. Indeed, the Canadian government rapidly understood that to undermine Quebec's argument for independence, it would have show that one could live as a
francophone anywhere in Canada and that one could live as a francophone on Quebec's terms, that is, as a monolingual (at least regarding
matters within the limits of state control).

The Official Languages Act of 1968 put French on a footing of equality
with English as an official language and committed the federal government to providing federal services in both official languages. The government also began to set up programs to support the teaching of French as
a first language outside Quebec, and as a second language across the country, through transfer payments to the provinces, even though education
remains under provincial jurisdiction. Finally, it developed funding programs, largely through the culture ministry, for the maintenance and
development of French language, culture, and identity outside Quebec.

This new system required interlocutors at the level of what came to be understood as the francophone minority community. Organizations already existing at the local or provincial levels rapidly regrouped. These were, for the most part, associations dating from the late nineteenth or early twentieth centuries, devoted to specific causes (notably French-language education) or acting as organized regional groupings for the development of traditionalist nationalism.

In the Maritime provinces, the only other space in Canada where a Quebec-style movement might have been imaginable, it took a number of years for a focused strategy to develop. The older Société nationale de l'Acadie, in existence (under various appellations) since 1881, was associated with traditionalist nationalism and with a diasporic Acadie, spread out since the 1755 deportation across the Maritimes, New England, Louisiana, and France. The contemporary population concentration in northern and eastern New Brunswick served as the basis for the platform of the short-lived Parti Acadien, with its Parti Québécois–style politics of territorial state nationalism. (The party was founded in 1972, lost most of its support between 1978 and 1982, and officially disbanded in 1986.) In between lay provincial organizations that emerged alongside the SNA (the Fédération des Acadiens de la Nouvelle-Écosse in 1968, and the Société des Acadiens du Nouveau-Brunswick in 1973), maintaining a tension still felt today between diasporic and state-territorial ideas of Acadie.

In 1968, the Association canadienne-française d'éducation de l'Ontario (ACFÉO), which had been formed in 1910 to resist provincial pressure to ban the use of French as a language of instruction, dropped "education" from its title, allowing it to take on the role of provincial interlocutor and lobby group for francophone rights. Other provinces followed suit, as did the Yukon and Northwest Territories (as well as, much later, Nunavut, once it was established in 1999 as a separate jurisdiction), setting up a full complement of province-based lobbying organizations representing francophone minority communities both in discussions with their provincial legislatures and with the federal government. In 1975, these organizations grouped together as the Fédération des francophones hors Québec (FFHQ: Federation of francophones outside Quebec), with headquarters in the federal capital, Ottawa. In 1991, the FFHQ decided it now wanted to define itself not in terms of where it was not (Quebec) but, rather, in positive terms, and renamed itself the Fédération des communautés francophones et acadiennes du Canada (FCFA: Federation of francophone and Acadian communities of Canada).

This ambivalent organizational process also played out on the terrain of nomenclature. Some associations retained the older terms *Canadien français* or *Acadien*, specified through the addition of the name of the province in question (Association canadienne-française de l'Ontario, Association canadienne-française de l'Alberta, Fédération acadienne de la Nouvelle-Écosse, Société des Acadiens du Nouveau-Brunswick), while others invented new appellations (Société franco-manitobaine, 1968;

Fédération des Franco-Colombiens, 1971). Members of the elite contemplated what terms might replace *Canadien français*; the best-known debate was probably the one which occurred in Ontario (which, after all, did account for half the francophone population "outside Quebec"). In a well-known article published in 1980, Danielle Juteau rehearsed the full panoply, from *Canadien français* to *Franco-Ontarien* to *Ontarois* (Juteau-Lee 1980), the latter term having been invented in 1979 by Yolande Grisé, a professor at the Université d'Ottawa, in eastern Ontario (Grisé 1982). (Gaëtan Gervais, a professor at the Université Laurentienne, in northern Ontario, invented a Franco-Ontarian flag in 1978.) The 1970s, in other words, was a moment of debate over reimagining the nation in the wake of Quebec's Quiet Revolution, and nomenclature was a key terrain.

Over time all these terms became increasingly contested as exclusionary on the basis of gender or ethnicity, and the federal government, as we will see in the following chapters, has shifted its investment under the influence of neoliberalism; but the federal funding structure has remained influential and has allowed for the persistence of this quasi-national, province-based form of organization. The FCFA remains a key interlocutor at the federal level today.

5.2 EDUCATION AND INSTITUTIONAL TERRITORIAL NATIONALISM

Much of the energy of these associations from the 1960s to the 1990s was devoted to struggles over French-language education. This was scarcely a new issue, although it took on renewed significance in this period.

Indeed, the use of French as a language of instruction was an issue enmeshed in the process of constructing the Canadian state, in which both language and religion were battlegrounds in the imagining of Canada. In Canada as elsewhere, schooling was a central terrain of state formation in the nineteenth and twentieth centuries, as the state progressively took control over education away from religious institutions and used education as a means for constructing citizens and preparing them for the industrial and bureaucratic workforce of the liberal democratic and capitalist nation-state (Bourdieu and Passeron 1977; Bowles and Gintis 1977). The question for Canada was how it would handle both linguistic and religious duality.

The legislation constituting Canada in 1867 (the British North America Act) guaranteed the right to Catholic education, but said nothing about languages of instruction. In fact, Catholic education was organized and provided by the Church, both in English and in French (albeit in separate institutions). Irish and French embroiled themselves in struggles over control of the Church in Canada, and over its educational establishments, largely through struggles over language (Choquette 1977, 1987). The

Protestant establishment, which was the architect of state-controlled and -centralized schooling, had reservations about Catholic education, of course, but its hands were tied. Its concerns about language of instruction waxed and waned, although in Ontario, at least, both German and French were used as languages of instruction in the nineteenth century. However, in 1885, English instruction became obligatory, and as of 1890 other languages could be used only when students spoke no English. Francophones took refuge in the claim that this was the case for their children, and in the protection afforded them by the francophone Church.

In the early twentieth century, as European tensions mounted, so did defense of the Empire (British, of course) and suspicion of the Other. German was no longer tolerated as a language of instruction, needless to say, and francophones, with their deep resistance to mobilization for Britain, were also increasingly suspect. Manitoba outlawed the use of French as a language of instruction in the late 1800s; Ontario followed suit in 1913. Most historians of francophone Ontario agree that this move had, almost predictably, an effect opposite to what was intended: rather than forcing francophones to accept the domination of English once and for all, it served to spark political resistance (Choquette 1977, 1987; Gaffield 1987)—we have already seen how l'ACFÉO served as the basis for forms of political organizing that remain active today. Thus, repression produced resistance, and the early-twentieth-century struggles over French-language education are now part of the mythology of the long struggle against anglophone domination in Ontario. I will turn to the particular case of that province, partly because it serves as a good and often precedent-setting example for the rest of Canada outside Quebec, and because the specific case I will discuss in this chapter is located in that history.

Ontario stopped actively enforcing the prohibition of French as a language of instruction in 1927 (its inspectors possibly exhausted at having to chase after teachers and students who systematically hid their French books and hauled out English ones when they heard the inspector was coming), although it did not take the corresponding regulation off the books until 1944. By the 1960s, francophones in Ontario, as in Quebec, were largely educated in French-language Catholic schools.

However, in Ontario, Catholic high schools were funded by the government only through grade 10 (at which point students are usually about fifteen years old). As a result, there were also some bilingual programs in public high schools, especially in areas where francophones formed a significant portion, if not the majority, of the local population. Otherwise, further education took place in convent and seminary schools (*collèges classiques*), for which parents had to pay, except in cases where students were recruited by their parish priest as potential priests or nuns. (And it was in those seminaries, the breeding ground for the francophone elite, that young men were often recruited for the OJC.) As we have seen, this system produced an undereducated francophone population, and the political modernizing mobilization of the 1960s took aim at precisely this problem by arguing for democratized access to education, and specifically to French-language education. The argument was that francophones were disadvantaged in English (or even bilingual) schools, through the difficulties of learning in a language not their own and through the marginalization of their identities and their interests in those institutions (Churchill et al. 1985).

In Ontario, as in other provinces, this put the struggle for French-language state-funded education front and center. Bowing to pressure from the federal government, in 1968 the government of Ontario agreed to fund French-language education through the end of high school (in Ontario at that time, grade 13, or ages eighteen to nineteen), with one major condition: it was not prepared to fund all Catholic schools, French or English, to that degree, so while French-language elementary schools could be Catholic (usually called "separate") or not (usually called "public"), high schools had to be public.[1] The immediate result was the conversion of French-language high schools, including the *collèges classiques*, into public schools, necessarily within local or regional school boards dominated by anglophones.

These schools were understood to be both a crucial means of facilitating francophone access to higher education and hence to socioeconomic mobility (as it was also argued in Quebec) and a space for reproduction of francophone identity. Since minority francophones had no hope of establishing political control over territory, they turned to institutional spaces as a means of constructing a privileged market and ensuring social, cultural, and linguistic reproduction. In keeping with the foundations of Romantic nationalism, it was widely understood that this reproduction depended on primary socialization within the family and secondary socialization in schooling. The job of the French-language minority school was thus to provide a homogeneous, unilingual francophone space in which francophone youth could be socialized as francophones speaking the kind of French ideologized as normal (as a whole, bounded, autonomous system mobilizable for all possible forms of human activity), and thereby, free of anglophone domination, realize their full intellectual and social potential and acquire the kinds of scientific and technical knowledge required for access to the modern world.

This struggle was conducted systematically across the country and has extended from education to other institutions, notably health care. It has been a struggle, in fact, on two fronts: against an anglophone majority reluctant to provide francophones with any institutional power base, and against (mainly working-class) francophones fearful of not having access to the kind of schooled English social mobility depends on. Over the years, however, the mobilized, educated, modernizing francophone elite has largely succeeded in establishing not only French-language schools, but also French-language school jurisdictions. This takes its most developed form in New Brunswick, where the francophone and anglophone school systems run parallel to each other all the way through to distinct sections within the Ministry of Education.

In the struggle, the new francophone elite has buttressed its claim with academic work in sociology and social psychology. Raymond Breton's early work on "institutional completeness" provided a theoretical framework and a language for the argument that minorities cannot be considered emancipated until they have under their control the full range of institutions regulating modern life (R. Breton 1964); for this reason, it seems to me that the best way to juxtapose the nationalism of francophone communities with that of Quebec is to talk in terms of *institutional* versus *territorial* nationalist movements, recognizing that in both cases, the key locus of control is the state. Social psychologists have developed the idea of normality through the concept of "ethnolinguistic vitality," arguing that it is not just emancipation but also the ability to reproduce and to flourish that depends on this institutional completeness (Landry and Allard 1989). Collective life remains linked to ideologies of the nation as an organic and homogeneous whole.

For all these reasons, it was clear to me when I arrived in Toronto in the early 1980s that to explore the issues of language and nationalism that had been my concern in Quebec in the 1970s, the obvious place to start following the thread was in educational institutions. One new colleague discouraged me, saying I would never be allowed to do ethnographic work in French-language schools because, to put it bluntly, I am not "Franco-Ontarian." However, I was able to gain permission from both the school board and a local Catholic primary school, by simultaneously following the board's bureaucratic regulations (meeting the person responsible for the board's French-language schools and filling out its application forms) and meeting with a school principal, who kindly allowed me to meet with her teachers at their weekly staff meeting. This dual approach was important, because the board insisted it would not impose any research program on any school, while the school affirmed that I had to have board approval to conduct research there.

Thirteen years of subsequent research were largely made possible by one teacher, who agreed to let me enter his grade 7–8 classroom. As an immigrant from France, the only male teacher, and the teacher of the highest grade in the school, he had high status, and nothing to lose. Once I began to visit the school three full days a week, I got to know the other teachers, who invited me to their classrooms one by one. After six months in this school, my credentials were established for the rest of the system, and I was able to easily navigate the rest of Toronto's French-language schools.

In 1984, I became head of the Centre de recherches en éducation franco-ontarienne (CREFO), a research center devoted mainly, but not only, to educational and linguistic issues of the Ontario francophone population. CREFO's history is part of the growth of francophone minority institutions across Canada discussed above, and my position there inserted me right into the discursive space of francophone Ontario, and especially of its educational system. In addition, in 1989, my eldest child started to attend the local francophone day-care system; having children in the system has also been an important element of my relationship to it (although I have kept away from them, their teachers, and their classmates as direct participants in my research projects).

Between 1983 and 1996 I spent a great deal of time in French-language day-care centers, elementary schools, and high schools, both Catholic and public, and have been in contact with school board– and Ministry of Education–level administrators and elected councillors and with professional associations of francophone educators.[2] Most of the time, this was in the context of research projects funded by the Ontario Ministry of Education, the Multiculturalism Directorate of the Canadian Secretary of State (now Heritage Canada), and the Social Sciences and Humanities Research Council of Canada. I sometimes conducted this fieldwork alone, but I also often worked in the company of CREFO colleagues and graduate students; the kind of distributed knowledge generated by team fieldwork I hoped for in the brewery became more easily realized in the context of educational institutions (where, among other things, people mostly didn't care which of us was sitting in the back of the class or hanging around the cafeteria, or if they did, they had no problem with the knowledge that we worked together). The rest of the time, my participation was the result of my role as a parent or, as head of CREFO, in invited involvement in such activities as community roundtables, public debates, or committees, or taking part in media broadcasts on francophone issues. As a politically constituted discursive space, francophone Canada creates reflexive, often self-critical, communicative events. It also has an investment in creating legitimacy through democracy and transparency, in ways that can be understood to be the legacy of the assemblies held by the OJC, but now working at being broadly consultative and public.

The rest of this chapter will be based on the last of the studies I conducted during this period, from 1991 to 1996, in a Toronto-area high school. Almost everything I will say about this one school corresponded (although of course not in the smallest details) with the fieldwork I had conducted in other schools in the same area. For many years, people told me that this was problematic—that Toronto, as a southern urban environment, was not in any way typical of "real" francophone communities, which were, to their minds, much more stable and homogeneous, not to mention being linked, ideologically, to the rural life that Romantic nationalism constitutes as authenticating. In my view, Toronto represented the edge of social change, a kind of first glimpse at what francophone Canada might be becoming. Since then, urbanization, tertiarization, and mobility have indeed spread, and today Toronto looks more typical than anomalous.

I look first at the discursive constitution of the school as a homogeneous francophone space, the kind of institutional nation francophone activists fought for through the 1960s and 1970s. I will then examine how students position themselves with respect to their engagement with this

institutional commitment. In particular, I will show that the school's legitimacy as a national space, devoted to the reproduction of language, culture, and identity, is challenged by the growing value of French-English
bilingualism as a commodified skill and a form of capital of distinction
(Bourdieu 1979).

Multilingualism is prized by francophones, anglophones, and immigrants alike as they jockey for privileged access to the francophone market
constructed in Quebec, the bilingual market constructed by the state in
response to Quebec's regional power, and the emerging importance of
French and English in the globalized new economy. Here we see how
mobilizing the language of rights to close off a segment of the market
produces debates over who counts as a francophone and what counts as
good French. Francophone spaces get caught in a tension between nationalist ideas of authentic identities, and preferences in increasingly competitive markets for measurable commodities and for forms of symbolic
capital that can be seen to constitute added value.

5.3 CONSTRUCTING AN "OASIS"

The school, which I have called l'École Champlain, was one of the earliest
to be founded after the 1968 legislation allowing for French to be used in
public schools throughout high school. In 1994, in a document published
on the occasion of the school's twenty-fifth anniversary, it described itself
as a "véritable oasis culturel au sein d'une société principalement anglophone" (a veritable cultural oasis in the midst of a mainly anglophone
society). In the course listing of the previous year (extracted below), it
insisted on the linguistic dimension of the constitution of this "oasis" (lines
1–5 and 10–13), linking the individual practice of French (lines 5–10) to
the development of the community (lines 15–17), and taking a strong line
on how the development of whole, bounded, linguistic systems is necessary
not only to healthy communities but also to fully realized cognitive capacities (lines 17–21), in a discursive move reminiscent of the discourse
of linguistic deficits and bilingual confusion that flowed out of the nation-
state's insistence on homogeneity and standardization (Tabouret-Keller
1988; Heller and Martin-Jones 2001; Heller 2007b).

1	Usage du français: L'École Champlain	Use of French: Champlain School is a
2	est une école de langue française. Toutes	French-language school. All activities,
3	les activités, qu'elles soient purement	whether strictly academic, cultural or
4	scolaires ou qu'elles soient culturelles ou	recreational take place in French. We
5	récréatives se déroulent en français. On	also expect of you that you speak in
6	attend également de vous que vous vous	French to your teachers and fellow
7	adressiez en français à vos enseignant-e-s	students; in class and during all school
8	et à vos condisciples; en classe et pendant	and extracurricular activities. The Law
9	toutes les activités scolaires et	on Education stipulates that in a
10	parascolaires. La loi sur l'éducation	French-language school the language
11	précise que dans l'école de langue	of administration and communication is

12 française la langue d'administration et French. A French-language school, in
13 de communication est le français. Une addition to being a teaching institution
14 école de langue française, en plus d'être is also a source of extension of this
15 une maison d'enseignement est aussi un language and of the culture it transmits.
16 foyer de rayonnement de cette langue et No human being can develop in
17 de la culture qu'elle véhicule. Aucun harmony, can develop his or her full
18 être humain ne peut se développer potential if he or she does not master
19 harmonieusement, se réaliser pleinement perfectly this tool of thought and of
20 s'il ne maîtrise pas parfaitement cet communication. Each teacher and each
21 outil de pensée et de communication. department will have a policy aimed
22 Chaque enseignant-e et chaque secteur at encouraging you to use only French
23 auront une politique visant à vous in school and in the classroom.
24 encourager à n'utiliser que le français à
25 l'école et dans les salles de classe.

(École Champlain course listing [*Répertoire des cours*] 1992–1993, p. 3)

The image of a culturally—and linguistically—homogeneous space is supported and framed at the level of the Ontario Ministry of Education, whose first explicit articulation of the mandate of the French-language school in 1994 (extracted below) included explicit reference to the school as an exclusively French-speaking space (lines 17–19), in juxtaposition to identity and community (lines 11–16 and 39–41). It deals with the problem of the remaining value of bilingualism by defining it (in terms provided directly by social psychology; Lambert 1972; Landry and Allard 1996) as good if it is "additive" (that is, a form of parallel monolingualisms), or as harmful if "subtractive" (in which parts of a linguistic system are putatively replaced by another; see lines 30–33). The ideal student is therefore a monolingual francophone who will learn English, but in ways which keep that language safely on the other side of a boundary protecting French and the francophone milieu. L'École Champlain's reference to the value of standard language is also echoed here (lines 20–29), although the ministry is careful to avoid devaluing linguistic forms that are not the focus of schooling, by referring to "decontextualized language" linked to school success:

1 Énoncé de principe: Le mandat des écoles Statement of principle: The mandate of
2 franco-ontariennes Franco-Ontarian schools
3
4 —Favoriser la réussite scolaire et —Promote the school success and
5 l'épanouissement de l'ensemble des personal development of all students,
6 élèves, filles et garçons, dans le respect girls and boys, respecting their
7 de leurs caractéristiques—physiques, characteristics, be they physical,
8 intellectuelles, linguistiques, ethniques, intellectual, linguistic, ethnic, cultural,
9 culturelles, raciales et religieuses—sans racial or religious, and whatever their
10 égard au statut socio-économique. socio-economic status.
11 —Favoriser chez les élèves le —Promote the development of
12 développement de l'identité personnelle, students' personal, linguistic and
13 linguistique et culturelle et le sentiment cultural identity as well as their sense
14 d'appartenance à une communauté of belonging to a dynamic and pluralist
15 franco-ontarienne dynamique et Franco-Ontarian community.
16 pluraliste.

17 —Promouvoir l'utilisation du français	—Promote the use of French in all
18 dans toutes les sphères d'activités à	spheres of activity at school as well
19 l'école comme dans la communauté.	as in the community.
20 —Élargir le répertoire linguistique des	—Widen students' linguistic
21 élèves et développer leurs connaissances	repertoires and develop their
22 et leurs compétences en français, en	knowledge of and competence in French,
23 acceptant et prenant comme point de	while accepting their spoken French and
24 départ leur français parlé. Cette	using it as a point of departure. This
25 compétence acquise dans l'usage	acquired competence in the
26 décontextualisé du français leur	decontextualized use of French will
27 permettra de poursuivre avec succès leur	allow them to successfully pursue
28 apprentissage toute la vie durant, quel	learning all their lives in whatever
29 que soit le domaine d'études choisi.	field of study they may choose.
30 —Permettre aux élèves d'acquérir une	—Permit the students to acquire a good
31 bonne compétence communicative en	communicative competence in English,
32 anglais, dans des conditions qui	under conditions which promote
33 favorisent un bilinguisme additif.	additive bilingualism.
34 —Encourager le partenariat entre les	—Encourage a partnership among
35 écoles, les parents, les différents groupes	schools, parents, different community
36 de la communauté ainsi que le monde	groups as well as the world of business,
37 des affaires, du commerce et de	commerce and industry.
38 l'industrie.	
39 —Donner aux élèves les outils	—Give students the tools necessary to
40 nécessaires pour participer à l'essor de la	participation in the development of the
41 communauté franco-ontarienne et pour	Franco-Ontarian community and to
42 contribuer avec succès à la société, sur les	successfully contribute to society,
43 plans social, politique, économique et	whether in the social, political,
44 scientifique.	economic or scientific domain.

(*Aménagement linguistique en français: Guide d'élaboration d'une politique d'aménagement linguistique* [Ministry of Education and Training of Ontario, 1994], p. 9)

These discursive assertions hint, of course, at the difficulty of constructing the oasis. Students in French-language schools often spend hours getting to and from school, a much more arduous life than attending the neighborhood English-language school; the fact that they do it is testimony to their investment. But in a place like Toronto, children learn early about the relevance of English to their lives, no matter what language they speak at home. In addition, by the time they are about nine or ten years old, they learn to orient to the peer group as a world in which to build selves separate from the world of adults. The only other people in their environment who really understand what it is like to navigate the worlds of French and English are their schoolmates, who are also exactly the people with whom they construct the modes of resistance to adult authority that in North American society are the hallmarks of healthy adolescence. When that adult authority insists on exclusive use of French, an obvious means of creating an alternative world is to speak English.

The upshot is that in the school, teachers walk around insisting "Parlez français! Parlez français!" (Speak French! Speak French!). They also embed the use of French in the disciplinary processes of maintaining social order, thereby tying French to both the moral and the social order, and upping the stakes in the struggles between adults and youth. Before we turn, in the next section, to student responses, I will examine here the modes of construction of the link between French, social order (mainly in turn-taking), and moral order (mainly through the concept of "respect").

This tie is evident in the following text, a guide to key foci for the discipline of students:

1	Aux enseignant-e-s: Veuillez évaluer	To teachers: Please evaluate
2	dans les domaines indiqués	in the areas indicated
3	—Travaille de façon concentrée et ne	—Works with concentration and does not
4	perd pas son temps	waste his or her time
5	—Parle que lorsqu'elle est invitée à le	—Talks only when invited to
6	faire et cela avec respect	do so and with respect
7	—Écoute attentivement et	—Listens attentively and
8	respectueusement lorsque son	respectfully when his or her
9	professeur ou un autre élève parle.	teacher or another student is speaking.

(Disciplinary evaluation sheet [*Feuille de route quotidienne*], 1994)

This sheet also hints at another crucial dimension of the ways in which francophone oasis-making is part of the constitution of the order of the school: it links conventions of turn-taking to being a good student-citizen, and it makes no distinction between conforming to conventions of turn-taking and the language in which those turns are taken. The well-known Initiation-Response-Evaluation (I-R-E) sequential structure of classroom talk turns out to be the bedrock of school culture (Sinclair and Coulthard 1975; Mehan 1979), not only because it allows for the reproduction of an ideology of learning and teaching focused on the individual accumulation and mastery of knowledge transmitted and validated by the teacher (Philips 1983), but also because it allows for the surveillance of the circulation of bodies and artifacts, and their Foucauldian disciplining into appropriate social subjects (Foucault 1975). The key word here is "respect," the moral regulation and legitimation of a specific institutional social order of schooling, the oil of the mechanism of social selection (Bourdieu and Passeron 1977).

We can see how this discursive assemblage works in a number of ways in everyday life at school. The most explicit example turned up in one class Laurette Lévy and I observed (each of us once a week) for the first semester (September through January) of 1991. This was a particularly difficult class, grade 10 French, taught at what was then known as the "general" level, that is, with a curriculum oriented toward postsecondary entrance into the workforce or vocational training (as opposed to the university-entrance-oriented "advanced" level). The students were either working-class whites, mainly ethnolinguistically francophone Canadian in origin, with a track record of low grades; or Somali-speaking refugees who had entered Canada the previous summer with no papers and who were placed at the general level (to their fury, since most of them had attended elite French schools in their country of origin). The teacher, Lise, albeit originally from Quebec, had grown up in the Toronto area and thus knew exactly what it meant to be in a multilingual English-dominated environment; in addition, she was in fact not principally a French teacher at all, but was involved in physical education and counseling, both areas where teachers typically have a less hierarchical relationship with students (at least in Canadian high schools). On every count, therefore, she was probably the least likely teacher to invoke discipline.

However, the force of the conventional social and moral order, in the face of students unlikely to profit from investing in it, caused regular interactional breakdown. Students spoke at the same time, to each other and to the teacher, or refused to speak when called upon to do so (when they came to class, which did not happen on a regular basis either); they also kept their coats or jackets on in class, or listened to their Walkmen, in a kind of refusal to really be present. Saïd, one of the Somali students, regularly challenged the legitimacy of her pedagogical practices, arguing that a "real" class would have things like *dictées* (those dictations which serve to inculcate the standard language in traditional French pedagogy), not the projects and presentations which Lise seemed to favor (and which were of course mandated by a curriculum aimed at "meeting the needs" of general-level students, with the effect of ensuring that those students would never learn what they might have needed to know in order to move up to the advanced-level class). By October, Lise was exhausted and exasperated, complaining that in her class "ça manque de respect" (there is no respect), but struggling with how to deal with it. One day, she became so angry with Saïd that she sent him to the principal's office, then embarked on a meta-lesson on respect and turn-taking as essential conditions for engaging in teaching and learning activities. She makes her point about respect most forcefully in lines 1, 20, and 28 below.

1	Lise:	Le respect selon moi vous me	Respect in my opinion you'll
2		direz si vous êtes d'accord ou	tell me if you agree or
3		non, il y a trois respects très	not, there are three very
4		importants que tu sois à	important respects, whether
5		l'école, que tu sois au travail,	you're at school, at work,
6		que tu sois à la maison.	at home.
7		Premièrement, si tu veux te	First, if you want to
8		respecter toi-même	respect yourself
9	Nathalie:	Oui, la première chose	Yes, the first thing
10	Lise:	Te respecter toi-même, ça veut	Respect yourself, that means
11		dire faire attention à toi,	paying attention to yourself
12		ça veut dire	that means
13	Mohamud:	C'est contrôler	It's controlling
14	Lise:	(xx) que ton hygiène	(xx) that your hygiene
	Female	C'est contrôler	It's controlling
15	student:		
16	Mohamud:	C'est contrôler alors	So it's controlling
17	Lise:	C'est te contrôler, contrôler tes	It's controlling yourself, your
18		colères, contrôler tes peines,	anger, your sadness,

19		contrôler tes joies, c'est aussi	your joys, it's also
20		respecter autrui, c'est-à-dire	respecting others, that is
21		respecter les autres, ça veut	other people, that means
22		dire lorsqu'une personne qui	when a person is
23		parle, tu dois apprendre à te	speaking, you have to learn
24		taire	to be quiet
25	Mohamud:	La dernière chose c'est	The last thing is
26		bon pour (xx)	good for (xx)
27	Leïla:	(laughs)	(laughs)
28	Lise:	Tu dois aussi apprendre à	You also have to learn to
29		écouter l'autre qui parle	listen to others when they
30		(pause) okay tu dois aussi	speak (pause) okay you also
31		apprendre à ne pas fesser	have to learn to not hit
32		l'autre parce qu'il vient de	another person because he's
33		dire quelque chose que	just said something that
34		t'aimerais pas. Pis la	you wouldn't like. And the
35		troisième c'est respecter tout	third is respecting all
36		ce qui est matériel, c'est-à-	material things, that is
37		dire c'est pas parce que t'es	it's not because you're
38		fâché que tu vas envoyer un	angry that you're going to
39		pupitre sur le tableau, par	throw a desk against the
40		exemple, il y a d'autres	board, for instance, there are
41		façons de régler	other ways to settle
	Female	Madame, c'est bien (xx)	Madame, that's fine (xx)
42	student:		
43	Lise:	Il y a trois respects selon moi,	There are three respects in my
44		toi, l'autre, puis matériel	opinion, me, you, and material

(Tenth-grade *Français général* class, October 1991)

The day after that, Lise wrote on the board:

1	—Interruptions non-nécessaires	—Unnecessary interruptions
2	—Comportement peu désiré:	—Little desired behavior:
3	——Parler sans raison	——Speaking for no reason
4	——Impolitesse	——Impoliteness
5	—Parler une autre langue que le français	—Speaking a language other than French

(Tenth-grade *Français général* class, October 1991 [from field notes])

The examples I have given above are the most explicit, but there were other forms of surveillance of self and other, too, that occurred on a daily basis. The I-R-E and other interactional formats were regularly used to comment not just on content but also on linguistic form, and teachers also self-corrected on a regular basis. Almost all of these were about "pure" French versus French contaminated by influence from English, although in a few cases the issue was standard versus vernacular French. Below, I provide a few examples of each.

The next extract is the canonical format, exploiting the I-R-E format for purposes of linguistic control. Martine, the teacher of the advanced-level grade 10 French class, is preparing the students for the next module focused on a reading activity, by generating a discussion about reading. Her response to Michel's contribution, though, is about form rather than content.

1	Martine:	Pourquoi lit-on?	Why do we read?
2	Michel:	Pour relaxer	To relax
3	Martine:	Pour "se détendre," "relaxer"	To "se détendre" [relax],
4		c'est anglais	"relaxer" is English

(Tenth-grade *Français avancé*, 1991)

In the next extract, Lise takes up a contribution from Stéphane to a collective storytelling format, in which each student provides the next element in the string of events (in this case, someone has stolen a car and is driving off). Lise provides the "good" "French" term for a flat tire (*une crevaison*), although the word "flat" is quite integrated into Canadian French (along with a lot of other car-part terminology, as I had learned long before in my strolls among the garages of Montreal in 1978).

| 1 | Stéphane: | Elle a un *flat* | She has a *flat* |
| 2 | Lise: | Elle a une crevaison | She has a flat |

(Tenth-grade *Français général*, 1991)

In the following extract, Julien is giving a presentation in accounting class on the financial difficulties of his favorite hockey team, the Quebec Nordiques (indeed, because of those difficulties, they are now the Colorado Avalanche, although their sweater remains iconic of Québécois nationalism and, fifteen years later, is still sold). Thérèse's comment is not about the team or their finances, but about the form of the word *irréalistique*.

| Julien: | Ça veut dire que, lui s'embarquer là-dedans c'est vraiment un risque pour lui. Perdre son poste puis trouver une somme d'argent aussi énorme, ça ça sera le euh très le c'est comme un peu irréalistique pour la ville de Québec | That means that for him to get involved in that, it's really a risk for him. To lose his job and find such a large sum of money, it it will the uh very the it's a bit unrealistic for the city of Quebec |
| Thérèse: | [. . .] Les mots en -*ic* hein? c'est des mots souvent anglais, "realistic," (xx) il y a plusieurs qui l'utilisent comme ça. C'est *réaliste*, euh *réaliste*, *idéaliste*, et cetera, mais il y a beaucoup d'élèves qui utilisent ces mots-là avec la la terminaison -*ic*, ça n'existe pas en français, ça c'est de l'anglais | [. . .] Words ending in -*ic* eh? they are often English words, "realistic," (xx) there are many who use it like that. It's *réaliste* uh *réaliste*, *idéaliste*, et cetera, but there are many students who use those words with the the ending -*ic*, it doesn't exist in French, that is English |

(Eleventh-grade *Comptabilité*, 1994)

In the next extract, Lise self-corrects her use of *timé* (timed), again, despite the fact that the term is in quite current usage in everyday conversational Canadian French (she is preparing the students for a specific exercise).

1	Lise:	Alors ce qu'on va faire	So what we're going to
2		aujourd'hui, on va sortir les	do today, we're going to take
3		textes que vous avez eus hier	out the texts which you got
4		sur le futur dépasse souvent la	yesterday on the future often
5		technologie [...] ça va être uh	overtakes technology [...] it
6		*timé*, moi je pense c'est	will be uh *timed*, I think it's
7		vraiment le le (*pause*)	really the the (*pause*)
8		*chronométré* je devrais dire,	*chronométré* I should say,
9		mot anglais, okay t'as ton	English word, okay you have
10		texte	your text

(Tenth-grade *Français général*, 1991)

We found these practices most often, not surprisingly, in French classes, given the ideological load that subject bears in a school devoted to the language's "normalization" (to borrow a term from Catalanist sociolinguistics). They were also widespread in classes heavily focused on linguistic expression, such as geography or history. We found them less often in science and math. In science classes, pedagogy at that time was built on the idea that school-based knowledge should be arrived at through careful scaffolding from practical knowledge of the everyday world. As a result, most modules included elicitation of that knowledge. But the science teachers knew, of course, that in a place like Toronto the chances were that knowledge would be acquired in English. They therefore had regularly to handle the discrepancy between the two legitimate forms of knowledge: everyday knowledge in English and school-based knowledge in French. They used two strategies to do this: the same kind of simple substitution of one word for another in the sequence of talk as used by *Français* teachers (as in, say, the tenth-grade *Français général* class quoted above), and alternately through the discursive separation of public, unified, teacher-controlled talk in French, from "offstage," student-dominated talk, which the teacher simply ignored if it wasn't in French (as in the talk among student groups doing lab work).

In the end, then, rather a lot of interactional, communicative, and discursive work went into making the school fit the image of what it was supposed to be: a francophone "oasis" in an anglophone environment (well, the implication is clearly "desert"). Part of the lack of fit, of course, came simply from the fact that the world of the school was dominated by English; it was even part of an English-language school board until a major centralization of school governance undertaken by the provincial government in 1996 resulted in a reduction in the numbers (and increase in the size) of boards across the province, and, concurrently, the creation of French-language boards for which francophones had long fought (and which the government found itself acquiescing to as an unintended and unforeseen consequences of their centralizing reforms).

The other part, however, had to do with the complicated trajectory of the school's students, in terms of what this meant both for their linguistic repertoires, and for their interest in investing in the school as a site for access to symbolic resources. Investment also meant collaborating with the school's social construction of linguistically and culturally homogeneous space oriented to facilitating francophone access to school success and hence to socioeconomic mobility. In the next section, I explore some of these positionings, and the tensions that flow from them over two competing ideologies of language: language as emblem of authentic ethnic identity, and language as a commodity exchangeable, notably, for jobs on the new labor market at both national and international levels, where communicative skills in general, and French and English skills in particular, have new value.

5.4 IDENTITIES AND COMMODITIES

Just as schools like Champlain (or territories like Quebec) are only fictively bounded and homogeneous, so are the populations supposed to be found in those spaces. The ideal citizen, or student, has to be made. But the nature of heterogeneity is always historically contingent, so the details matter. In the case of Champlain (and, for that matter, the rest of francophone Canada), the rise of the francophone middle class and the construction of its privileged market (centered on Quebec, but with global ambitions riding on the coattails of the lost French Empire) account for a number of forms of heterogeneity that are important to this story.

First, not only the state but also the anglophone middle class had an interest in reassessing its relationship to French and to francophones. While, predictably (and as we have seen in the previous chapter), many did their best to preserve the market conditions favorable to them, or at least to find corners of the market that they could hope might remain unchanged, many responded by seeking to invest in French as way of maintaining their class status (and the Canadian state structures on which that status largely depended).

This took the form, most famously, of the invention of French immersion, the use of French as a language of instruction for anglophones, in English-language schools. The French immersion movement began in the Montreal suburbs in 1965, in an initial experimental program closely followed, and legitimated, by a social psychologist and a neurologist from McGill University (Rebuffot and Lyster 1996). From the beginning, parents were clear that they were concerned about their children's access to jobs, and, as with French-language minority schools, the program has remained attractive largely to the middle class (Heller 1990).

However, for many anglophones, French-language schools have presented an even better alternative—a kind of super-immersion allowing for a deeper, more "authentic" experience—as well as constituting political support for the francophone community. In places like Toronto, this support was critical to the possibility of French-language schools, since their opening had to be voted on by English-speaking school councillors and since the commitment of resources to a new school required, by law, a higher enrollment threshold than the francophone community itself could actually muster.

The second major trend was the social and geographic mobility of francophones, who not only became more attractive as spouses outside the working-class networks where francophone intermarriage with other Catholic working-class families had long been established, but also moved more and more beyond their traditional networks, encountering non-francophones along the way. (For example, many of the francophone parents married to non-francophones whom I have interviewed over the years told stories of having come as a single young person to learn English with no intention of staying, but then having met someone and settled down.) This resulted in more bi- or trilingual families, for whom French-language schooling, along with bilingual home life, formed part of a strategy of accumulation of linguistic capital.

The third was the direct result of the class-mobility-related declining birth rate among francophones. Immigration became a necessity, and as Quebec gained control of elements of its immigration policy, greater numbers of francophone immigrants entered the country. Some have stayed in Quebec, but many have left, especially in periods when Quebec's economy has significantly underperformed those of Ontario, Alberta, and British Columbia. Many now come directly to those and other provinces, and most francophone communities across the country, in alliance with the federal immigration authorities, began in the early 2000s to develop their own strategies for attracting francophone immigrants, especially to rural areas losing employable youth to the cities (see chapter 6).

The population of schools like Champlain shows traces of all these forms of diversity. Indeed, from the very beginning, Champlain's motto was "L'Unité dans la diversité" (Unity in diversity). The only monolingual francophones there tend to be very recent arrivals from francophone Europe, or from areas of Quebec, New Brunswick, or northern Ontario where francophones are a majority and where social conditions (often of poverty) keep francophones away from English. Everyone else speaks at least one other language, frequently English, but often Haitian Creole, Arabic, Polish, Russian, Romanian, or a language of sub-Saharan Africa (Somali, Lingala, Kinyarwanda, and Kirundi are currently among the most frequently spoken). Of course, the longer students live in Toronto, the more likely they are to learn English.

These kinds of students are all found in schools like Champlain because outside Quebec until 1982 (and in Quebec until 1972) there were no constraints on student admissions. Article 23 of the 1982 Charter of Rights and Freedoms now stipulates that minority-language schools are only required to accept students with at least one parent whose first language learned and still understood is the language of the minority; who were themselves schooled in a school using the language of the minority; or who already have a child enrolled in a minority-language school. Beyond that, the schools can accept whomever they want. In practice, however, the need to distinguish themselves from immersion schools ensures selection practices (and a concomitant degree of contention over what they should be). Schools remain under pressure to remain democratic, to maintain enrollments at levels that ensure access to resources (numbers of students are related to access to all kinds of resources, from speech therapists to librarians to extracurricular activities), but also to remain somehow recognizably francophone. The result is a student population with diverse resources and interests.

The only students who really correspond to the profile of the idealized student on whose behalf middle-class francophones fought are the monolingual working-class Canadian-born. As I have mentioned, however, many of these families are highly concerned about gaining access to English, and many prefer immersion schools to French-language ones, since they are closest to their ideal of bilingual schools. Those who were present at Champlain complained vehemently about the normative pressures the school exerted on their French, saying that their teachers corrected both the bilingual practices that are common for them (and by no means derail their attachment to an idea of belonging to a francophone collectivity) and the vernacular forms that, for one reason or another, are not part of the normativized lexicon or phonology (the areas in which Canadian French shows the greatest distance from European French). Some of them dealt with this by moving to an English school (where any deviance from the norm could be explained by the fact that English is not their first language, and where the normative stakes are in any case not so high, given the dominant unmarked status of anglophone spaces); others stayed at school but avoided situations (like class) where they would have to perform. If the school pushed their backs to the wall, as it once did to a group of friends in Lise's class, forcing them to take part in a show of literary texts, they picked a song. One of the girls in that group managed to put off her oral presentation for over a month, until Lise finally agreed to let her do it in private, not in front of the class. (Of course, the complex ambivalent engagement or disengagement with schooling was not caused by nor confined to the terrain of language; I simply wish to show here how language became available in this way in the slow, and often agonizing, process of exclusion experienced by these students.)

Francophones who came to the school with no English, whether from Quebec, France, or eastern Africa, tended to be shocked at the widespread use of English and at the strikingly different variety of French most students spoke. One of them said that on his first day, trying to find his way to the cafeteria, he convinced himself that he must be in the wrong school. Nationalist Québécois (usually dragged to Toronto kicking and screaming by parents seeking employment or promotion) refused to engage in the social life of the school; Africans and Europeans often felt rejected by students who clearly spoke French (they heard them in class) but who for some reason chose not to as soon as they left the classroom. Where possible, monolingual francophones often formed small peer groups across age

grades (normally friendship ties remained within age grades, extending perhaps up or down one year because of kinship, romance, or shared extracurricular interests like sports or music). Africans usually were able to constitute
groups with a shared other language, but their own postcolonial histories
and the racial politics of Toronto also contributed to the rapid establishment of a race consciousness across African and Caribbean student groups.

The students who, more or less literally, occupied center stage at the
school came from a wide variety of backgrounds; they all had in common
an experience of living across French and English, and an investment in
doing well at school. They came to class on time with their homework
done, spoke French to the teachers, ran for student council, got the best
lockers, and on warm days sat outside the front of the school, chatting or
playing soccer (the working-class smokers were relegated to a space
behind the school, where they went even in the depths of winter; other
marginal students would hang out in the parking lot, in the cafeteria, or
off-site altogether). But they also whispered in English in the back of the
class, their heads down, leaning over; or passed notes and pens and bottles
of liquid eraser to each other; and in the corridors, during lab work, or in
other spaces they controlled they spoke mainly English, with some French
every now and then (and more on the city bus after school or in sports
competitions in board or city leagues, where the relevant concern was
distinguishing themselves not from school authorities but from students
in English-language schools).

The identity dimension of the school certainly added value to the linguistic resources distributed there. Students could argue that they were
bilingual in ways students in French immersion could never hope to be. At
the same time, they all shared an interest in using the homogeneous space
of the school not to reproduce homogeneous spaces, and to keep English
(and anglophones) at bay, but rather to construct a bilingual (or multilingual) repertoire of higher value than anyone else's. The paradox is that a
key element of the value of the commodity is its authenticity, and the
source of authenticity is participating in an institutional site constructed
as authentic on the basis of essentializing ideologies about its population,
but the population needs the school in order to authenticate itself. The
complications of managing this paradox (sometimes frogs on gym shorts
just aren't enough) are only worsened by the problem of aiming at a bilingualism in which at least the francophone element looks like a performance that only a monolingual could possibly produce.

The field is therefore open to struggle among students who all seek to
build a minimally bilingual French-English repertoire, who all need the
school for the valued resources of French, but who struggle over whose
French is actually the most valuable. They also struggle over whether it is
legitimate to ask French-language institutions like the school to facilitate
access to English. But most important, new market conditions turn both
identity and language into commodities that can be traded together, but
also separately.

5.5 CRAWLING TO NEOLIBERALISM

In this chapter I have taken the story from the beginnings of modernizing ethnonationalism through to an encounter with some of its inherent contradictions, most notably the ever-present impossibility of realizing both uniformity and equality. I have documented some ways in which social actors on the ground work hard, every day, to neutralize the tensions; the legitimacy of their social position depends on it. From being principally the province of the clerical and professional elite, francophone nationalism came to benefit a secular middle-class population in both the public and the private sectors and to attract people who had little or no claim to ethnonational membership.

The processes unfolding here are in many ways simply the logical unfolding of the ways in which ethnonationalism has been connected to the relationship between the state and the bourgeoisie in controlling expanding markets. In the following chapters we will see that the state's response to increasing expansion, in the form of neoliberalism, in combination with the shifting political economy of expansion, has a major impact on modernizing nationalism. The delocalization of manufacturing and the globalization of primary resource extraction have led to a growth in the tertiary sector and a shift in state–private sector relations. The kinds of interest in language as skill and as capital of distinction we saw emerge at Champlain have become ever more important in the regulation of the field of *la francité*. In the next few chapters we will take a closer look at what that might mean for ethnonationalism and for our institutionalized and normalized understandings of how language, identity, nation, and state add up.

In order to understand the social changes I gathered a sense of at Champlain and to explore what they meant for modernizing nationalism, I joined forces with colleagues in Ontario, Acadie, Europe, and eventually also Quebec and Alberta to see how things looked in important spaces for production of national and linguistic ideology beyond schooling.

Already, school processes had led me to approach the spaces where discourses about Franco-Ontarian education were emerging in the Ministry of Education, in the school boards, in associations of educators, at professional conferences, in the media, in the courts, and in sociolinguistics, just to mention the most salient (sociolinguists, including me, have been involved in Franco-Ontarian educational language policy and curriculum development since the 1970s; see Heller 1994b, 1996, and 2007c). In our next phase of work, we sought to understand links between the economic basis of discursive reproduction, the role of the state and its agencies, and the other central domain of production of ideas about *la francité canadienne*, the so-called *milieu associatif*.

6

Neoliberalism and *La cause*

Modernizing Nationalism at Its Limits (Lelac, 1997–2004)

6.1 THE *MILIEU ASSOCIATIF* AS DISCURSIVE SPACE

By the time I was ready to take a look at the network of institutions and volunteer associations known as the *milieu associatif*, it was quite well-developed. Building on the political lobbying associations of the French Canadian traditionalist elite and the social, charitable associations they founded (see chapter 3), francophone activists in the 1960s and 1970s took seriously Raymond Breton's (1964) injunction to develop "institutional completeness." In this they were aided and abetted by the federal government's construction of the francophone community as one of two pillars of "linguistic duality." The network had spread through Quebec and across the so-called *milieu minoritaire* and comprised what was left of older institutions like the Church, schools, social clubs, and political lobbying associations; and newer ones like associations of francophone gays and lesbians, immigrants, and recording artists.

As a result, we attended community consultations and assemblies and went to local chambers of commerce, credit unions, insurance companies, professional conferences, state activities, a tremendous number of committee meetings, spectacles of various kinds, festivals, shops, more schools, markets, government agencies, restaurants, cemeteries, churches, arenas, daycare centers, health clinics, radio stations, seniors' residences, fishing docks, cultural centers, artists' workshops, literacy centers, libraries, bookstores, transportation hubs; to associations devoted to seniors, children, sports, and businesspeople; even, when it was absolutely necessary, to beaches—but in case you get the wrong idea, let me assure you that this fieldwork has also involved a lot of scraping ice off windshields. We heard masses, a space opera, political speeches, all kinds of music, committee deliberations, radio and television broadcasts; we read legislation, reports, grant applications, local newspapers, advertisements, minutes of meetings. We met hundreds of generous people and didn't get lost as often as you might expect.

Much of this work has been reported in French, in edited collections bringing together thematically linked papers by team members working in various combinations (see Heller and Labrie 2003; Heller and Boutet 2006; McLaughlin et al. 2009). This is a frank political commitment, as well as an outgrowth of the ways we managed team resources and commitments, and partly a reflection on the vagaries of trying to work across both francophone and anglophone intellectual worlds. (Though many of us have presented in English at conferences, often together, getting that work out collectively in English in print has so far escaped us.) I am conscious here of the attempt to speak with my own, single voice, to provide an explicit frame for understanding the results of a collective enterprise of a large group of people (all of them named in the acknowledgments).

This chapter is devoted to exploring the changes we caught glimpses of at Champlain, which can broadly be described as a shift from talking about rights to talking about community economic development, from constructing language and identity as inalienable heritage to constructing them as sources of added value. I begin by pulling together some of the things we found out about how the state and the *milieu associatif* responded to the economic changes affecting francophone Canada in that period. I look at ways in which the state's general neoliberal strategies, focused on individual worker skills development and privatization, were modified to accommodate commitments to "linguistic duality," in the form of programs supporting "community economic development." I will also briefly touch on another, related set of recent initiatives that seek to bring in immigrants where young people cannot be retained, or where the population is diminishing simply because people are having smaller families.

That section is based on data collected through interviews with municipal, provincial, and state-level government agents, participation in community consultations during the period in the 1990s when the federal government was redefining its relationship to the institutionalized francophone community, and examination of reports produced by (or commissioned by) government agencies and the *milieu associatif*. (Since we live in a regime in which the state must account for how it spends taxpayers' money, much of this material is publicly available.)

We will see that this compromise not only preserved the idea of ethnonational collective entities that modernizing national discourses had established, but also retained the much older focus on rural traditional bastions as the legitimating core of those collectivities. "Community economic development" turns out to mean finding new ways to support the reproduction of rural heartland regions through development of tertiary-sector activities (often heritage tourism) and, where necessary, the recruitment of workers through immigration.

The final part of the chapter is devoted to a closer look at how this shift happened in one particular heartland area with which we are becoming familiar: Lelac, a town that in many ways resembles the stereotype of the French Canadian rural settlement. I was first invited there in the early 1990s, by a student from a nearby town who had grown up in the area and taught in its original French-language school, and she introduced me to some of the people most active in the modernist political movement. They helped us understand how the francophone community was organized. I spent a lot of time there between 1998 and 2004, piecing together the area's history and closely following how its associations and institutions responded to the economic and political shifts felt in Lelac as elsewhere across francophone Canada. In the end, Lelac became one of our best vantage points for discovering what it means to live in a traditional bastion in the twenty-first century.

6.2 FROM RIGHTS TO PROFITS: CANADA'S NEOLIBERAL TURN

Francophone mobilization, while aimed, in my view, at socioeconomic mobility—indeed, specifically at free participation in the private-sector economy—was framed and legitimized in the language of a nation's rights to political power and to the expression and practice of its own cultural values. The Canadian state's response, as we have seen, was equally political: the 1968 Official Languages Act.

One immediate result was the establishment of funding programs, largely through the culture ministry, for the support of French-language artistic and cultural activities. The numerous associations that sprang up in the 1970s as interlocutors (and funding recipients) for the federal government learned how to develop grant applications and project reports in order to undertake a variety of such activities, often at the local level. Seasonal labor (for example, in fishing and lumber) also depended on income supplements through various kinds of employment insurance or welfare programs. However, by the late 1980s, both the state and the community associations it supported lost faith in this approach, since it failed to address the economic crises that were threatening the existence of the communities as they were ideologically understood.

The federal government of Canada adopted neoliberal policies similar to those of most First World countries. One immediate consequence, which is particularly important for our purposes, was the termination of the funding programs that earlier had been a major signal of state investment in the francophone community (along with the termination of the welfare programs that had sustained seasonal workers, among which Acadian fishermen were well-represented). Indeed, the Official Languages Act itself was overhauled.

The following text (Section 41, Official Languages Act, 1988) represents the most significant change in this regard. In italics (mine), we find the new phrasing that will turn out a few years later to make all the difference:

> The Government of Canada is committed to (a) enhancing the vitality of the English and French linguistic *minority communities* in Canada and

supporting and assisting their development; and (b) fostering the full recognition and use of both English and French in Canadian society.

[Le gouvernement fédéral s'engage à favoriser l'épanouissement des *minorités* francophones et anglophones du Canada et à *appuyer leur développement,* ainsi qu'à promouvoir la pleine reconnaissance et l'usage du français et de l'anglais dans la société canadienne.] (Section 41, Official Languages Act, 1988)

The juxtaposition of the terms "communities" (or *minorités*) and "development" laid the basis for channeling state funds toward an identifiable collectivity, thus maintaining the criteria of inclusion and exclusion. The question of who belongs counts.

More generally, the Canadian government turned to programs to develop the tertiary sector, aimed at producing workers adjusted to the new economy (that is, with the literacy and numeracy skills, self-reliance, and "flexibility" that the new economy requires). It also turned more to the private sector and to individual initiative to provide economic expansion, turning away from its welfare-state role of providing protection for its citizens, and toward the neoliberal role of encouraging citizens to produce (Silva and Heller 2009).

Meanwhile, the francophone association network took stock of the economic devastation of its traditional bastions. In the late 1980s, the Fédération des communautés francophones et acadiennes du Canada (FCFA) undertook a nationwide consultative process that produced the conviction (repeated time and time again since the OJC) that a priority had to be placed on economic development.

The early- to mid-1990s saw a drawn-out process of dialogue between the association sector and the federal government about the role the state should play; during that time, they experimented with a number of different formats for sustaining funding. Francophone institutions (creatures, we must remember, of the 1960s Canadian welfare state) were not interested in disappearing; they had everything invested in finding new ways to reproduce the francophone nation. They were therefore deeply threatened by the neoliberalizing government's focus on the individual. This is expressed most explicitly in the following extract from a report commissioned by the FCFA during a period when the federal government put forward a series of reforms to funding programs aimed at worker training:

In the proposed reform bill, preference is given to an approach favouring the individual which seems to neglect the universal nature of the programs. [. . .] We fear that the individual approach will favour the decisions made by the majority for the majority.

[Dans le projet de la réforme proposée, on privilégie une approche favorisant l'individu et on semble vouloir délaisser le caractère universel des programmes. [. . .] L'approche individuelle, on le craint, risque d'avantager des motivations faites pour la majorité et par la majorité.] (*Plan directeur de l'adaptation de la main d'oeuvre de la francophonie canadienne* [Formatel Consultants 1995: 70])

The FCFA proceeded to argue that the 1988 version of the Official Languages Act (cited above) obligated the federal government to support not just individual workers, but collective francophone minority community development. The result was the 1998 establishment of the Réseau de développement économique et d'employabilité du Canada (RDÉE; Economic Development and Employability Network of Canada), which is still in existence (see Silva and Heller 2009 for a detailed description and analysis of the relevant discursive and institutional shifts through the 1990s and into the 2000s, and Forgues 2007 for a chronology).

The RDÉE is set up as a partnership between the federal government and the francophone "community" sector (represented by the FCFA) under a co-presidency. On the federal government side, the 1988 legislation was used to distribute responsibility for official languages across all government ministries (rather than concentrating it in the hands of the ministry of culture), most of which are at the RDÉE table. The period 1998–2003 saw continued shifts in the definition of the RDÉE's mandate and in its organization, as the federal government sorted itself out. In 2003, the government produced a new Action Plan for Official Languages which stabilized the orientation and funding basis of the RDÉE. By 2005, the RDÉE had produced a clear statement of its goals:

> RDÉE Canada, in collaboration with its provincial and Territory partners, promotes economic development and job creation in the francophone and Acadian communities of Canada.
> [. . .] *It is relevant to underline that more than a million francophones live in linguistic minority contexts in Canada* [emphasis in the original]. Their impact on the economy of the country is important. Their presence in business adds value to exchanges and allows for a greater diversification of economic activity. The RDÉE acts as a link among these francophones of the country.
> RDÉE agents are involved in four sectors:
>
> • Rural development
> • The knowledge economy
> • Tourism
> • The integration of youth into economic development

> [RDÉE Canada favorise, en collaboration avec ses partenaires provinciaux et territoriaux, le développement économique et la création d'emplois dans les communautés francophones et acadiennes du Canada.
> [. . .] *Il est pertinent de souligner que plus d'un million de francophones vivent en situation linguistique minoritaire au Canada.* Leur impact sur l'économie du pays est important. Leur présence dans le domaine des affaires ajoute de la valeur aux échanges et permet une plus grande diversification de l'activité économique. Le RDÉE sert de maillon entre ces francophones du pays.

Les agents du RDÉE interviennent dans quatre secteurs:

- Développement rural
- Économie du savoir
- Tourisme
- Intégration des jeunes dans le développement économique] (*Réseau de développement économique et d'employabilité du Canada* mission statement, from the RDÉE's Web site [www.rdee.ca]; accessed February 2, 2005)

I would like to draw attention to the three dimensions of RDÉE's focus: the insistence on community economic development (over the development of individual job skills, otherwise the dominant trope of neoliberal federal policy); the target population (rural youth); and the economic sectors involved (tourism and the knowledge economy). This can be seen as an effect of efforts to save the nation as it was constituted under disappearing political economic conditions—that is, to shore up the rural traditional bastions of francophone identity by reinventing their economic basis, thereby retaining a population that otherwise leaves to seek employment elsewhere, whether in the oil sands of northern Alberta or the tertiary-sector job markets in the city.

Just to give an idea of how essential the ideology of the rural heartland is to francophone Canada, I quote an extract from an interview I conducted with two civil servants in Ottawa closely involved with the policy and program changes outlined above. Both agents find it unthinkable to support the francophone community any other way, since for them (as for Romantic nationalists since the nineteenth century; Williams 1973; Heller 2005a), the city is where the individual trumps the collective, where francophones go to assimilate to the dominant, profit-oriented, English-speaking capitalist world.

> CAROLE: For the francophone communities, the young people that leave, go to the big cities from the rural communities and assimilate themselves to the majority / so they really lose [community] members, the next generation perhaps will not speak French
> DANIELLE: And we have statistics on that
> CAROLE: They don't go to Calgary saying me, I'm francophone I'm going to try and keep my, my francophone identity, they say me, I'm looking for a job [. . .] If it's in an Anglophone environment, that's not a problem I'm bilingual, after that [. . .] when they choose the person they'll marry, once again their goal is not, you know, it's not *la francophonie canadienne*, it's just to have a, a husband, a wife, then to have kids, so not everyone thinks about the survival of the francophone minority community
> DANIELLE: Sometimes love is stronger than survival (*laughter*)
>
> [CAROLE: Pour les communautés francophones, les jeunes qui s'en vont, vont vers les grandes villes des communautés rurales et s'assimilent à la

majorité / alors ils perdent vraiment des membres, la génération d'après ne parlera peut-être pas le français

DANIELLE: Puis on des statistiques là-dessus

CAROLE: Ils s'en vont pas à Calgary en se disant moi je suis francophone je vais essayer de garder ma, mon identité francophone, ils disent moi je suis à la recherche d'un emploi [. . .] Si c'est un milieu anglophone, c'est pas un problème je suis bilingue, après ça [. . .] en choisissant la personne à qui ils veulent se marier, encore une fois leur but à eux c'est pas de, t'sais c'est pas la francophonie canadienne, c'est juste avoir un, un époux, une épouse, puis de faire des enfants, puis c'est pas tout le monde qui pense à la survie de la communauté minoritaire francophone

DANIELLE: Des fois l'amour est plus fort que la survie (*rire*)] (Interview, federal civil service, 2004)

Although the neoliberal turn might have undermined the idea of nation more radically than it did, it nonetheless had a major impact on the reproduction of the idea of *la francité*. Most important, it shifted the grounds of legitimacy from a discourse of rights to a discourse of economic development. Francophone associations had to learn new ways of seeking funding, had to build new networks with ministries that in the past had been irrelevant to francophone community activity, and, crucially, had to reshape their activities into profit-making enterprises. But the legitimacy of the traditional bastions as the heartland of francophone Canada remained unchallenged, as did the traditional idea of the importance of reproducing those heartland communities biologically. Keeping young people in the region became the focus of resources and energy.

Failing that, rural francophone minority communities have become involved in the recruitment of francophone immigrants, in direct alliance with the federal ministry responsible for immigration. That ministry sends delegations overseas to recruit francophone immigrants, and members of the *milieu associatif* have begun to accompany them. The ministry has also set up a body constructed similarly to the committee on human resource development that became the RDÉE, that is, as a state-community partnership, with co-presidents. New forms of immigration call into being new community structures, as well as framing scholarly work on what it means for francophone communities, since those communities that have long understood themselves as ethnonational collectivities must now come to terms with highly educated, skilled people who choose other ways of being francophone, in Quebec as well as elsewhere (we will discuss this further in chapter 7; see Korazemo and Stebbins 2001; Jedwab 2002; Madibbo and Maury 2002; Quell 2002; CIC 2003, 2005; Farmer et al. 2003; Laperrière and Beaulé 2004; Gallant and Belkhodja 2005; Belkhodja 2006; Jacquet et al. 2008). To maintain francophone communities, there must be francophone bodies present; to recruit and sustain them there has to be a local economy. The notion of recruiting francophone immigrants to do francophone heritage work strikes no one as a contradiction, although public debate does focus on the "problem" of how to attract immigrants to rural areas in general, and francophone ones in particular. There is also a great deal of concern about what francophone communities mean by "integration" and how prepared they really are to deal with ethnocultural difference (see chapter 8).

In the next section, I return to Lelac, a community that represents the ideal of the heartland and that has been living through most of the processes described so far. We will see how its *milieu associatif* approached the discursive shift from *la cause* to *valeur ajoutée* in ways that left the lines between them quite blurred and raised important questions about how to do being a francophone community as a commodity.

6.3 LELAC: POTATOES, MILK, TREES, TOURISTS, AND THE HIGHWAY

Lelac lies in the middle of a peninsula, in a rural region of fields, lakes, and forests in central Ontario.[1] It is the only francophone village in the area, although the village just to the south is bilingual, and many francophones live in the two nearby towns. While there is no direct historical continuity between New France and the contemporary community, the region's founding myth focuses on the arrival in the region of Champlain and his scout, Étienne Brûlé, in the early 1600s. Just outside Lelac stands a monument to the first Catholic mass celebrated in the area. The echoes of Champlain's presence provide a powerful sense of historical legitimacy and are frequently evoked in texts and oral accounts of the region's history.

A short-lived Jesuit mission was established nearby and is now the site of a living museum, open to tourists in the summer months (and a source of summer employment for local students). The mission took in converted members of the local indigenous population and was destroyed by non-converts, probably in alliance with the British (the French and the British mobilized local populations on a regular basis in their struggle for imperial domination; Wolf 1982). The surviving converts retreated with the Jesuits back to Quebec City, where their descendants still live today. Other indigenous groups moved in, until the British removed them from land allotted to agricultural immigrants.

Today's francophone population stems from the in-migration of French Canadian farmers from Quebec in the mid-nineteenth century, onto land that was available because the regional indigenous population was kept away from it (the descendants of that later wave of indigenous settlement remain in the region, many of them on a reserve just off the shore of the lake near which Lelac sits). The community the Québécois settlers established represents almost an archetype of the traditional French-Canadian community: rural, isolated, Catholic, homogeneous. The area was mainly farmed (subsistence, dairy, and potato monoculture), but farming existed side-by-side with, and was often supplemented by, fishing and lumber-jacking. The first families to arrive settled the most fertile land, in the center of a peninsula; later arrivals were relegated to poorer soil closer to the water's edge.

The local elite, drawn from well-off farming families, began to organize itself around the parish in the late 1800s and early 1900s. The Catholic Church actively promoted the development of this elite, providing elementary education, arranging for promising youth to be sent away to convents and seminaries for higher education, and organizing discussion circles that can be seen as embryonic forms of later community associations (all strategies used throughout French Canada). In Lelac as elsewhere, these circles established the groundwork for community activism—for example, in the form of the local OJC *commanderie*, as well as the founding of insurance companies and credit unions, which were essential for the financial stability of the community. This process produced major clerical and lay figures of importance today, such as a bishop, and a lawyer responsible for suing the province in the mid-1980s in a landmark lawsuit over francophone rights.

Those who were unable to make a living from agriculture or a combination of agriculture and forestry or fishing went to work for anglophones in nearby English-dominated towns, at first in sawmills, and later in other manufacturing industries. These families were marginal to the major sites of discourse production in the francophone community; they had fewer means of producing a traditionalist discourse, and fewer reasons for doing so. They are still held up by activists as examples of the ravages of assimilation.

The early part of the twentieth century saw the development of a property-based tourist industry, in which local skills in construction (and, for females, cooking) were seasonally put to use by rich anglophones from Toronto or the United states seeking to build weekend and summer retreats (on lakeside land farmers once considered worthless). Agriculture became untenable as a family-based business in the 1960s as a result of mechanization and industrialization of production systems within a much more centralized, government-controlled system of production. Displaced sons either followed their uncles into town or became entrepreneurs in the cottage tourist industry; the latter is a major source of male employment to this day, creating conditions that allow networks of relatively poorly educated but often highly skilled male francophones to reproduce language and local identity without participating in the structures and discourses of the elite. Some women work in towns, in industry, shops, or health care; many turn their own country skills to profit by selling baked goods, preserves, and crafts and by providing various other forms of services (such as cleaning) to tourists in the summer.

The area was galvanized in the late 1970s by a struggle over French-language education. Because of the school reforms we discussed in the previous chapter, the local "continuation" (francophone Catholic) school in Lelac was closed in the early 1970s, and a bilingual program was introduced in the nearby town, to accommodate both that town's anglophone high school students and the francophones from Lelac and the surrounding area. Lelac students began to be bussed into the nearby town for high school, moving from their local village French-language Catholic elementary school to the big high school twenty minutes or so away. Members of the local elite lobbied for the school to be divided into separate French and English schools. The struggle was fierce, both between the elite and the school board and within the francophone community; people talk about it to this day. The elite was ultimately successful, and the struggle has entered local (indeed provincial) lore. It also laid the foundations of the local community association.

By the early 1980s the community had its own high school, as well as a community center right on the main street of the town. Lelac youth still had to come into town for high school, whichever high school they opted for, but it seemed like a compromise that would facilitate access to the French-language school for francophones from the whole region.

However, in the following decade the regional industrial base was greatly eroded. By the late 1990s, attempts to develop heritage and environmental tourism began to replace it, marrying the region's undeniable natural beauty to its complicated English, French, and indigenous history and its identity as "country." In the mid-1990s, there was an explosion of interest among certain francophones in the Métis heritage their ancestors had vigorously denied, testifying to the changing organization of social categorization and inequality. In the late 1990s, a nearby urban center experienced tremendous economic and demographic growth, drawing many people south and attracting francophones from other parts of the country, who had different ideas about being francophone and speaking French. The new globalized economy has produced a new crop of wealthy people (from farther and farther afield, as far as Germany and Russia) seeking to build country estates, touching off a small construction boom. Finally, technology and better roads also brought new people into the community, including educated francophones seeking a place to retire, to work out of home offices, to develop as writers or musicians, or to establish an alternative, eco-friendly economy. Some are people with local roots who left for higher education and have now returned.

The cultural association that was born out of the school struggle (although it can also be traced to the discussion circles and OJC cell of the 1950s and the still-existing social club founded by the OJC) was necessarily caught up in these changes. In the next section we will take a closer look at how the shifts in state funding models described in section 2, and the local manifestations of economic changes described here and in section 1, progressively constrained the association's course of action. What we witnessed in the period between 1998 and 2000 was a shift in legitimating ideology. An association founded to defend a nation's rights turned into an association at the service of its community, devoted to community development and the promotion of French language and culture.

6.4 FROM CULTURAL SURVIVAL TO ADDED VALUE

We began following the local community center, interviewing members and sitting in on the monthly meetings of its executive committee. The council's membership had generally been drawn from the local elite; in the 1990s and 2000s, it began to draw less from local families (although they too remained present) and more from active and retired professional educators, as well as other professionals from the public sector, a few entrepreneurs, and some members from outside the community altogether. It does not include, for example, industrial, farming, or construction workers, the unemployed, or the poorly educated (this is scarcely a surprise, but it bears repeating.) The Church collaborates but does not participate directly: this is a modern, lay association.

Its director, Bernard, played an important role in the school crisis. For him it was a moment of conversion; as he tells it, he had been a staunch believer in bilingualism. The school crisis radicalized him; he became the media spokesperson for the French-language school forces, and later spent many years as an elected school board trustee. His position at the center involved being the local representative to the province-wide lobbying association (itself in turn a member of the FCFA). Together with his school board activities, Bernard's entire life focused around *la cause*.

In his work, he had cultivated relationships with federal civil servants responsible for the management of francophone minority community arts and culture funding at both the provincial and federal levels, and he knew how to fill out the grant applications for the concerts, festivals, day camps, and other linguistic and cultural heritage activities that were the center's major concerns. Executive committee meetings mainly consisted of his accounts to the volunteer members on the state of play of his various applications, reports, and upcoming events and, where necessary, staff and infrastructure issues (for example, the state of the building housing the center).

In the late 1990s, things started to fall apart. The funding programs Bernard was used to were disappearing; it was much harder than before to get funding for planned activities. The shifts I described above were being felt at the local level, and for Bernard, at least, they were bewildering. The executive committee realized that things had to change.

From 1998–2000 it embarked on a makeover in quite intense fashion, not only hashing things out in meetings, but also circulating draft documents for commentary between meetings, and frequently consulting by telephone or in person. It focused on the development of a more bureaucratized regime, drawing up job descriptions for paid staff and contracts for them to sign. Activity that, although paid, had emerged out of volunteer labor for *la cause* was turned into wage labor in a service economy. The council also focused on its own role and on the mandate of the organization, introducing the new understanding of itself as a service organization. I next discuss three moments in how this shift unfolded.

The first is from a council meeting held in early 1998. At this meeting, the council debated what kind of council it wanted to be, based on management training documents the members had studied and discussed in order to prepare themselves for the changes they understood they had to undertake. The models provided for varying degrees of power to be concentrated in the hands of the council or the director and therefore were closely linked to the specific relationship between this council and its particular director, Bernard. As the discussion unfolded, one member raised the issue of this relationship and how to handle it in the context of broader ideological orientations. Specifically, the problem that the council raised was the possibility of curtailing the director's independence for reasons that they described as bureaucratic and democratic (better to have elected members make decisions; a council remains, but directors come and go; a council is legally responsible for the organization in ways the director is not) and that certainly would have the effect of concentrating power in the hands of the (elected) council. However, Bernard, who, as everyone knew, had a different view on how things should be run, was sitting in the meeting. One council member, Richard, makes it clear in the course of the meeting that it is not a question of not having confidence in Bernard, but an association planning for its future cannot count on the eternal presence of one director. (In the exchange below, Denis is another council member.)

> RICHARD: We can choose a structure which has to do with us [or which fits us]. The DG [Director-General] which we have right now or if ever the DG came to change, we wouldn't have a choice, y'know? We wouldn't be able to revise what kind of structure we want. So
> DENIS: Yes
> BERNARD: Okay but seeing as how
> RICHARD: Well yes we can [have?] lots lots of confidence as it is now with Bernard, we can choose a model, you know, a simpler one. But if the next one who replaces him, we can't trust him, well we wouldn't want the same one either
> DENIS: But that could change
> RICHARD: Yes?
> DENIS: If we adopt a structure isn't that what we're looking for right now? A fixed structure for the council? We aren't going to start changing every time we have a different DG
>
> [RICHARD: On peut choisir la structure qui se rapporte à nous. Le DG qu'on a tout de suite ou si jamais le DG venait à changer, on aurait pas le choix, t'sais? On ne pourrait plus réviser quelle sorte de structure on veut. Donc
> DENIS: Oui
> BERNARD: Bon mais vu que

RICHARD: Bien si on peut [faire?] beaucoup beaucoup de confiance
   comme c'est là à Bernard, on peut choisir un modèle, tu sais, plus
   simple. Mais si le prochain qui va le remplacer, on ne peut pas le faire
   confiance, bien on ne voudra plus avoir le même non plus
DENIS: Mais ça ça pourrait changer
RICHARD: Oui?
DENIS: Si on adopte une structure c'est pas ça qu'on cherche en ce
   moment? Une structure fixe pour le CA? On n'est pas pour com-
   mencer à changer à chaque fois qu'on a un différent DG] (Executive
   committee meeting, cultural association of Lelac, 1998)

In addition to the facework accomplished here to further the council's
goals, other dimensions are worth commenting on. The actual discursive
work is accomplished by Richard and Denis, who thereby provide a basis
for the council to present itself as united and democratic, and not under
the thumb of its president, François, or any other individual member.
Indeed, earlier in the transcript, François lays the groundwork for both
supporting the particular model Richard and Denis are hinting at, namely
a fixed structure independent of the particular personalities involved, and
building a consensus in support of such a structure. He does this explicitly: "J'aimerais plus un consensus que consensus ouais? / au lieu d'un vote
majoritaire" (I would prefer a consensus to consensus yeah? / rather than
a majority vote). He also does this through control over turn-taking and
topic introduction and through the frequent use of personal disclaimers
that situate the decision as a collective rather than individual one. He
frequently uses *je* (I) and framing devices such as "suggesting" and "giving
my opinion" as a means of stating his own position, which he makes available to the group without imposing it. He does not position himself as
speaking for the group. In this excerpt, the building of the consensus is
taken over by Richard and Denis, who do the actual framing of the models
to be discussed and the facework needed to accomplish a collective
decision with Bernard's consent.

   The next turn in the sequence is taken by François; he speaks at length
about the importance of arriving at an informed collective decision. A few
minutes later, he calls for a motion. Richard responds: "Mhm, qu'est-ce
que tu veux que je dise?" (Mhm, what do you want me to say?). It is François who formulates the formal motion that will then be reiterated and
entered into the minutes as having been proposed by Richard and sec-
onded by Denis. The association moves toward a more bureaucratized
organization, less dependent on the charismatic leadership characteristic
of the battles of the modernist discourse, more focused on service to the
community than fighting the community's battles with the dominant anglophone majority. Significantly, it does so by eschewing charismatic
models of leadership, preferring to accomplish its goals as a consensual
bureaucratic organization.

   Not surprisingly, the process in which interactions such as this played
a central role did not sit well with Bernard. Unable to shift his frame from

rights to development, he did his best to resist. In the end, a few months after the meeting discussed above, Bernard was dismissed from his position by the council, whose members one evening asked him for his keys and escorted him outside the building (the building which, it will be recalled, had served as headquarters for the school crisis of 1979–1981 in which Bernard had played such an important role).

By January 2000, the now director-less executive committee drafted a new mission statement, which it published in a consultation document leading up to a public consultation: "L'[association] est un organisme catalyseur au service de la communauté francophone" (The association is a catalyzing organization at the service of the francophone community). It is significant that the group, now identifying itself as an association, even felt the need to publish a mission statement, a genre with origins in the private sector. Such a statement makes the most sense in the context of the discourse of public service and accountability that is typical of the new economy. And of course the content points directly to the same notions of service. Thus, in what is probably the most significant single sentence for the establishment of its orientation, the association sent a clear message about its new orientation.

The document also illustrated what kinds of services might be involved in the association's new vision of itself. While the association still aimed to focus mainly on social and cultural activities, it also began to use a discourse of "community development." In the text this "community development" is framed as being designed to develop and maintain pride in francophone identity, but also as concerning the advancement of shared interests (indeed, this is one of the ways the association's consultation document actually defines "community"; the other defines "community" as a collection of people with shared resources).

In addition, the association helped set up a separate small organization in collaboration with a man of local origin who had just returned to the area in his retirement. Having had a long career with a federal government agency promoting economic development in Africa, he was interested in applying his expertise in community development to his birthplace. This new organization gave itself the mandate of "développement de biens et de services novateurs et de création d'entreprises et d'emplois" (development of innovative goods and services and creation of companies and of jobs) (as cited in an article in the local French-language newspaper, January 20, 2000).

The discourse of goods (*biens*) and services is shared by both organizations. In this discourse, language is less about identity and pride, about rights and struggles, and more about market value. In the same text, the sentence about resources and services ends thus: "d'entreprises et d'emplois qui montrent la valeur ajoutée des francophones et des bilingues de la [region] où l'on reflète leur impact considérable sur la vitalité de la région" (of companies and of jobs that show the added value of the francophones and the bilinguals of the [. . .] region where their considerable impact on the vitality of the region is reflected). French is important because it will help the entire region emerge from its economic slump. French is important because it has economic "added value." And francophones are important because without them, the region would have no claim to being able to provide that added value.

The crisis of the association, triggered by changing political and economic conditions (the withdrawal of the neoliberal state and the shift from primary- and secondary- to tertiary-sector economic activities, respectively), was resolved in an organizational shift embedded in a discursive one. The association reinvented itself as a service organization linked to activities that are marketable and that indeed can be seen as providing the authenticity which the tourist industry can effectively exploit (as well as contributing to the maintenance, even to the sense of maintaining, the bilingual linguistic proficiency that internationalized markets value). It hired a new director, who hired new staff members, all with job descriptions and contracts. And while the center still hosts concerts and get-togethers, it has directly and indirectly inserted itself into a variety of activities, from running a community radio station to working with other groups to establish a seniors' home in Lelac, a museum of local francophone history and an eco-educational center, and to undertake other activities that fit more comfortably under the rubric of "development."

It also lends staff to a new group of volunteers who took the lead in tourism development in 2001. Specifically, since the community realized it would have to fund its museum project on its own, ways had to be found to raise money. Some members of the local activist group (Bernard called them the *TLMs—Toujours Les Mêmes*; Always the Same Ones) decided to come together, with association support, to start a summer festival. That festival became a site where local activism met the commodification of authenticity, and where traditional claims to legitimacy began to be challenged.

6.5 LE FESTIVAL DU VILLAGE

The idea of a local community festival was of course scarcely original. Across North America, communities have drawn on older traditions such as Winter Carnival/Mardi Gras and harvest festivals to develop activities that draw locals and tourists alike. Ontario boasts a provincial association (Festivals and Events Ontario) that draws on such expertise to help communities (such as Lelac) that are new to the festival scene to pick an attractive theme, bring together the necessary resources to pull it off, and market it adequately to a well-targeted population.

We visited the festival in 2002, 2003, and 2004, and spent the interval between the 2002 and 2003 editions interviewing members of the organizing committee, attending its monthly planning meetings (held in the Lelac office of the local newspaper, which was run largely by a local high school teacher; we recorded eight of the nine meetings held between January and July 2003), and following up the links between the local festival, the broader organization of community festivals within the provincial tourism development infrastructure, and other local development projects (such as the seniors' residence opened in 2009). With the exception of newly hired association staff (two educated young women from the region), we had previously met all the participants through some form or another of community associative life. The ones you will meet here include the volunteers Gilles (the president); Pauline, his wife (both are from old local families); Henriette (it is on land carved out of the former farm of Henriette's husband's family that the seniors' home is being built); Nina (a professional translator who recently moved back into the area with her two young sons); René (a retired educator originally from Quebec who had for many years worked in Toronto); and paid organizers or support staff: Mario (a singer-songwriter of folk-rock and volunteer fireman, who came into the region as a child and whose 1992 song about the indigenous history of the region made his name); and Sylvie and Louise (young local women working with the association).

The theme was found by Gilles, a retired educator from an old Lelac family, president of the local chapter of the club that is what remains of the OJC, and regular columnist for the local newspaper (writing under the guise of an old-timer, with a pseudonym culled from the repertoire of distinctive, rather florid first names typical of late-nineteenth- or early-twentieth-century French Canada). He drew on one of the founding myths of Lelac, which can be traced back to a leaflet published in 1955 by the parish priest, himself a scion of one of the village's most prominent families, and the founder of the discussion circles of the 1950s. The story claims to be a simple written version of a true story that has been transmitted orally since the events in it took place, sometime in the early twentieth century (one version places the events in 1900). It also served as the basis for a play, written and directed by the priest, which several community members (including Jacques and Clément, whom we met in chapter 3) remember having participated in.

According to this text, one winter the village was beset by a wolf. Night after night it raided farms, terrorizing the entire village. No one seemed able to stop it. The priest urged the villagers, whose quarrels between rich and poor had divided the village in the years prior to the wolf's appearance, to set aside their differences in order to unite against this common enemy. In the end, it was one-eyed Théophile, one of the poorest men in the village, who was able to shoot down the wolf through divine intercession.

This 1955 version is clearly aimed at building solidarity against a common enemy through an appeal to Catholic values; in that sense, it is an excellent example of traditionalist nationalist discourse. While the text does not reveal what the wolf symbolizes, we may speculate that it combines features of the Others of the era: from the harsh climate, to the indigenous population displaced by white settlers, to the dominant anglophone community surrounding Lelac, and even to the city-dwellers buying up the lakeshore. In 2002, what community members found appealing was not so much the Catholic values (although, as we will see in chapter 7, those values still prevailed in the orientation to commodifying themes elsewhere in francophone Canada) as the figure of the wolf, which symbolized community solidarity and community attachment to the world of lakes and forests in which it had established itself.

The theme settled, a program had to be developed for the festival, which in 2002 was held in a variety of locations and in 2003 was moved to the village recreation hall (used as a skating rink in the winter) and a couple of adjacent undeveloped fields. It was not difficult to decide on a

Figure 6.1 This sculpture of the wolf symbol stands at the entrance to the village church. It was created for the festival by a local woodworking artist and furniture-maker who had moved to Lelac from southern Ontario. Photo by Emanuel da Silva.

program structure. For its first edition, in July 2002, the festival opened on a Friday night, in the recreation hall, with a version of a traditional format for francophone socializing, the *party de cuisine* (kitchen party). These are impromptu parties held in farmhouse kitchens, dating from the times before radio and television provided alternate sources of entertainment; at these parties, family, friends, and neighbors gathered to play traditional music on fiddles, accordions, spoons, and washboards (in a musical tradition shared with much of eastern North America), to sing, and to dance square dances, reels, and jigs (the latter presumably learned from the Irish). (See figure 7.6 in chapter 7 for a representation of the *party de cuisine* constructed for a exhibit of nativity scenes in rural Quebec.) For the 2003 edition of the festival, the *party de cuisine* was changed to a *party de grange* (barn party) in order to take advantage of the space afforded by the local arena.

GILLES: And the other thing I'd like to suggest for Friday night [. . .] I was wondering for the kitchen party / or the party could take place in the arena / and we would have a place for the dance there could be folkloric dances there too

MARIO: I would change that / instead of having a kitchen party have a barn party and put bales of hay there

GILLES: Well that would be ideal

NINA: *Barn dances*

MARIO: Yeah it eats it would kill the sound a bit because of all the iron in there / if we put in bales it would absorb the sound a bit so it would help the sonority too

RENÉ: Ah you're talking about the arena here

MARIO: Yes the pavilion

GILLES: The pavilion

MARIO: Because we'd have a lot more room there / eh we were packed like sardines

[GILLES: Puis l'autre chose que j'aimerais suggérer pour le vendredi soir [. . .] je me demandais pour le party de cuisine / ou le party pourrait se passer à l'aréna / et on aurait un endroit pour la danse / y pourrait avoir des danses folkloriques là aussi

MARIO: Moi je changerais ça au lieu d'avoir un party de cuisine avoir un party de grange pis mettre des bailles de foin là-dedans

GILLES: Ben ça serait idéal

NINA: Des *barn dances*

MARIO: Ouin ça mange ça tuerait un peu le son à cause de tout le fer là-dedans / si on mettrait des bailles ça absorberait un peu le son fait que ça aiderait au niveau du sonore aussi

RENÉ: Ahh toi tu parles de l'aréna ici

MARIO: Oui le pavillon

GILLES: Le pavillon

MARIO: Parce [que] là on aurait ben plus de place / ey on étaient paquetés comme des sardines] (Meeting of the festival organizing committee, January 2003)

Saturday was given over to an official opening, with speeches from dignitaries and a blessing from the priest; to exhibitors inside and outside the hall (mainly representatives of government programs and educational institutions); and to a series of outdoor performances, culminating in an evening concert. Sunday began with a special Mass in the church across the street, followed by a series of child-centered events that families could take part in. The gymnasium of the elementary school next to the church held a collection of exhibits representing the core of what was intended to eventually become the collection for the local heritage museum, for which the festival was raising funds. These exhibits included displays from the local genealogical society, tracing the history of Lelac families through records of baptisms and marriages; a photo and text display of notable community members past and present (for the most part, educators, health professionals, clergy members, and politicians); old farm implements; artifacts of the wolf legend (such as the gun supposedly used to kill the wolf, and photographs of a taxidermically preserved wolf); and documentation of the local indigenous population.

Three areas of program content proved more difficult to grapple with; they were the subject of some discussion over the months of planning in 2002–2003 and showed signs of change over the three editions of the festival we attended. The first had to do with the choice of music for the Saturday evening show. Since Friday night was an opportunity to showcase local artists (including Mario), Saturday was meant to have groups with a broad reputation from elsewhere. The federal funding programs available to finance such invitations tend to constrain choices; in particular, they usually insist on representation from outside the province of the proposed event. In addition, the committee faced a dilemma around musical tastes; as Mario commented, if the committee were to simply cater to local tastes, the program would contain nothing but country music, and this did not accord with his sense of what the festival should be promoting, namely francophone Canadian contemporary music, much of which falls somewhere along the line from folk to rock (with more recent incursions into other genres; see chapter 7). In the years we attended the festival, Saturday night's headliners were indeed drawn from that genre.

The second had to do with language. In many respects, the committee acted in ways consistent with modernist politics; in their deliberations, most of them spoke fairly standard French, although sometimes they threw some English around, and Mario quite consistently opted for more vernacular variants. (I understand this to be a question of the different kinds of legitimacy at stake for people from inside or outside the village, and with or without an investment in education, or, conversely, in popular culture). Already in the previous extract we saw a certain amount of interactional work done around what to call the arena: Is *aréna* a proper French word? Should it be called *pavillon*?

In the following extract, the committee members work at finding an appropriate French term for an item they want to include as a souvenir for sale. (Natalie is one of my research assistants.)

HENRIETTE: Hmmhmm / I'm going to show you this stuff here (ahhhh) even if they'd sell for $3.98 in stores I suggest we sell them at $4 / and also (ahhhh) I need your help I need your help to find a term in French for the pinchers

LOUISE: Oh my god

HENRIETTE: And they would sell for $4.98 but I'd suggest selling them for $6 because I only have twelve / I didn't expect them to be so cute because I would have gotten twenty-four

GILLES: How do you say it in English?

HENRIETTE: In English you say pinchers

MARIO: What?

HENRIETTE: Pinchers so in French what are we—

(Through the next four lines many people are talking at once)

MARIO:—biters gobblers pincers uh (x)

HENRIETTE: Something (x)

MARIO: A wolf bites

GILLES: The *louette* [wolfie?] or the *loupette* [wolfette?]

RENÉ: The wolfette *(laughter)* we've just decided that it's going to be called a *loupette*

HENRIETTE: Ahhh a *loupe* [magnifying glass; the feminine of *loup*—wolf— is *louve*] *loupette* is a little magnifying glass

RENÉ: Okay then a uh a *poussette* [a baby carriage] *(laughter)*

NINA: It's called a pincer-wolf

MARIO: A wolf-pincer

HENRIETTE: A cruncher *(laughter)* what would you call it Natalie?

NATALIE: Uh I thought of biter / but I like what you just said

NINA: A *croque-loup* [wolf-cruncher]

NATALIE: No no the *pince-loup* [wolf-pincher]

NINA: *Loup-pince* [pincher wolf]

NATALIE: Yes

GILLES: Yes the pincher wolf

NINA: It's like (x)

MARIO: It's the pincher wolf

HENRIETTE: We couldn't call it Théophile [the name of the man who supposedly killed the wolf in the legend]?

GILLES: Yes *(laughter)*

NINA: Have you had your (x) today?

MARIO: Anyway I don't think we need to worry about its name / no one will ask what it's called

HENRIETTE: But we have to we have to put something on the list

MARIO: Ahh on the list

NINA: Pincher wolf

MARIO: Pincher wolf is fine

HENRIETTE: Okay if we find something better we (x) if you are okay with six dollars / you don't have a choice I've decided

[HENRIETTE: Hmmhmm / je vais vous montrer ces bébelles ici (ahhhh)
   même si dans des magasins ils se vendraient à $3.98 je propose qu'on
   les vendent à $4 / puis aussi (ahhhhh) j'ai besoin de votre aide j'ai
   besoin de votre aide pour trouver un terme français pour les pinchers
LOUISE: Oh mon dieu
HENRIETTE: Pis eux ils se vendraient pour $4.98 mais moi je propose les
   vendre pour $6 parce que j'en ai juste douze / je pensais pas qu'ils
   étaient si cute parce que j'en aurais eu vingt-quatre (ahhhh)
GILLES: Comment tu dis en anglais
HENRIETTE: En anglais tu dis des pinchers
MARIO: Des quoi
HENRIETTE: Des pinchers alors en français qu'est-ce qu'on va—
(Through the next four lines many people are talking at once)
MARIO:—des mordeurs gobeurs pinceurs euh (x)
HENRIETTE: Quelque chose (x) là
MARIO: Un loup ça mord
GILLES: La louette ou la loupette
RENÉ: La loupette (*rires*) nous on vient de décider que ça va s'appeler la
   loupette
HENRIETTE: Ahhh une loupe loupette c'est une petite loupe
RENÉ: OK alors une euh une poussette (*rires*)
NINA: Ça s'appelle un loup-pince
RENÉ: Pince-loup
HENRIETTE: Un croqueux (*rires*) toi comment t'appellerais ça Natalie
NATALIE: Euh j'ai pensé à mordeur / mais j'ai aimé aussi ce que tu viens
   juste de dire
NINA: Un croque-loup
NATALIE: Non non le pince-loup
NINA: Loup-pince
NATALIE: Oui
GILLES: Oui le loup-pince
NINA: C'est comme (x)
MARIO: Là c'est loup-pince
HENRIETTE: On pourrait pas l'appeler Théophile?
GILLES: Oui (*rires*)
NINA: As as-tu eu ton (x) aujourd'hui
MARIO: Oui en tout cas je pense qu'on a pas à s'inquiéter du nom / il y a
   personne qui va demander c'est quoi son nom
HENRIETTE: Non mais il faut faut mettre quelque chose sur la liste
MARIO: Ahh sur la liste
NINA: Loup-pince
MARIO: Loup-pince c'est beau
HENRIETTE: OK si on trouve quelque chose de mieux on (x) si vous êtes
   d'accord avec six dollars / vous avez pas le choix j'ai décidé (Festival
   organizing committee meeting, July 14, 2003)]

The activity is obviously pleasurable for everyone; they all talk at once,
laugh frequently, play around with puns. Mario suggests that maybe it
doesn't matter whether they have a name for it in French, until Henriette
reminds him that it has to be written "on the list." The fact that it figures

in writing, and for communications among people directly involved in running the festival, seems legitimate to Mario.

In other meetings, the committee runs into similar terminology problems, as illustrated in the following three extracts. Here they search for a term for "craftsmen."

> MARIO: We have to find pieces we have to find some *craftsmen* people who make
> NINA: *Artisans*
> [. . .]
> GILLES: So for the kiosks / you have the exhibitors the artisans you have the sellers of crafts you have the creation of databases you have sales of what other stuff
> MARIO: The *artisans* that that's the *craftsmen*
> GILLES: Yes
> MARIO: It's the people who make
>
> [MARIO: Faut trouver des œuvres faut trouver des *craftsmen* des gens qui font des
> NINA: Des artisans
> GILLES: Donc pour les kiosques / t'as les exposants les artisans t'as les vendeurs d'artisanat t'as la creation de bases de données t'as la vente de quoi autre chose
> MARIO: Les artisans ça c'est les *craftsmen*
> GILLES: Oui
> MARIO: Ça c'est ceux qui fabriquent]

Here they search for a word for "remote."

> GILLES: See if the the / *remote* in French it's not *télécommande* it's something else uhm it it's
> PAULINE: It's called a *remote* yeah I don't remember the word
> GILLES: The *poste* the *portable* the the *radio*
> PAULINE: Yes the *diffusion* uh
> GILLES: On the field
> MARIO: (xx)
> PAULINE: Uh your question is uh
> GILLES: No dictionary here
>
> [GILLES: Voir si le le / *remote* en français c'est pas télécommande ça c'est autre chose uhm ça c'est
> PAULINE: On appelle ça un *remote* ouin je me rappelle pas du mot
> GILLES: Le poste le portable le le radio
> PAULINE: Oui oui la diffusion euh
> GILLES: Sur le champ
> MARIO: (xx)
> PAULINE: Uhm votre question c'est uh
> GILLES: Pas de dictionnaire ici]

Finally, here they search for a word for "marquee."

> SYLVIE: We should put a sign indicating saying welcome to the festival or something like that

NINA: Well wasn't there / wasn't there that big sign
GILLES: Well there's there's the *marquee* how do they call that in French a
    marquee
NINA: Just there the flowers
GILLES: Yes yes how do you say that
HENRIETTE: The *pancarte*
SYLVIE: Ah okay change the letters for
GILLES: Yes
RENÉ: Nina must know
NINA: I'm a walking dictionary eh
GILLES: Yes
NINA: The *marquee*
GILLES: The *marquee*
RENÉ: The *marquee*

[SYLVIE: —faudrait mettre une affiche qu'indiquait qui disait bienvenue
    au Festival ou quelque chose comme ça—
NINA: —ben il y avait pas le / y avait pas la grosse affiche là /
GILLES: Ben / y a / y le *marquee* / comment ils appellent ça là en français
    un *marquee* /
NINA: Juste là / les fleurs
GILLES: Oui oui / comment on appelle ça—
HENRIETTE:—la pancarte
SYLVIE: Ahh OK changer les lettres pour—
GILLES:—oui—
RENÉ:—Nina doit savoir—
NINA:—je suis un dictionnaire ambulant hein
GILLES: Oui
NINA: Le *marquee*
GILLES: Le *marquee*
RENÉ: Le *marquee*]

This traditional attention to making the internal space homogeneously
francophone encounters its limits, however, when it comes to the audience, or, more precisely, the consumers. The following example consists
of extracts from a long discussion about how to manage the limits of
uniformity (I have indicated where material has been cut; each cut consists of three or four turns at talk, about 30 percent of the material provided below).

NINA: The signs on the site
SYLVIE: The signs
NINA: The signs on the site / you wanted to talk about them
SYLVIE: Ahh yes sorry on the site I thought you were talking about the
    Web site // uhmmmm I was talking last week with Mary Caron from
    the chamber of commerce and and uhm so that they take some (x)
    cards and she asked a couple of little questions about the festival / and
    she asked me if our intention was to have not only francophones but
    also the anglophone community
NINA: We want only francophones and Chinese to the exclusion of any
    other party (x)

MARIO: What does she mean by do we want (x)

NINA: Honestly

SYLVIE: It's because she received some some uhmmm I don't remember anymore what the word is in French *"complaints"*

NINA: Ahhhh "plaintes"

SYLVIE: Last year / because seeing as how we had in the pamphlet it was English-French they thought everything was going to be bilingual / and they were mainly talking about the signs on the site that it was all in French so

NINA: Like *"parking"*

SYLVIE: So she asked me if it could be bilingual mainly on the signs uhm the signs that will be on the site uhmm

[. . .]

RENÉ: Well here we're talking only about signs / we aren't talking about when there is a group playing music that there should be someone translating

SYLVIE: No no no no

MARIO: No but

NINA: We'll add fifteen thousand dollars in simultaneous translation there

[. . .]

SYLVIE: And he also talked about the workshops to have uhmm maybe people who speak French and English

[. . .]

NINA: But somewhere people come for a bit of immersion in the culture and the language and

MARIO: Yes if they ask a question in English we aren't going to say "We don't speak English" (*laughter*) (x)

[. . .]

?: Are the workshops going to be bilingual?

NINA: No listen where are we going to draw the line there

?: The spoons when we do the spoons

MARIO: *"We're going to play the spoons now"* (xx) (*laughter*) by the music

[. . .]

NINA: Well it seems to me that that will be part of the interpersonal skills of each person who responds to requests for information that's all / that's that's that's that we should have tact and a little politeness and we will use all the signs of courtesy which are included in regular customer service that are offered in all companies no matter whether a customer wants to speak to us in Swahili / well we'll tell him "Speak English" because we are sure he doesn't speak French you know and we will be able to answer him / that's just life skills

SYLVIE: No because I think it's just for the announcements because that's what she asked me / what is who is your audience who do you want to be there

[. . .]

SYLVIE: No I told her that well of course the francophones / but also I told her also that we want to show francophone tradition to the anglophone community

MARIO: And that we exist

SYLVIE: Yeah

MARIO: It's important that they know it

NINA: Well you're always going to get people who are going to complain

MARIO: Yeah no no but you want to be as accessible as possible without really you know going to the point where you're on stage translating the songs well that would be going to extremes / but the signs we can make arrangements in fact with symbols or so everyone can understand

RENÉ: And it's difficult and this is not being ironic it's difficult to get francophone culture across in English you know / like I know people they asked me too for the kiosks it's the same thing / I told them well if you speak in English you speak in English / your product whether it's a bar of soap or a and that's all / if people want to speak in English they speak in English

[. . .]

SYLVIE: Uh uhm but the only thing that's important is the signs to have them translated

MARIO: Well translated / I like the idea of the symbol myself

SYLVIE: Yeah but we can't put symbols

MARIO: Symbols are even better / and anyway that way it isn't just the anglophones who will come it will be Poles Germans who understand neither English nor French

[. . .]

MARIO: And anyway we promote it like come see what francophone culture is

NINA: Well I think it could be part of a press release you know we can include it like uhm a little open-mindedness

MARIO: (*laughter*) (xx) Ah people *c'mon* eh a little open-mindedness

?: (x)

NINA: C'mon there / six / new business / we discussed political issues if there is no new business we will move on to ending the meeting

[NINA: Les affiches sur le site

SYLVIE: Les affiches

NINA: Les affiches sur le site / tu voulais en parler

SYLVIE: Ahh oui excuse sur le site je pensais que tu parlais du site web // uhmm je parlais la semaine passé avec Mary Caron de la chambre de commerce pis uhm pour qu'ils prennent des (x) cards pis elle m'a demandé un couple de petites questions sur le festival / pis elle me demandait si notre intention était d'avoir pas seulement des franco-phones mais aussi la communauté anglophone

NINA: On veut rien que les francophones et les chinois à l'exclusion de quiconque (x)

MARIO: Qu'est-ce qu'elle veut dire par est-ce qu'on veut (x)

NINA: Voyons

SYLVIE: C'est parce que elle a eu des des uhmm je m'en souviens plus c'est quoi le mot en français "*complaints*"

NINA: Ahh "des plaintes"

SYLVIE: L'année passée / à cause vu qu'on avait dans le dépliant c'était anglais français ils pensaient que c'était pour être tout bilingue / pis ils parlaient surtout des signes sur les lieux que c'était tout en français donc

NINA: Comme *"parking"*

SYLVIE: Donc elle m'a demandé si ça pourrait être bilingue surtout sur les signes uhm les signes qu'il va (y) avoir sur les lieux là uhmm

[. . .]

RENÉ: Ben là on parle des affiches seulement / on parle pas de quand il y aura un groupe qui joue de la musique là que il y a quelqu'un qui traduise

SYLVIE: Non non non non

MARIO: Non mais

NINA: On va rajouter 15 mille dollars service d'interprétation là

[. . .]

SYLVIE: Pis il a parlé aussi des ateliers d'avoir uhmm peut-être d'avoir des personnes qui parlent français anglais

[. . .]

NINA: Mais à quelque part les gens viennent pour un peu d'immersion dans la culture pis la langue pis

MARIO: Oui si ils posent une question en anglais on n'est pas pour dire "On parle pas l'anglais" *(rires)* (x)

[. . .]

?: Est-ce que les ateliers vont être bilingues?

NINA: Non écoute où est-ce qu'on met la ligne là

?: La cuillère quand on fait de la cuillère

MARIO: "We're going to play the spoons now" (xx) *(rires)* par la musique

[. . .]

NINA: Ben il me semble que ça va faire partie du savoir faire de chacune des personnes qui répondent aux demandes des renseignements c'est tout / c'est c'est c'est qu'on ait du tacte pis un peu de politesse pis on va utiliser tout les signes de courtoisie qui est là dans le service à la clientèle régulier qu'on offre dans toutes les entreprises peu importe si un client veut nous parler en Swahili / bon on lui dira parle anglais parce qu'on est sûr qu'il parle pas français t'sais pis on va être capable de lui répondre / c'est juste du savoir vivre ça

SYLVIE: Non parce que je pense que c'est juste pour les annonces parce que c'est ça qu'elle m'a demandé / c'est quoi c'est qui votre audience c'est qui que vous voulez soit là

[. . .]

SYLVIE: Non je lui ai dit que ben c'est sûr les francophones mais aussi je lui ai dit aussi qu'on veut montrer à la communauté anglophone la tradition francophone

MARIO: Pis qu'on existe

SYLVIE: Ouais

MARIO: C'est important qu'ils le sachent

NINA: Ben tu vas toujours avoir des personnes qui vont se plaindre

MARIO: Ouin non non mais tu veux être aussi accessible que possible sans vraiment t'sais à aller au point où t'es sur la scène en train de faire la traduction des tunes ben là tu irais à l'extrême là / mais des signes on peut s'arranger justement avec des symboles ou pour que tout le monde puisse comprendre

RENÉ: Pis c'est difficile pis c'est pas l'ironie là c'est difficile de faire passer de la culture francophone en anglais t'sais / comme je sais que les gens

moi aussi ils me l'ont posé pour les kiosques c'est la même chose / je
leur ai dit ben si vous parlez en anglais vous parlez en anglais / votre
produit que ça soit une barre de savon ou que ça soit et là c'est tout / si
les gens veulent parler en anglais ils parlent en anglais
[...]
SYLVIE: Euh hum mais la seule chose qui est important c'est les signes
    d'avoir qu'ils soient traduits
MARIO: Ben traduit / moi j'aime l'idée du symbole
SYLVIE: Ouais mais on peut pas mettre les symboles
MARIO: Les symboles c'est encore mieux / pis de toute façon les de cette
    façon là c'est pas juste les anglophones qui vont venir ça va être des
    Polonais des Allemands qui comprennent pas ni l'anglais ni le français
[...]
MARIO: Pis de toute façon on le promouvoit comme venez voir c'est quoi
    la culture francophone
NINA: Ben je pense que ça peut faire partie d'un communiqué de presse là
    t'sais on peut l'intégrer comme uhhm un peu d'ouverture d'esprit
MARIO: (*rires*) (xx) Ah les gens c'mon hein un peu d'ouverture d'esprit
?: (x)
NINA: C'mon là / six / affaires nouvelles / on a discuté affaires politiques
    si on n'a pas d'affaires nouvelles on va passer au lever de séance]
(Festival organizing committee meeting, June 9, 2003)

Here the committee has to struggle with feedback from the community. A request that signs and announcements be in both languages feels a
lot like the old strategies of domination against which Lelac activists have
long struggled. At the same time, the new conditions turn those anglophones into customers, who should be treated, as Nina points out, according to the basic principles of customer service. René and Mario, however,
argue that bilingualism actually diminishes the value of the product they
are trying to promote—a product, moreover, which continues to have
political significance for them. As Mario says, this is not just about selling
culture, this is about showing anglophones that the francophone community exists. And not only anglophones: anyone else who comes along
is just as important. In the end, Nina opts for the high road: vaunting their
bilingualism as proof of the kind of open-mindedness they wish the
anglophone community would more often display. And indeed, the committee works hard at getting its publicity materials out in both French and
English, and in sites where anglophones will encounter them (although at
the same time, they rely on other bilinguals to help them accomplish
this.)

    The third domain of discussion had to do with who might be invited to
do what, and specifically, what definition of "francophone" needed to be
invoked in setting those criteria, if any. The protocol for the Saturday
morning opening required inviting local officials, not all of whom spoke
French. This was handled by the Master of Ceremonies, with a deft series
of switches back and forth between French and English, bridging the
English of specific officials with the francophone frame of the event.

More difficult was the realization that, while the festival could legitimately ignore the anglophone history of the region, it was much more difficult to ignore the role of the indigenous population, given the importance of New France as a founding myth and its vexed relationship with the indigenous population that left for Quebec, as well as with the one driving past the village every day on their way from the island into town. This is a tension that emerged strongly across francophone Canada in the early 1980s, when a crisis over land development in a Quebec town pitched indigenous activists against the Quebec state police (other crises shook Acadie in disputes over fishing rights at around the same time). By the time the Festival du Village came along, it had been clear for at least a decade that francophone claims to primacy on the grounds of having settled the land before the British paled next to indigenous claims not only to precedence but also for redress against European violence, whether French or English. This hit close to home in Lelac, and undoubtedly explains the sudden interest in identifying with the Métis population, which had emerged here (and in other francophone communities as well) a few years earlier. At the same time, of course, neither the local indigenous population nor most members of the Ontario Métis nation spoke French.

The result for the festival was a conscious effort to include indigenous groups, an effort encouraged by government funders. A local chief was invited to bless the festival in a sweetgrass ceremony at the official opening;

Figure 6.2 The Franco-Ontarian and Métis flags beside the outdoor stage. Photo by Mary Richards.

Figure 6.3 A French Canadian folklore duo performing. Note the *ceinture flechées*, the *tuques*, and the plaid shirts. Photo by Mary Richards.

Figure 6.4 Performers from Wendake on stage. Photo by Mary Richards.

Figure 6.5 Performers from Wendake dancing with audience members. Photo by Emanuel da Silva.

the Métis flag was flown alongside the Canadian, Ontario, and Franco-Ontarian flags; local indigenous history was included in the museum; and indigenous and Métis artisans began to show up among the exhibitors on the festival grounds. In 2004, the Wendat community from Quebec, the descendants of the converts from the Jesuit mission, were invited, and in 2004 a local indigenous group performed and taught ritual dances during the Saturday afternoon program.

Finally, in 2004, the Saturday afternoon program also included an African dance troupe from Toronto. Once opened, the issue of francophone diversity continued to expand, displays of tradition and rallies for *la cause* giving way to entertainment for local families, for their children and grandchildren who could combine a trip home with a weekend spent between festival and beach. It was hoped, too, that the festival would offer enough of interest to attract people with no ties to the community.

The commodification of Lelac, however, was less than successful in financial terms. The festival has suffered from financial woes from the beginning, and had to be cancelled completely for 2006. The tension between community pride and commodification is not easily resolved.

The organizing committee solved the problem partly by carving out a francophone space for their own activities and trying to fence them off from the linguistic compromises they had to make in order to open the festival up to participants from outside. Sometimes, as Mario suggested,

Figure 6.6 Members of an African dance troupe from Toronto. Photo by Emanuel da Silva.

this could be done with symbols (P for parking lots, flags) or through nonverbal means (sweetgrass, dance); however, sometimes languages other than French simply could not be avoided. At the same time, despite explicit inclusion of elements of traditional French Canadian culture, the festival also opened itself more and more to other ways of being francophone. Finally, holding such a festival raised questions about who gets to decide what that francophone content is, and what kind of linguistic wrapping it requires—questions the organizing committee was never able to clearly answer for itself. The commodification of identity turned out to be a bit more complicated than the community's prior political experience had prepared it for.

The next chapter takes up some of these complications: tensions between inalienable trait and measurable skill or between community pride and economic development; and tensions over boundaries and over legitimate language. Here we have seen how modernist strategies and frames are challenged in the *milieu associatif*. In the next chapter, we will explore some of the economic activities most central to francophone Canada's entry into the globalized new economy.

7

Selling the Nation, Saving the Market
(All Over the Place, 2001–Present)

7.1 AUTHENTICITY AND LANGUAGE
IN THE NEW ECONOMY

The Festival du Village was not the only festival of its type to be developed in the late 1990s and early 2000s, reflecting the general growth of the tertiary economy, particularly its tourism sector (Urry 2002; Jaworski and Pritchard 2005). However, while anglophone towns mainly looked to themes more or less connected to local traits (from pumpkins to Disneyland), francophone areas tended to concentrate on combinations of heritage and environment. Quebec had already begun to organize its tourist market in this way, capitalizing on an older tourist infrastructure aimed at wealthy English-speakers from Montreal, Quebec City, and the large urban centers of the northeastern United States. More recently, Quebec has actively cultivated a market in francophone Europe, for which francophone North America represents breathing space, the possibility of self-reinvention, some nostalgia for lost empire, and contemporary Romantic environmentalism. Quebec also mobilized the representations of memory and tradition that emerged out of the mobilization movement of the 1960s (Handler 1988), reworking them for both local and far-flung audiences. The RDÉE helped other parts of francophone Canada to do the same.

In addition to local festivals, we saw broader attempts at marketing regional histories and identities, as well as specific tourist products like large-scale heritage pageants, various kinds of stage and musical shows and festivals, and so-called "living museums" (re-creations of historical sites). Quebec has organized its tourism marketing by carving up the province into distinct "regions," each of which is marketed in campaigns mainly directed at the United States and France as offering something different. In 2004, the Chambre économique de l'Alberta published a tourist guide called *L'Alberta: L'autre belle province*. Through its reference to Quebec's traditional label as *la belle province* (the beautiful province; this was on Quebec license plates until it was replaced with *Je me souviens*, or "I remember"), the title aims at both Québécois tourists and tourists who usually go to Quebec. The guide orients tourists to places where services in French are offered, but also, crucially, to parts of the province where tourists can explore francophone history and contemporary life (Roy and Gélinas 2004; Moïse et al. 2006).

While Quebec and parts of Acadie are enjoying some success, this is not always the case elsewhere. For example, in the late 1990s, members of the local francophone elite in the Welland region of southern Ontario looked into tourism to provide an alternative to the collapsing steel and textile industries, hoping this might be an area where francophones could develop as entrepreneurs, not just service providers. Welland is near Niagara Falls, so getting people into the region is not a problem; the problem, historically, has been with keeping them there. The area used to be devoted to tobacco farms until many people stopped smoking; in the 1970s and 1980s it was converted to fruit and, notably, to vineyards and an emergent wine industry. Around these new activities, complemented by a casino in Niagara Falls itself and theater festivals in two nearby towns, has grown a vibrant tourist industry based on inns, restaurants, wine-tasting, theater, a little gambling perhaps, and a look at the falls. However, regional officials and entrepreneurs simply fail to see the added value either of the Welland population's bilingualism in French and English or its local (working-class) history. There are plenty of tourists: the francophones come anyway, and Franco-Ontarian history is not what they come for. Tourism as a strategy is widespread, but sometimes it works and sometimes it doesn't. It occupies complicated territory between political mobilization and self-objectification, and, perversely, while aiming to control regional products and markets, it can also deliver that control into the hands of state authorities who distribute infrastructure resources in ways highly reminiscent of the industrial economy (Where do the roads get built, the airports remodeled? How do you raise capital for your museum?). In addition, consumers do not share the same set of interests as producers. Tourism raises the issue of authenticity in this sector of the new economy. Authenticity adds value to tourism products, but may also cede authority to new hands—or, at the very least, allow new actors to penetrate.

We see this both in the development of tourist "products" such as festivals and pageants and in one of the major ways in which the distinctiveness of regions is developed: through the concept of *terroir*. The idea of *terroir* was originally pioneered by France to safeguard the value of its high-end niche agroalimentary industry. The term refers to the unique characteristics of locally circumscribed areas of land, which lend local agricultural products distinctive and unreproducible qualities. In Canada, Quebec was the first to exploit this concept, developing a high-quality organic meat production industry for veal and lamb in the Charlevoix (a picturesque region east of Quebec City, developed for Anglo-Canadian and American tourism as a retreat for nature, art, and folklore already in the 1920s), and an artisanal cheese industry across the province. Quebec's products are currently the most successful in tying Romantic nationalism to local production, with product names drawing on local toponymy and local heroes, and clear regional branding. For example, in 2005, my local Toronto supermarket put in a separate dairy case just for "artisanal" cheeses from Quebec; in Quebec supermarkets Charlevoix veal is labeled as such and placed in a different part of the meat case from other kinds of veal; and in 2008 a shop called "A Taste of Quebec" opened in a tourist district of Toronto, offering not only authentic products but also cooking classes and a space for private functions. Indeed, artisanal cheese production has become such good business in Quebec that an association of independent cheese producers recently lobbied for label distinctions between their (truly authentic) products and those now produced by big industrial conglomerates that have invested in the artisanal cheese market.

The concept has spread to other parts of francophone Canada, especially the Maritimes. Indeed, as I write (2009), the Assemblée communautaire fransaskoise and the Institut français of the University of Regina are joining forces to further the idea of *terroir* in Saskatchewan. The project's Web site (www.terroirsk.ca, accessed February 25, 2009) invites participants to a symposium titled "Terroir: Identité et seduction" (*Terroir: Identity and Seduction*; (R)romantic nationalism indeed), with the goal of facilitating discussion among participants, "government representatives, entrepreneurs and farmers" as "a first step toward a better awareness of the immense potential of the *terroir* as an alternative approach to rural development." In addition, while the products designated through the term *terroir* are largely related to food (although related products such as creams, soaps, and textiles are also involved), the realm of arts, folklore, and culture is equally relevant.

In this chapter, I discuss two forms of commodification of identity: the heritage pageant and the circulation of authentic artifacts, based on fieldwork conducted in Ontario, Quebec, New Brunswick, and francophone Europe (France, Belgium, and Switzerland). Our questions focused on what kinds of products were being constructed, for what kinds of consumers, and how they were being marketed. In each case, the product (whether comestible, viewable, livable, or anything else) is constructed as unique and authentic by nature and tied to a francophone history, relation to the land, and sensibility: all the hallmarks of Romantic nationalism. But the role of language in the construction of this authenticity ends up acting as a double-edged sword: it carves out a niche and serves as a guarantee of authenticity, but potentially constrains the market's reach. In addition, the marketing of culture evokes complicated emotional responses; not everyone is comfortable selling oneself as a living piece of folklore. Branding authenticity sometimes involves shaping authentic objects in ways that begin to feel, well, inauthentic. All these tensions are present.

The second part of the chapter focuses on the other major dimension of francophone Canada's entry into the tertiary-sector economy:

communication-heavy production of knowledge. We will look first at
the areas of multimedia production and environmentalism as they
developed in Montreal in the 1990s and 2000s. Quebec (as well as, for
that matter, New Brunswick) engaged directly in the development of
the tertiary sector in ways that were completely consistent with the
modernizing efforts to increase francophone control over the private
sector. For Quebec, the economic dislocations of the 1980s opened up
ground for support for small and midsized companies (the so-called
PMEs, or *petites et moyennes enterprises*).

The construction of the regional francophone market in Quebec thus
laid the basis for the service economy that grew up around it, providing
for the first time an employment sector where the bilingualism of minority francophones was actually valued (although, as we shall see, this turned
out to be more complicated than economic developers thought; bilingualism turns out not to just simply be bilingualism). It also provided the
opening for Quebec to exploit the trilingualism of its immigrant-origin
population (Lamarre and Dagenais 2003) and to move into communica-
tions- and service-related sectors, especially those involving a clientele
spread across the Americas and Europe.[1]

Based on fieldwork in a multimedia company (carried out in 2004
mainly by Stéphanie Lamarre; see Lamarre and Lamarre 2006a,b) and a
fair-trade environmentalist NGO (carried out in 2003–2004 mainly by
Emmanuel Kahn; see Kahn and Heller 2006), we will see how the nature
of the knowledge economy and its geographic expansion raise questions
about how to maintain the privileged francophone market niche that earlier political mobilization had created, and still serve a multilingual clientele in ways consistent with the logic of the product and of consumer
capitalism.

The third part focuses on one particular dimension of the knowledge
economy, the so-called "language industries" (communications, such as
call centers; language learning and teaching; translation and interpretation; speech technologies). New Brunswick famously went after the call
center industry, laying fiber-optic cable, promising tax breaks, and vaunting the bilingual skills of Acadians. So successful was this effort that
Moncton became the call center capital of Canada; by 2005 it had about
forty call centers, employing around five thousand people (Dubois et al.
2006). Other bilingual zones of Canada, such as Montreal and parts of
Ontario, also sought to capitalize on a bilingual labor pool in this way.
Welland provides one example; the following text (collected by Sylvie
Roy) is from a municipal effort to attract the call center industry (an effort that was largely successful, unlike its attempts to enter the tourism
sector; see Roy 2003).

> [The city] is not just heavy metal any more. [The city] is poised to challenge
> winds of technology as they breathe life into a new world economy based upon
> rivers of information through its call centre facilities. An old hand at capitalizing
> upon waterways of opportunity, [the city] is perfectly positioned geographically

to be Canada's high-tech alternative. [. . .] Fifteen percent of [the city's] population is English/French bilingual and many are multilingual, with Italian being the third predominant language spoken. The benefits of this francophone and ethnic presence are not lost on any employer doing business in French-speaking Canadian communities or in a global marketplace. (Municipal government marketing materials, early 1990s)

In all of these places—Montreal, Moncton, Welland—francophones historically were marginalized members of the working class whose French served mainly to keep them from economic mobility and class solidarity with other, mainly Irish or more recent immigrant working-class groups. The only thing the state had ever made of their Frenchness was to construct it as a problem that somehow had to be resolved. Now, the state, at various levels, regards it as something to sell.

At the federal level, the government of Canada also turned to the language-based tertiary sector as a way to meet its commitment to the development of linguistic duality, hitherto managed within the framework of the welfare state. Building on Canadian expertise and infrastructure created largely for the management of bilingualism in the federal public service, the minister responsible for official languages, Stéphane Dion, targeted this sector in the official languages development plan he was required to submit in 2003, widely known in francophone Canada as the Plan Dion (Canada 2003).

Previous plans had focused largely on actions undertaken directly by the government. The Official Languages Act had created a large market for translation, interpretation, and language teaching (see Yarymowich 2005 regarding the language teaching sector, LeBlanc 2008, 2009 regarding translation). Since the mid-1980s, much of the translation and language teaching work that had been done in-house by government employees and large companies was being increasingly outsourced to self-employed individuals or private firms; by 1994 almost 50 percent of the government's translations were being outsourced (Canada 1994: 477). A major downsizing of the civil service in the early 1990s called government expenditures on language training into question. Activities earlier framed around the discourse of rights, and understood as part of the cost of functioning bilingually, were recast as profit-making potential, as a means to commercialize the expertise the state had created but could no longer pay for.

In this spirit, the Plan Dion provided seed money for five years for an association called the Association des industries de la langue/Language Industries Association (AILIA). AILIA's Web site (www.ailia.ca; accessed February 24, 2009) indicates that its structure covers three sectors: the translation and interpretation sector, the language training sector, and the language technologies sector. An earlier version of the Web site (accessed November 16, 2005) provided this narrative:

Mission: To join forces and be the voice of the Canadian language industry in order to make Canada a world leader in this area.

Backgrounds [*sic*]
1996: The Canadian Translation Sectoral Committee is established. Final report submitted in 1999.

May 2002: Industry Canada sponsors a symposium on the language industries. Approximately 100 stakeholders agree on the priorities for developing businesses working in this area of activity.

June 2002: At the instigation of the NRC [National Research Council] and Industry Canada, the Canadian Language Industries' Technology Road-map Committee is established. The aim is to identify the stakeholders in this area and determine their profile, pinpoint growth sectors, take stock of Canadian research in those fields, and suggest measures to be taken to ensure a leadership position at the international level.

[...]

Spring 2003: The Canadian Language Industries Network (CLIN-RCIL) becomes AILIA (Canadian Association de l'industrie de la langue/Language Industry Association).

March 2003: The Canadian government launches its *Action Plan for Official Languages*. This plan allocates $20 million in investments. There are three main measures affecting the language industry:

1. Consolidating the industry fundamentals
2. Creating a strong image
3. Research and development in language technologies (Association des industries de la langue/Language Industries Association [AILIA] Web site, 2005)

This section is based on fieldwork in call centers in Moncton, Welland, and the Lelac area, and interviews with human resources personnel and employment agencies in Toronto and Ottawa. The fieldwork was undertaken between 1998 and 2004, with the major part of the fieldwork in Welland carried out by Sylvie Roy and in Moncton by Mélanie Le Blanc.

Together, the emergence of both commodified identity and commodified language reveal an impasse unresolvable within a modernist nationalist framework. This impasse has to do with the ways in which the legitimacy of the privileged ethnonational markets that francophone Canada spent over fifty years trying to establish is called to account by the logic of that market. Successful entry to this market means dealing with the consequences of its expansion, which, by turning the linguistic and cultural bases of that ethnonational legitimacy into a commodity, undermines its political power. Commodification disconnects language from identity and therefore destabilizes the logic of ethnonationalist politics, which require them to be intertwined. At the same time, the value of commodified resources depends on the legitimacy of the nation whose authenticity those resources represent.

In the rest of this chapter, we will look at how people have struggled over this impasse in various ways, in two major sectors of the tertiary economy: tourism and authentic artifact-related consumption; and the knowledge economy, particularly the language industry. In both, we see participants work to maintain the relative gains of the past fifty years while attempting to overcome some of their perverse effects. First, we turn to a historical pageant in eastern Ontario, and to the circulation of authentic goods and performances on the European circuit.

7.2 TOURISM, *TERROIR*, AND THE PERFORMANCE OF IDENTITY

For two years (2003–2005) we carefully followed the development of a summer theater heritage pageant in eastern Ontario. Local activists turned to the development of summer theater as a way to reinvent identity maintenance after the neoliberal turn of the state. Drawing on the expertise of a local historian who had long been contributing to the cause of Franco-Ontarian political consciousness-raising; his son, a longtime community organization activist; the regional school board drama teachers and infrastructures; and the new provincial provisions for *animation culturelle* (cultural identity construction activities aimed at students in Franco-Ontarian schools), a group of local activists gained government funding for the development of a historical pageant recounting the major episodes of Franco-Ontarian history. This pageant was funded on the basis of a five-year business plan, on the premise that it would serve as a catalyst for the development of the tourist industry in a region historically dependent on a combination of dairy farming and the lumber industry.

The pageant drew on the successful precedents of *Le puy du fou* in France (www.puydufou.com) and *La fabuleuse histoire d'un royaume* (www.fabuleuse.com) in the Saguenay region of Quebec for the shape of its narrative and the mode of its production. It depended on large open spaces, typically outdoors, and the mobilization of large numbers of local volunteers. It recounted regional history as a saga of the heroic resistance of a marginalized minority against the forces both of nature and of politically dominant centers. And it uses the dark of night to dramatic effect. (For reasons having to do with both the climate of the Saguenay region and the institutionalization of the pageant, *La fabuleuse histoire d'un royaume* is presented indoors, in a purpose-built theater on the site of a former skating rink.)

The Ontario pageant organizers initially hoped to construct a set in the forest, but in the end settled for constructing a set with seating for over a thousand people on the site of a former apple farm, whose owners had already turned it to local tourism use (it was the kind of place where school groups and families could go to pick apples in the fall and have a meal, or, if the weather was good, a picnic and hayride). Three hundred local volunteers were mobilized to do everything from sewing costumes to selling tickets to taking leading roles. Rehearsals and other preparatory activities took place nights and weekends throughout the year in the local school.

As a consciousness-raising activity, the pageant was very successful. Most people in the region saw it, and it was adopted as the newest manifestation of local pride. Indeed, the narrative followed the already well-institutionalized unfolding of the history of Franco-Ontarian struggles. The founding myth shows us Champlain (again Champlain, always Champlain, unless it's Jacques Cartier) warmly received by the indigenous population, producing a mixed race ("Nous sommes tous des Métis"—We are all Métis) with inalienable ties to the land, although also with unfortunate tendencies toward killing indigenous people, locked in conflict with the British and their Anglo-Canadian descendants, fighting for their schools and their rights to full citizenship. The period of modernization is dealt with in one breathless scene, in the form of a parade, in which each float represents some aspect of modernity (television, the space race, popular music). The show ends with an interpellation of the audience as actors of their own history, through the projection on a large screen of a series of famous figures of Franco-Ontarian history, followed by a projection of an image of the audience itself as it watches the screen.

The business plan required by the funding agencies projected an ever-increasing catchment area for the audience. It was expected that people would come in from Ottawa (about forty-five minutes away by car), and eventually from Montreal (about two hours away), and that tour buses operating out of those regions would include the show on their itinerary. However, that audience failed to materialize. One obvious problem was an infrastructure Catch-22: the show was supposed to trigger development (for example, inns, cafes, and restaurants), but the clientele for them would not come to the show unless they were already there. Otherwise, you find yourselves, as we did, out in the country, navigating in the dark.

But the other problem was ideological: framed as a regional francophone story, it had little attraction for the region's anglophones or for francophones from elsewhere, especially francophones from Quebec who had a well-internalized narrative about the impossibility of francophone life outside Quebec. Even the introduction of some English into the voice-over introduction (Welcome to our English-speaking audience! Even if you don't speak French, the show has lots of special effects and music, so you'll enjoy it!), the downplaying of the didacticism of the first scripts, and the heightening of "entertainment values" (a full-scale mobile model of Champlain's ship, fireworks, live galloping horses, big musical production numbers) failed to improve ticket sales. Every year since 2004 the show has been about to collapse; the community has rallied around it as its new cause, management has been shuffled and reshuffled, and bankruptcy declared. I ran into the historian at a meeting in Ottawa in early 2008, and we had a chance to catch up on recent events. He assured me that the problems were "simply" financial, not at all related to the quality of the product: the show would go on.

Efforts in Quebec and Acadie have, on the whole, been more successful. One reason for this is that both regions can draw on an established

tradition of tourism involving their own regional populations, other Canadians, and Americans. They have also been more successful in attracting
tourists from francophone Europe.

The policitized Québécois music and theater scene of the 1960s and
1970s paved the way for a continuing tradition of interest to all these
consumer groups, covering exactly the kinds of music that were at issue
for the Festival du Village. Theater, music, food, and history, all mobilized
in the context of the Quiet Revolution (Handler 1988), remained available as tourist products.

This tradition was expanded to an Acadie that could tie itself more
legitimately to France than even Quebec could, since Champlain established his settlement there four years before he founded Quebec City, and
since the Acadians of the mid-eighteenth century were deported from
their lands for refusing to swear an oath of loyalty to the British Crown.
(Actually, they simply wanted to remain neutral, but it is the refusal part
that has become salient.) The Saguenay's *Fabuleuse*, which first opened
in 1989, inspired other pageants, including two in Acadie. Both are pre-
sen ed in the context of "living village"–type tourist sites.

(ne, in northeastern New Brunswick, brings together original building: from different moments of the region's history, from about the late
1700s to the 1930s (the moment at which the pageants and historical
revues also begin to have difficulty maintaining the thread of the historical narrative of the community; this is where the breathless parade of
modernity begins). Employees from the area work there in the summer,
portraying the kinds of people who might have lived there at the time.

The other, *Le pays de la Sagouine*, was opened in 1992 (www.sagouine.
com). It has a theater that presents performances of *La Sagouine* (Maillet
1974), a fictive monologue in Acadian French by a washerwoman that
casts Acadian history in the form of a biblical epic. When it was first performed and published, it was well-received (and Maillet herself later won
the Prix Goncourt for another text); this helped legitimize Acadian
French as a language of literature and a terrain of political consciousness-
raising. The site of *Le pays*, developed for a *Sommet de la Francophonie*
held in Moncton, contains re-creations of the buildings of the kind of
fishing village in which *la Sagouine* is supposed to have lived, sometime in
the eighteenth or nineteenth century. It also has a restaurant where you
can eat traditional Acadian food, and a boutique where you can buy traditional Acadian things.

In addition, both Quebec and Acadie regularly send performers to
France, to big-city stages and to the many festivals held in French regions
in the warmer months of the year. In 2004, Acadie was even the special
guest region at the Festival interceltique held every summer in the Breton
town of Lorient, their parallel regional, maritime linguistic minority status
apparently overcoming any potential objection that Acadians are not only
not Celts but even claim their descent from the enemy (France). France,
of course, represents the most obvious first step toward expanding a

Figure 7.1 Reenactment of nineteenth-century Acadian rural life at the Village Acadien. Photo by Jeremy Paltiel.

market for cultural products; even Céline Dion went to France before trying her luck in Las Vegas.

Other kinds of products also circulate in France. I began to notice this in December 2001, when I happened to be in the Normandy city of Rouen at Christmastime and took the opportunity to visit the outdoor Christmas market (one of many held across Western Europe). One stall-holder tried to sell me a polar fleece jacket with a small red maple leaf (like the one on the Canadian flag) embroidered on it, speaking in what was to me, at the time, a bewildering mix of fairly typical European French and exaggerated Canadian French features (familiar *tu* rather than *vous* as second-person-singular address form, /t/s and /d/s affricated before high front vowels for so long I thought he would run out of breath, vowels diphthongized to within an inch of their lives). I tried to explain that it made no sense to try to sell me, a Canadian, a jacket that was supposedly warm enough for Canadian winters, since (a) I already had one, although it was true that the one I had bought in Canada had no flag on it; indeed, the only place you can buy fleeces with flags on them in Canada is at the airport; (b) as a Canadian, I happen to know that fleeces do you no good on their own when it's really cold out. As it happens, the only other place I have since seen such a jacket was in a store in Beijing.

Shortly after that encounter, however, I came across a stall with Canadian maple syrup for sale. The vendor was a young man whose French careened much less wildly around variables and who claimed to be from eastern Quebec, on an annual selling tour around European markets. A

few years later, one of our collaborators, Claudine Moïse, noticed that
Canada was the special guest country at a number of commercial fairs and
markets in France (and, as it turned out, also in Belgium and Switzerland),
so several team members went to do more serious fieldwork. Having
country themes seems to be a product of French cultural policy (the year
I was in Rouen, the guest country was in fact Finland), and since either
2004 or 2008 commemorated the four hundredth anniversary of New
France (depending on whether you count from the first, short-lived Acadian settlement in 1604 or the longer-lived Quebec settlement of 1608),
there was a fair amount of money available from French, Canadian, and
Québécois sources for celebrating francophone Canada in France in that
period.

What we discovered was a small network of entrepreneurs, some based
in France and some in Canada, organizing a circuit of vendors and their
products. Most of the products were of the *terroir* variety: lots of maple
syrup and smoked salmon, along with wild-berry-based products, goat
milk soap, and emu oil, all of it the result of small-scale production in
rural Quebec. (Emus are not indigenous to Canada, of course, but the
logic of the *terroir* makes it possible to blur the line between local authenticity, environmentalism, and other dimensions of alter-globalization.)
The vendors either were Québécois living in France (many of them students), or were brought over for the season. Most of them were dressed
for the occasion in a combination of costume elements indexing the figure of the lumberjack (red-and-black-checked wool shirt, or *chemise à
carreaux*) and the *voyageur* (a woven sash called a *ceinture fléchée*, or
arrowed belt, after the pattern woven into it), or both (a *tuque*, a wool
cap, usually red).

The following two examples are from an interview conducted by Claudine Moïse and Emmanuel Kahn with Éric, one of the major Quebec-
based organizers. In the following extract, Éric insists on the importance
of authenticity in the evaluation of their product's quality. (Elsewhere in
the interview he makes the same points about maple syrup that he does
here about salmon.)

EMMANUEL: Where does the smoked salmon come from?
ÉRIC: It's Atlantic salmon and Pacific salmon
CLAUDINE: Both yes
ÉRIC: Both yeah and wild / because you know we can't (x) and that's my
    next challenge / is to get people to understand / I say this and it isn't
    pejorative / I want to make sure we understand each other / because
    here in France / they go through 40,000 tons of smoked salmon a year
CLAUDINE: Yes
ÉRIC: It's all farmed salmon

[EMMANUEL: Le saumon fumé d'où il vient?
ÉRIC: C'est du saumon de l'Atlantique et du saumon du Pacifique
CLAUDINE: Les deux oui

Figure 7.2 A stand at the Christmas market at Montbéliard. Note the *chemise à carreaux* on the vendor. Photo by Mary Richards.

Figure 7.3 An exhibit at the Foire de Montpellier. Note the maple sugar, the *chemise à carreaux*, and other items indexing rural francophone Canada. Photo by Mireille McLaughlin.

Figure 7.4 A stand at the Christmas market in Strasbourg, 2007. Note the signs for salmon (*saumon*) and maple syrup (*sirop d'érable*). Photo by Claudine Moïse.

ÉRIC: C'est les deux ouais et sauvage / parce que vous savez nous on peut pas (x) et ça c'est mon prochain défi / c'est de faire comprendre / je dis ça puis c'est pas péjoratif / je veux bien qu'on se comprenne / parce que ici en France / ils passent 40,000 tonnes de saumon fumé par année

CLAUDINE: Oui

ÉRIC: C'est tout du saumon d'élevage] (Interview, Montbéliard, France, 2005)

In the following extract, Éric links this authenticity to language: being able to provide a (largely linguistic) performance of francophone Canadian-ness was a major dimension of the symbolic added value of the products.

CLAUDINE: And how do you choose your vendors for the / for the fair?

ÉRIC: Well like / my vendors / except for two people they're all Québécois [masc.] // Québécoises [fem.] // uh / the two French people are excellent / that's why I used them / they know the product very well and uh / like the Christmas market well / I work with the Web page often with the Association France-Québec / the vendors (x) the Québécois or Québécoises need a job / they call there / ah / or Promotion canadienne needs [someone for a] Christmas market / they send their CV / young people all go through the Internet / they send it / two pages / no more / I take a look / yeah / okay / if it's good we go to the ne[x]t stage and then

EMMANUEL: They're all francophones?

ÉRIC: Pardon?

EMMANUEL: Francophones or are there anglo-Québécois or?

ÉRIC: No / they're Québécois / Québécoises / it's (x) I have to say / the accent as they say

EMMANUEL: Yeah

ÉRIC: Often we get there / no / no / we buy / speak to us / speak to us

CLAUDINE: (*laughs*)

ÉRIC: We capitalize on that accent also (x) it's [the] business / eh / it's

[CLAUDINE: Et comment vous choisissez vos vendeurs là sur le / sur la foire?

ÉRIC: Ben comme / mes vendeurs / à l'exception de deux personnes c'est tout des / des Québécois / des Québécoises / euh / les deux Français sont excellents / c'est pour ça que je les ai utilisé / ils connaissent le produit très bien et puis euh / comme le marché de Noël bien / je travaille avec le Web page souvent avec l'Association France-Québec / les vendeurs (x) les Québécois ou Québécoises ont besoin d'un emploi / ils appellent là / ah / oui Promotion Canadienne a besoin marché de Noël / ils envoient leur CV / les jeunes passent tous par Internet / ils envoient ça / deux pages / pas plus / je regarde / ouais / ok / si c'est bon on va l'étape plus loin et puis

EMMANUEL: C'est tout des francophones?

ÉRIC: Pardon?

EMMANUEL: Des francophones ou il y a des anglo-québécois ou?

ÉRIC: Non / c'est Québécois / Québécoises / c'est (x) il faut l'admettre / l'accent comme ils disent

EMMANUEL: Ouais

ÉRIC: Souvent on va arriver / non / non / on achète / parlez-nous / parlez-nous

CLAUDINE: (*rire*)

ÉRIC: On capitalise sur c't accent-là aussi (x) c'est la business / hein / c'est] (Interview, Montbéliard, France, 2005)

While the products themselves required some authentication, organizers contributed not only through the provision of linguistic packaging
(with, it must be noted, the active involvement of either the state, here in
the form of Promotion canadienne, or the *milieu associatif*, here in the
form of the Association France-Québec), but also through visual elements, such as insisting that vendors wear traditional costume, and
through juxtaposing the commercial side of the fairs with entertainment,
food, and exhibits. (Chantal White reports exactly the same combination
in the mise-en-scène of selling hooked rugs at a cooperative in Nova Scotia, where the authenticity of the rugs is packaged in performances of
hooking, and where repeated exchanges with French tourists focused on
specific features rendered salient as distinguishing the local variety of
French, the kind rug-hookers speak, from the French spoken by tourists.
Tourists can also eat typical food at the local restaurant, go whale-watching
in boats formerly used for cod fishing, and, if they can find them, buy

hooked rugs with more contemporary motifs sold by a small group of younger women kept out of the cooperative because their work does not use traditional designs; Moïse et al. 2006.)

One of the exhibits at Montbéliard was a collection of *crèches* (nativity scenes) on loan from Rivière-Éternité, a small village in the Saguenay region of Quebec. Mireille McLaughlin and I went there in the summer of 2006 and encountered the people responsible for the collection, most of which was housed in the basement of the parish church (exactly the kind of place where most OJC cell meetings were held, especially in rural areas like this).

The collection had its origin in an attempt on the part of municipal authorities to counteract unemployment-related depression and alcohol abuse in the town, which was suffering from the decline of the lumber industry and had been overtaken by the neighboring village in competition for state funds for building tourism-related infrastructure. In 1989, they asked for the help of a local activist turned "bénévole en développement touristique" (tourism development volunteer) in his retirement. He said that to be successful, all such efforts needed to draw on the two universal themes of tourism: nature and culture. He suggested building a program around a theme drawn from those domains, and suggested four: decorated eggs, bears, wild berries, and nativity scenes. The municipal council chose nativity scenes.

The town's attempts to build both local morale and an alternative source of income through tourism began with a townwide Christmastime competition among households for the best outdoor nativity scene. This grew to the establishment of a collection of indoor and outdoor scenes (the outdoor ones are now housed in a nearby park), featuring regional artists, more prominent Québécois artists, and scenes produced around the world. The plan is to open a museum that will be open year-round. In the context of the four hundredth anniversary of New France, state funding was available to send municipal representatives with a traveling collection to France. By the time Mireille and I got there, there was no longer any money for personal accompaniment for the exhibit, and the local authorities were planning to bring the traveling exhibit home.

The crèches of Rivière-Éternité are part of the Saguenay region's efforts to maintain an economic base, not just in the face of troubles in the lumber industry, but also with respect to problems related to the production of aluminum (the major regional employment sector) and to out-migration of the region's youth, especially those who leave in search of higher education. The region has a strong sense of identity: it calls itself the Kingdom of the Saguenay (hence the title *La fabuleuse histoire d'un royaume*—The Wondrous History of a Kingdom). This sense has long provided solid political support for Quebec independence, bolstered by a combination of francophone working-class solidarity (the lumber mills and aluminum smelters have historically been owned by members of the Quebec anglophone elite, based in Montreal and Quebec City)

Figure 7.5 A small selection of the interior exhibit of crèches, Rivière-Éternité. Photo by Mireille McLaughlin.

Figure 7.6 An exhibit of a model of a *party de cuisine*. Photo by Mireille McLaughlin.

Figure 7.7 Part of the exterior exhibit of crèches. Photo by Mireille McLaughlin.

and francophone elite intellectual leadership (this region held a major concentration of OJC cells). Declining population has been somewhat offset by francophone outsiders coming in to develop tourism and tourism-related *terroir* activities (the goat milk soap sold at Montbéliard came from the same region, and the area is famous for its blueberries), but most recently the Saguenay has joined the ranks of the francophone traditional bastions actively seeking to recruit immigrants from Europe or from other former French colonies. A local NGO, Portes ouvertes sur le lac (Open doors on the lake, or Doors open onto the lake), sends out a regular electronic bulletin recounting its efforts to recruit newcomers and to make them feel welcome.

Many traditional francophone bastions across Canada are moving in the same direction: commodifying authenticity in order to keep people at home, thereby attracting consumers who introduce linguistic and cultural variability (especially English), and, as the population declines (if only because of falling birth rates), requiring the importation of immigrants to keep the new economy from failing to take off.

My favorite story is this: An Acadian couple received funding under a tourism-development envelope to start a soap production site, using traditional soap production methods even though the soap base was olive oil (not indigenous to Acadie, but associated with health). The product was packaged as organic and local (one soap package has a picture of the seashore and an Acadian flag on it), and the site marketed as an interesting place to visit—indeed, chosen in part for its location by the sea. At one point, the enterprise looked to a shopping mall in nearby Moncton to better its distribution. When Annette Boudreau and I visited the new store in the mall one day, we were greeted by a young gentleman in a bathrobe, offering to let us try their product; he was approaching all ladies unaccompanied by men, rubbing cream into our hands, and vaunting the qualities of the product. Annette recognized him: he was a former student of hers, from Madagascar. Eventually, the company was forced to close its shopping mall site or forgo state funding, since the funding was contingent on the enterprise's tourism activities. It closed the site and turned instead to the development of entertainment activities. Local billboards advertise its new spectacle, called "Le Bain Show." This is a semi-bilingual pun. *Le bain chaud* means "the hot bath," clearly appropriate for a soap-related spectacle. As it happens, *chaud* is homophonous (almost, anyway) with "show," which, while obviously originally from English, is also widely used in vernacular Canadian French to mean, well, "show."

In many ways this story points to ways in which people are dealing with the consequences of commodifying the cultural and linguistic forms constructed under conditions of nationalist political mobilization. The tensions between the authentic and the spectacle break out in a slow but steady stream of puns (bilingual and otherwise; see Lamarre 2009), wise-cracks, ironic meta-commentary, and promotion of the ordinary and unspectacular. I will follow this up in chapter 8.

In the next section, I will look at some of the tensions that emerge in other kinds of new-economy sectors, where language becomes a zone of tension between nationalist modes of constructing markets and new-economy techniques of managing language as a skill. Here the link between language and identity becomes even more problematic.

7.3 BOUNDING FRANCOPHONE SPACE

If any one sector characterizes the rebuilding of Montreal's economy after the crisis of the manufacturing industries, it is the multimedia sector. This sector is interesting for my purposes not just because it is one of the spaces to which Montreal has turned, but also because it represents the kind of value-added, symbolic, communication-intensive work that is so typical of the new economy.

It was able to find fertile ground in Montreal in part as a result of the downsizing of the federally funded and Montreal-based National Film Board, which has long been a hub of the Canadian film industry, in both French and English. In the early 1980s (roughly 1981–1985) much of its work was allotted to the private sector or outsourced (in a move typical of the neoliberal trend of the era; see www3.onf.ca/a-propos/historique.php). This downsizing released onto the market a large number of people with skills that were of value in the expanding digital communications sector; they turned into the core of a Quebec-based small-scale video technology industry, run by francophones and staffed by francophones.

One of our case studies in Montreal focused on one such company in the multimedia postproduction sector; we have called it Zone Grafix (ZG) (Lamarre and Lamarre 2006a,b). Aiming at the U.S. and Latin American markets, ZG sold itself as having symbolic added value derived from local specialization in the niche sector, the prestige of the National Film Board (a regular presence at the Academy Awards in Los Angeles, and hence on the American radar), and the aesthetic sensibility of a francophone culture. While most of the workers in the company were monolingual francophones, the company did need to have people with proficiency in English and Spanish; those people were found at the highest levels of the company, or in positions specifically defined for articulation with anglophone and hispanophone clients. Neither of the individuals in those latter positions was a francophone; one was from the Irish working class of Montreal (as were the superintendents in the brewery), and the other was an immigrant from North Africa.

The francophone employees often complained about being relegated to the production sector and kept far away from clients. In some ways, they represent even more of a success in modern nationalist terms than the Alberts of the brewery, insofar as they have interesting, well-paying jobs for which they do not need to learn English. At the same time, the industry they are in depends completely on an articulation with the world outside Quebec, most particularly a world in which English and Spanish play important roles. Those who are monolingual francophones, or at least have the ability to act like monolingual francophones, preserve the francophone cachet of the product and privileged control over the sector. But too much monolingualism restricts the opportunities open to individuals and creates privileged positions for bi- or multilinguals. This is the central tension produced by the tertiary sector.

Our second Montreal case study showed a similar tension around the costs and benefits of privileging a francophone regional market (Kahn and Heller 2006). Planète Juste (PJ), as we have called it, was founded in 1993 as a regional chapter of an international NGO, with the aim of promoting fair trade, ecological agriculture, sustainable and environmentally friendly modes of transportation, and energy efficiency.

All but one of its major staff members were Québécois francophones, although several spoke English or Spanish, picked up in their travels across the Americas through their involvement in social justice and green movements. PJ relied on its one anglophone employee for translations into English, and on temporary interns for local outreach in languages other than French. Despite self-criticism of its socially homogeneous profile (its director once said in a meeting that they were all, including him, "jeunes blancs d'origine catholique vivant sur le Plateau"—young Whites of Catholic origin living on the Plateau, a trendy Montreal neighborhood), PJ struggled with how to be more socially inclusive, maintaining its insistence on the importance of speaking and writing "good" French as a central recruitment and hiring criterion, and of developing a distinctive Québécois approach and practice in the struggle for social justice and sustainability.

This ideological tension also emerged clearly in struggles over the definition of the local. Most alter-globalization movements define locality through physical distance. In the case of Montreal, however, a 100-kilometer radius takes you into both Ontario and the United States, while leaving out most of Quebec. In a discussion about the promotion of "local" agricultural products, this tension came to a head. Jean, the person responsible for this sector of activities, noticed that his characterization of products as "québécois" had been changed to "locaux":

JEAN: What is this?
A CONSULTANT: Is this an issue of nationalism or of distance?
JEAN: Do we have to define a range? / for me it means *québécois*! I've heard people in the office say that New York is local!
THOMAS: If Quebec is local then New York and Toronto are local

[JEAN: C'est quoi ça?
UN CONSULTANT: C'est-tu une question nationaliste ou de distance?
JEAN: Est-ce qu'il faut définir un rayon? / pour moi ça veut dire québécois! J'ai entendu des gens dans la boîte qui disent que New York c'est local!
THOMAS: Si le Québec c'est local alors New York et Toronto c'est local]
(Field notes, strategic planning committee, 2003)

The issue for Quebec became how to balance the ways in which constructing a regional market was beneficial to francophones, with the integration of that market outside its borders (especially with the rest of North America), as well as with its commitment to democracy and social justice. Planète Juste is perhaps an extreme example of this commitment, but it takes up an important thread in the discourse of political mobilization of Québécois and other Canadian francophones. In its dilemma, it illustrates the problem of identity politics: Once you have successfully emancipated a group marginalized on the basis of social identity, how do you escape the confines of that categorization in order not to reproduce its stratifying effects? Conversely, if you leave that categorization behind, do you risk losing all you have gained?

7.4 PROBLEMS OF LINGUISTIC COMMODIFICATION

These questions become acute in the language industry sector, where the product, communication, allows an even greater separation of language from identity. I will examine that issue here by drawing on fieldwork conducted by members of our team in call centers in southern Ontario in 1998 and in southern New Brunswick in 2002 and 2003. I participated in fieldwork in each site, but the bulk of the data in Ontario was collected by Sylvie Roy, and in New Brunswick by Mélanie LeBlanc; Lise Dubois played a key role in the collection and analysis of the New Brunswick data as well (see Roy 2001, 2003; Dubois et al. 2006). Most of these call centers were what the industry refers to as "inbound," that is, agents take calls from clients. These are considered better jobs than so-called "outbound" centers, most of which are involved in telemarketing, exposing agents to people annoyed at having their evening meal interrupted by a sales call. (Also, inbound centers usually provide performance incentives based on service quality, while outbound centers look for service quantity, pressuring agents to work quickly and constantly.)

We have seen that both geographical areas placed an emphasis on the call center sector in attempts to revitalize regions hard-hit economically by the downsizing of heavy industry in northeastern North America. Both marketed the bilingual skills of the workforce in campaigns to sell the region to call center companies. And in both areas, managers found themselves responsible for staffing bilingual positions. The following is an excerpt from an interview conducted in 1998 with such a manager; she is the only person at management level to have any knowledge of French at all. It was not a language she had used much in most of her career, but it became useful once the call center expanded.

The switching between French and English in the interview is itself indicative of her slightly awkward position: she is being interviewed by two academics from an obviously francophone unit (our business cards and letterhead say "Centre de recherches en éducation franco-ontarienne") about the part of her job that requires her to manage the bilingual work of the company. At the same time, she rarely uses French in the course of her workday (or the rest of her life, for that matter), and for many years she did not use French at work at all.

> [We have a] very large base of French-speaking employees in our customer services areas specifically [. . .] Welland as a city / does compete with / you know / Moncton Fredericton and so on and so forth in trying to attract new business in the area // so / that's a real competitive issue there // there is a lot of many many benefits to being in Welland // especially the language // we are one of the biggest call centers in Canada [. . .] English is absolutely needed for every single transaction in every single job / so that one is like the baseline // but we also need French spoken / and also French written in some areas for a certain percentage of our customer interactions // so we currently have a very very large base of French-speaking employees in our customer services areas specifically [. . .] *on est très heureux d'être à Welland parce que / à côté / à cause de spécifiquement le côté francophone de Welland / c'est très important pour notre entreprise* [we are very happy to be in Welland because, besides, because of specifically the francophone side of Welland, it's very important for our company] [. . .] (Interview, manager, call center, Welland, southern Ontario, 1998)

Her only intervention in French may well be a formulaic phrase used for such occasions as this (although she stumbles over two different ways of saying "because," one more informal, *à cause de*, and one more standard, *parce que*). The content is also revealing: English remains the dominant language of the company, and French is confined to the customer-services area. What this means, concretely, is that bilingualism is really only found at the lowest rung of the ladder, among the employees who directly provide service in French to clients. This pattern (anglophone management, francophone labor) seems quite stable in the call center industry, from what we have seen elsewhere. It is, of course, one we have seen historically (see chapter 4); the major difference is that the workforce in the old economy was largely male, while today, the wordforce is more likely to be female.

Our interviews in Welland, Moncton, Toronto, and Ottawa with call center workers, managers, and employment placement agencies all point to the same set of paradoxes. Providing bilingual services means dealing with language for the first time as a commodity. Some workplaces continue to treat it as a talent people just happen to have; handling it this way makes it possible to avoid paying for it. Just as massive amounts of language work were accomplished with no concomitant reimbursement or recognition by the secretaries at the brewery, or by the other appointments clerks at an outpatient clinic where I had a summer job as a student, today people send out emails asking if anyone happens to speak Portuguese, because an order just got faxed in from Portugal that no one can read. (Duchêne's work at a major European airport documents an institutionalization of that practice, in which employees' linguistic repertoires get inventoried and shared, to be drawn on in just such emergencies, which are, of course, frequent in major airports; Duchêne in press.) The same is true for providing written translations; I cannot count, for example, the number of times English-speaking colleagues have interrupted my work to ask me to just quickly translate for them an abstract they need to submit in both English and French to a conference. We saw similar practices across all the sites we visited (see Djerrahian and Labrie 2009 for an account of a privatized biotechnology enterprise in the Ottawa region).

Finally, we see this kind of practice in employee recruitment and performance evaluation: management looks around for an employee who seems to speak French, and asks them to interview prospective employees (sometimes over the phone) or evaluate their work. These informal evaluators usually told us that they didn't have any specific set of criteria to use; what mattered was whether the person was or was not able to carry on a conversation with them in French.

However, many of the workplaces we encountered did treat language as a commodity in some way. The most frequent practice is to pay some kind of bonus, which around 2003 seemed to be in the range of about $0.25 to $1.00 CAN an hour; the federal government has long paid certified bilingual public servants a yearly bonus of about $800 CAN. These are not major sums. (In some markets, bilingualism is instead treated as an entry-level commodity, that is, a basic requirement for employment in that sector, and therefore something that potential workers need to invest in before going on the market; see chapter 5, note 1, and Duchêne 2009.)

In the call center in Welland studied by Sylvie Roy, flexibility was incorporated through the concept of "knowledge blocks": workers could devote time to training in the various areas of product and service provided by the company, each known as a "knowledge block." Having completed a training session, the new knowledge block would be added to a worker's profile, thus enabling management to identify which employees could be assigned to which sectors (and therefore also which shifts), according to the flux of client demand. Employees were compensated through a system that assigned value to knowledge blocks; they generally bought into the rationale that this would also help them accumulate expertise and gain control over their schedule. Within this system, speaking French was treated as one more knowledge block.

Where language was treated as something measurable in this way, employee recruitment and performance evaluation was usually conducted using standardized tests. I met several employees at placement agencies who spoke no French but whose files included recruiting bilingual call center representatives. They reported relying on widely available standardized tests, usually from Quebec. However, in one case, high school students working in a Toronto call center told Mary Richards and Philippe Hambye that there were so few francophones working in their center that the test they had to pass to be hired was in English (interview, 2008).

Everyone involved admitted to some degree of misfit. In the late 1990s, only a few years after the call center industry established itself in Welland in a serious way, employment placement agencies were claiming that they had exhausted the market. One recruiter told Roy that it was no longer possible to find candidates with adequate bilingual skills; she said that many people were claiming to be bilingual but that clients were not satisfied with their proficiency in French. In Moncton, the one thing management and agents all said posed a problem was the lack of fit between client expectations and employee linguistic proficiency.

In their search for a labor pool with bilingual skills, and their interest in the kind of low-ranking, "flexible" (read "unpredictable"), and not very well-remunerated positions offered by call centers, the industry has targeted a population whose bilingualism has two characteristics: the codes are usually not kept carefully separate as distinct codes, and the linguistic system bears the marks of lower-class position (in Canadian French these are most clearly found in the lexicon and phonology). This works perfectly well in interaction with clients from the same background, but that population represents a tiny portion of the market (only a million francophones live outside Quebec, and they now occupy a range of class positions). It doesn't work so well with monolingual francophones or with anyone whose French is shaped by schooling and middle-class normative expectations (and whose linguistic sensibilities regarding the "quality" of French are heightened by a combination of francophone hypernormative linguistic ideology and the ideological importance of French in the nationalist consciousness of francophone Canada). I should note, though, that the students interviewed in Toronto said that their outbound center was so little invested in the francophone segment of their work that in fact their French calls were rarely evaluated, unlike the high surveillance of English calls.

Finally, the constraints of call center work contribute to the contradictions. Oral work tends to be heavily script-supported, and scripted itself (Cameron 2001; Boutet 2008). Those scripts are always standardized in all senses; they fit poorly with the unpredictability of conversational interaction, and even more so with the variability of the vernacular. In many instances, conversation in French is supported by text in English. (While workers always claimed that this posed absolutely no problem for them, Dubois et al. 2006 documents cases where what this meant was the unavailability of lexical support in French when employee and client repertoires failed to match.) The Toronto students complained that the extreme insistence on keeping to the script impeded communication and was made worse by the often problematic translation from English to French—an issue they had no control over because, in classic Taylorist fashion, translation was outsourced:

AÏSHA: And it's badly translated also / the surveys are badly translated from English to French / it's badly translated / he says "I don't understand the question" / and you can't put that in your words / you have to read it exactly / *forbidden* / you have to read exactly
ZAHRA: You can't explain
AÏSHA: No you can't explain / you have to repeat the question again and again / until they understand
[. . .]
CATHERINE: You don't have like / sometimes / the supervisor who calls you to correct you she tells you "You didn't say this like you were supposed to" / but you're like
AÏSHA: That really gets to me / it's not even her language
CATHERINE: She tells you that you don't speak French well / and you can't say to her / otherwise you'll be kicked out right away / so you have to accept everything they they are telling you

[AÏSHA: Et c'est mal traduit aussi / les sondages sont mal traduits de l'anglais en français / c'est mal traduit / il dit "je comprends pas la question" / et tu peux pas mettre ça dans tes mots / il faut le lire exactement / *forbidden* / il faut lire exactement
ZAHRA: Tu peux pas expliquer
AÏSHA: Non tu peux pas expliquer / il faut répéter la question encore et encore / jusqu'à ce qu'ils comprennent
[. . .]
CATHERINE: T'as pas comme / des fois / le superviseur qui vous appelle pour vous corriger elle te dit "T'as pas dit ceci comme il fallait" / mais t'es comme

AÏSHA: Ça m'énerve ça / c'est même pas sa langue
CATHERINE: Elle te dit que tu parles pas bien le français / et tu peux pas
   lui dire / sinon tu vas être chassée directement / donc tu dois accepter
   tout ce qui on est en train de te dire] (Call center part-time workers,
   Toronto, 2008)

The result was that many call center employees were terrified to
answer calls from Quebec. It is impossible to predict from an area code
what linguistic stance a client is likely to take (although that is exactly
how call centers tend to manage the distribution of calls when they have
some monolingual employees), but everyone we spoke to talked about
the impossibility of getting it right, when a call from the same area code
could be coming from a monolingual or bilingual, anglophone, francophone, or allophone, normative or not. They also all agreed that the
majority of the explicit linguistic criticisms they ever received were about
their French (although the Toronto students were sometimes chided for
not following the English script properly).

In Moncton, one employee handled this by working hard at developing
a variety of guises, turning "Who am I?" into a kind of game (she won
when clients could not tell she was not from whatever part of North
America she claimed to be from for the purposes of the call). Another,
however, invented an English name for herself which she always used
(most agents in Moncton happened, not coincidentally for such a bilingual population, to have names like Julie or Anne-Marie, which are inter-
changeable in French and English); that way, all she got was praise for the
incredibly good French she spoke, considering that it was apparently her
second language.

At the same time, bilingual agents and their immediate supervisors
regularly deployed their vernacular in interaction among themselves, off-
line, and outside the surveillance of anglophone management. I think we
can read this as a strategy of solidarity aimed at protecting their share of
the job market, especially given their center's recent change in hiring policy: instead of only hiring bilingual agents, it had begun also hiring monolingual anglophones, to whom calls from western Canada and the United
States could safely be directed. The only other recourse for employees
was to frequently change jobs; indeed, for all the reasons one might imagine, the turnover rate in the call center industry does tend to be high.

Employers, on the other hand, did sometimes seek other avenues. The
Welland call center began to introduce French language classes for their
bilingual employees, that is, classes designed to help francophones better
fit their French to the expectations of the job, and operated along the
model of the other training courses within the "knowledge block" format.
The Toronto students quoted above represent another alternative: they
are all well-educated high school students from outside Canada (France in
one case and sub-Saharan African former French colonies in the others).
In Moncton, the call centers also drew on the local francophone university population.

For students, flexible hours are attractive, and the pay not bad for a part-time job. Catherine says: "Mais c'est trop stressant vraiment / on est juste là parce qu'on est élève et on a nos besoins aussi / et l'horaire qui est trop flexible pour nous ça nous arrange trop" (But it's really so stressful / we're only there because we're students and we have our own needs too / and the schedule is so flexible for us that's really convenient for us). Students and educated immigrants turn out to be an alternative labor pool, ready to accept the job conditions and possessing the kind of standardized linguistic skills call centers seek. They may well contest the legitimacy of call center managers' evaluations of their skills (a major problem when undereducated managers supervise overeducated employees), but since students at least are likely to move on, this form of resistance is not difficult to contain.

More difficult is the matter of what linguistic skills are worth. It is no surprise, then, to find economists now turning their attention to that question, trying to find formulas for making those calculations (Grin 1996, 2003; A. Breton 1998; Alonso 2006). The work I am reporting on here, however, suggests that that exercise may be impossible: the conflicting ideologies of language on the terrain resist Taylorization.

Nonetheless, in that one short phrase from Aïsha, "ça m'énerve ça / c'est même pas sa langue" (that really gets to me / it's not even her language), we see the core of a struggle on the terrain of commodified language skills: Who gets to define what counts as legitimate language? Is the evaluation of language skills something that requires linguistic ownership, or can it be done through standardized procedures? What matters more, being able to handle the unpredictability of conversation or sticking to the script? being a "native speaker" or having schooled knowledge? Should a translator be a human being with a native language into which she translates, as current dominant Canadian practice would have it, or can it be a machine? What kinds of people make the best language teachers?

Just as the personnel of Zone Grafix and Planète Juste struggle to balance saving the nation with conserving the market, selling their skills and entering the globalized world, call center personnel have to worry about who gets to decide what counts as linguistic competence, and therefore what the value of their capital is on the market of the new economy, and where that leaves them as Canadian francophones. The successful modernization of francophone Canada turns out to be full of unexpected consequences.

7.5 PARADOXES AND POTENTIALS

Language is now central to economic activities, both in the means of production and as a product itself.[2] In the tertiary sector, communication is the labor you sell. Your bilingualism might, just possibly, represent added value, which may gain you an edge in the competition for jobs, and possibly a few dollars an hour more for your work.

But that phenomenon produces some interesting and sometimes contradictory effects. Notably, there is a tension between efforts on the part of the service and information economy to standardize processes and products (they are easier to manage and to measure) and to allow for the flexibility and variability that attention to "meeting customers' needs" can require. The second important tension is between treating language as a technical skill (easier to measure and evaluate, but then also something that needs to be recognized, managed, and paid for), and as a kind of innate talent (hard to manage, but also something that does not require remuneration and allows room for worker adaptation to local conditions).

The use of certain forms of language guarantees authenticity, but these forms are necessarily bound up in new practices. Some older community-building practices are still possible when the clientele identifies with the authenticity being sold (when it comes to create itself through consuming itself, as it were); but market forces rarely permit the producers to limit their clientele in this way. In most of Canada, it is Americans, Germans, and Japanese who constitute the majority of tourists, however important Quebec and France may be. How is an enterprise to reach clients in search of authentic exoticism (a hallmark of current tourism) when they can't understand the authentic forms of communication that guarantee the legitimacy or the value of the product they are consuming?

I have provided here two examples of new economy activities that are far from specific to Canada, although they do, of course, have specific manifestations wherever they are found. Still, British and U.S. companies outsource call centers to India, and French companies outsource them to Senegal, hoping to capitalize on precisely the combination of language skills and joblessness that make Welland and Moncton attractive; and they encounter there the same paradoxes of norms and authenticity, of standardization and flexibility, that I have described above. Managers still have to figure out whether monolingualism or multilingualism is most helpful to the exercise of their supervisory tasks. And cultural or heritage tourism is an important growth area, as is the global marketing of authentic cultural artifacts, or their appropriation in more contemporary hybrid cultural forms. Language is both a technical skill and a symbol of authenticity in this new world, with all the paradoxes that flow from the combination.

Perhaps part of the problem is that we tend to think of new modes of production, and new products, as though they were old ones. We try to treat language as an assembly line or a chair, all the while asking it to do the new work of flexible adaptation to changing conditions. We use it to guarantee authenticity, while pretending it is a skill or a technical operation. But we also (perhaps conveniently) forget that language is actually much more than a skill or a talent, a means of production or a product; it is, as it has always been, a terrain for constructing both social difference and social inequality, a space in which to compete for jobs and markets and resources, both as individuals and as groups.

The space between paradoxes may open up new avenues for reimagining francophone Canada in ways that build on what has been gained without reproducing the structures of inequality political mobilization was intended to resist. As the ground shifts, new potentials open up. In the final chapter, we will look at the glimmerings of post-nationalism, which are appearing in the most unlikely places.

8

Paths to Post-Nationalism

8.1 LEAKING META-COMMENTARY

In August 2005, I went with Mireille McLaughlin, Sonya Malaborza, and Mary Richards to Caraquet, a town in northeastern New Brunswick that has always thought of itself as the capital of Acadie, although it now has to fight off the rivalry of upstart Moncton.

Since 2005 was the 250th anniversary of *le Grand Dérangement*, the deportation of Acadians by the British, it seemed like a good year to check out how history was being constructed, especially in the place that constructed itself as the authentic home of Acadian nationalism. It is the base of many Acadian institutions. Indeed, the OJC had been strong there (it was where we had interviewed Henri in 1998). The almost exclusively francophone regional population has long lived off the sea and the forest. One local institution is the Festival acadien, held in the weeks around the Acadian national holiday, the feast day of Notre-Dame de l'Assomption on August 15. Most Acadian towns have one, but Caraquet's has gained a special reputation.

The 250th anniversary edition promised to be particularly rich. But as soon as we got there we noticed something was up. We went to the historical pageant on the site of the nearby living-history museum. It had exactly the same structure as the one in eastern Ontario (Malaborza and McLaughlin 2008), only the narrative kept getting interrupted by ironic postmodernism. People still stood up to sing the *Ave Stella Maris* (more or less the Acadian national anthem), but then a segment on the OJC featured guys in 1950s suits, with slicked-back hair and sunglasses, and made fun of the secrecy that had been so sacred to the order: "Y'a des poignées de main secrètes / des rendez-vous en cachette / *La patente* / pour ne plus avoir de dettes / on a trouvé la recette / *La patente*" (There are secret handshakes / and secret meetings / *La patente* / to free ourselves of debt / we have found the recipe / *La patente*; Richard 2005). We saw the arrival of Champlain, the harmony with the indigenous population, the trauma of the deportation, the consciousness-raising of the *conventions nationales* of the early 1880s. We saw the political struggles of the 1960s and 1970s. And then at the end we were told: "Il n'y a pas de vérité / il n'y a que des histoires / suffit de les raconter / c'est à chacun d'y croire" (There is no truth / there are only stories [or histories] / it's enough to tell them / it is up to each person to believe in them; Richard 2005).

In town, in the brand-new theater near the docks, we went to a show that had been created for the 2004 commemorations of the four hundredth anniversary of Champlain's arrival in what became Acadie. This spectacle was meant to showcase Acadian music; its producers selected seven young performers from across the Maritimes and constructed around them a display of Acadian music from past to present, on a set that used a large back screen to project images of Acadie. Again, while much of the performance took place within the discourse of modernizing Acadian nationalism, there were interruptions.

One was a running joke about whether the performer from northwestern New Brunswick was really an Acadian or not (the area styles itself "la République du Madawaska" and claims a different genealogy and history). The other was a revival of a 1977 song by Angèle Arsenault called *Évangéline Acadian Queen*. *Évangéline* is the title of an epic Romantic poem written in 1847 by the American poet Henry Wadsworth Longfellow. The poem recounts the tragic separation of star-crossed lovers, Évangéline and Gabriel, in the deportation. Évangéline spends her life searching for her Gabriel. She finally finds him dying at the foot of a live oak in St. Martinville, Louisiana (you can visit the oak today, even if the story was made up). French Canadian priests appropriated it for purposes of nationalist consciousness-raising, translating it into French and distributing it across the Maritimes and Quebec; the religious, chaste figure of a woman devoted to her man, her religion, and her nation was the perfect gendered incarnation of Acadie. Indeed, Évangéline quickly became its symbol; on the occasion of historical pageants or parades, women and girls dress up in the costume invented for her (Caron 2007; there is usually a Gabriel or two around as well), and she figures in artistic renditions of Acadie on a regular basis. But her name has also been appropriated for an astonishingly wide range of purposes, serving as a brand name for products, services, and sites of all kinds. It is this proliferation that is mocked in the song revived by the show.

The lyrics can be read as a modern feminist rejection of the traditional submissive figure. In Arsenault's fairly vernacular version, when Gabriel dies, Évangéline, feeling liberated, says she is going home to invest in all the little enterprises that 150 years later will bear her name:

> Asteure que t'es enterré
> J'vais pouvoir m'en retourner
> Je m'en vais pour investir
> Dans les companies de l'avenir
> Afin que l'nom d'Évangéline
> Soit connu en câline
> [Now that you're buried
> I'll be able to go back
> I'm leaving in order to invest
> In the companies of the future

> So that the name of Évangéline
> Will be darned known]
> Évangéline Fried Clams
> Évangéline Salon Bar
> Évangéline Sexy Ladies Wear
> Évangéline Comfortable Running Shoes
> Évangéline Automobile Springs
> Évangéline Regional High School
> Évangéline Savings Mortgage and Loans
> Évangéline The only French newspaper in New Brunswick
> Évangéline Évangéline Acadian Queen ("Évangéline Acadian Queen,"
>   Angèle Arsenault, 1977)

We see here the valorization of the vernacular, of feminism, and of private enterprise that emerged in modernist nationalism and provides the basis for post-nationalist irony. The performance we saw in 2004 made the requisite lyrics changes (the newspaper no longer exists) and was delivered in high camp, with the women dressed up as beauty pageant contestants, complete with sashes and plastic tiaras.

Then we went to the center of town to inspect the preparations for the *Grand Tintamarre*, which would feature people crowding onto the main street making noise with horns, pots and pans, or anything else at hand. The space was decorated with large numbers of Acadian flags, or other decorations using the elements of the flag: invented at the first *convention nationale* in 1881, it has the blue, white, and red fields of the French flag, only it also has a yellow star in one corner: this is the *stella maris*, star of the sea and symbol of the Virgin Mary. (I should note that until 1963, the Canadian flag was the British Red Ensign, a red field with the Union Jack in one corner and the Canadian coat of arms in the other, so the Acadian use of the French flag is not so strange.) Needless to say, such decorations are also for sale along the parade route.

But we also encountered at one end of the designated Tintamarre space, as well as at a couple of places along the way, a few large papier-mâché heads.

They were a mystery, certainly not recognized by any of our long-term Tintamarrists, until Annette, Lise, and I went to interview the organizers of the Festival de Nice (France) the following spring. (Nice was yet one more of the towns featuring Canada as special guest, we discussed in chapter 7.) There we discovered that one of the organizers was a descendant of a family of float-makers for the festival (which traces its history back centuries, as do most such parades in the western Mediterranean area), and the *grosses têtes* (large heads) were a traditional feature of such floats. She had been invited to the francophone community college in the Moncton area a few years before and had taught the students how to make them.

We continued exploring the main street, coming across not just decorated houses, but decorated people, and artifacts for sale.

Figure 8.1 Mireille McLaughlin at a souvenir stand, Caraquet, 2005. Photo by Jeremy Paltiel.

Figure 8.2 A decorated house along the parade route. Photo by Mireille McLaughlin.

When the Tintamarre itself started, the street was crowded with Évangélines, flags, horns, and banners. But then a group of people carrying two banners caught my eye. The first one had the phrase we had become used to seeing in that anniversary year: "Après 250 ans . . ." (After 250 years . . .). But the second followed up with " . . . on ne sait pas où on va,

Figure 8.3 The author (162 cm tall), provided for scale, next to a *grosse tête* at one end of the parade route. Photo by Jeremy Paltiel.

mais on y va!" (. . . we don't know where we are going, but we're on our way!). That, I thought, pretty much sums it up. Especially since our camera ran out of batteries at exactly that point.

This kind of commentary now seems to be leaking out all over. In Acadie, it probably started in Moncton, Caraquet's emerging rival as capital of Acadie.

Moncton, as we have seen, has historically been the home of a minority francophone working class speaking *chiac,* a stigmatized version of the vernacular whose salient characteristic as far as nationalists are concerned is that it seems full of English. It is the classic country-versus-city confrontation. Indeed, that trope has been taken up as a basis for reimagining Acadie by a number of young intellectuals and artists, many of them produced by the Université de Moncton, which was founded in 1963 as part

Figure 8.4 Blueberries, muffins, and painted rocks for sale. Note the costumed vendor. Photo by Mireille McLaughlin.

of the modernizing movement of that era. In 2003, some members of this new university-trained group founded a chat space and called it Acadieurbaine.net (urban Acadie), throwing the contamination of the city right into the face of Romantic nationalism.

Other discursive spaces emerged in the city. In 2005, a cultural center held an exhibit of new ways of imagining the Acadian flag. Borrowing heavily from Magritte's famous surrealist picture of a pipe, *Ceci n'est pas une pipe* (This is not a pipe), the gallery's poster showed a picture of the Acadian flag titled *Ceci n'est pas un Acadien* (This is not an Acadian). Most of the alternative flags on display as part of the exhibit play on fragmentation, inclusion, and hybridity.

The same year, many of the same people started an event that was meant to counter the traditional festivities of August 15. Baptized SSNAP (Symposium des sons nouveaux dans une Acadie plurielle; Symposium of new sounds in a pluralist Acadie), the event was meant to be a little less militant, a little less straight, than the festivities they had grown up with. This alternative Moncton event was baptized Le quinze août des fous (something like "August fifteenth for crazies," only in French it rhymes; actually, the first year it was on August 12). Both these spaces (Acadieurbaine and SSNAP) have allowed for debate about what Acadie might be and whom it might include. As a virtual space, Acadieurbaine resolutely opts for a diasporic Acadie that can bring together pretty much anyone who wants to participate no matter where they are, although they have to have enough of a shared cultural and sociolinguistic frame to do so. In its early years, participants engaged in a great deal of discussion over whether

Figure 8.5 Participants and the flag. Photo by Mireille McLaughlin.

or not it was appropriate to use *chiac* there, repeating the normative discussions of language standardization reminiscent of modernizing schooling (see chapter 5). Not surprisingly, no consensus was reached, and participants use more or less standard French according to their politics and ideologies. In its first year, SSNAP provided the conditions for a face-to-face encounter between the highly articulate older generation of militants and the younger SSNAP organizers and participants. Challenged by the older generation to provide an alternative vision, the younger generation could only really point to the ways in which they felt the dominant ideology denied the heterogeneity, mobility, and multiplicity that the older generation's militantism had won them and that they wanted to see actively valued (White, personal communication).

Figure 8.6 The *Grand Tintamarre* begins. Photo by Mary Richards and Mireille McLaughlin.

Figure 8.7 Socialization into *acadianité*: the littlest noisemaker. Photo by Mary Richards and Mireille McLaughlin.

In Quebec this kind of commentary also exists, for example in the form of a spate of seemingly uncontrollable bilingual puns (Lamarre 2009) and the wildly popular *Têtes-à-claque*. The latter are a set of animated figures produced by combining bobble-head dolls with the features of real actors; the figures speak *joual*, that is, Québécois vernacular

Figure 8.8 Poster for *Ceci n'est pas un Acadien*. Photo by Mireille McLaughlin.

French, and parody a variety of aspects of ordinary life, from Halloween trick-or-treaters from hell to annoying television ads for "bargain-priced" complicated tools no one needs (see www.tetesaclaque.tv; they also make television appearances as well). These all pick up the threads of making peace with the ordinary and everyday, not letting English and the vernacular freak us all out, and taking a bit of distance from the high drama of nationalism. The online segments have also picked up a fan base in France, according to my colleagues and one particularly enthusiastic hotel desk clerk in Chinon, who was quite happy to struggle with the *joual* in order to get the joke.

Montreal, like other parts of the world with high immigrant populations (Alim et al. 2009), has also been producing rather a lot of multilingual hip-hop (Sarkar and Winer 2006; LeBlanc et al. 2007), but most of this is serious in tone. Although it joins the other popular culture forms we have seen in breaking down the purist norms of nationalist space, there is a militancy to its resistance and to its search for a centering of heterogeneity and multiplicity in the self-representation of the

Figure 8.9 Alternative visions of the Acadian flag. Photo by Mireille McLaughlin.

Figure 8.10 More alternative visions of the Acadian flag (the pig's head refers to an incident in the history of Acadian political mobilization). Photo by Mireille McLaughlin.

Figure 8.11 Poster for the first SSNAP. Note the participation of Acadieman. Photo by Mireille McLaughlin.

city. As a self-consciously urban phenomenon, it also adds to the contestation of the rural traditional bastions as the places where Quebec happens.

The impasse we saw emerging at the Festival du Village is clearly widely felt. While mainly that feeling remains a bit difficult to express, it is giving way to a search for a way out. At the moment, that search seems concentrated in the area of popular culture and involves a deep breath, a step back, and a bit of a giggle. Key features of what I want to claim as an emergent post-nationalist sensibility include embracing globalized heterogeneity and mobility, defanging English, playing with the vernacular and other hallmarks of Romantic nationalism, and making terrible fun of the purists. I'd like to consider here two artists whom I consider my poster boys of post-nationalism, although they don't know that and may well disagree.

8.2 THE POSTER BOYS OF POST-NATIONALISM

The first poster boy of post-nationalism is Dano LeBlanc, from Moncton. Born in 1968, he is a member of the first generation of children of the modernizing nationalists. He spent about ten years in Montreal, which sounds like a typical choice for minority francophones in search of a francophone space, but he spent many of his years there studying English literature in an English-language university. After returning to Moncton, in 2000 he launched a comic super antihero, Acadieman (see www.capacadie.com). Acadieman is skinny and wears a T-shirt with the Acadian flag on his chest, only instead of the star we find the skull-and-bones he adopts in his self-stylization as the *Pirate du chiac*, his preferred linguistic register. He exists in comic book form, in (so far) three seasons' worth of television episodes (released on DVD), and on the Internet through a blog called "Acadieman Diaries." Like the *Têtes-à-claque*, Acadieman comments on a variety of things he encounters in his everyday life: his call center job, noisy neighbors, interfering mother, crazy cat, and tendency to drink way too much coffee. But he also has things to say about Acadian identity and about language; in one television episode, for example, he too takes on Longfellow's *Evangeline*, this time through time-travel right into the events recounted therein.

Sometimes LeBlanc speaks as his alter ego Acadieman, sometimes as himself, sometimes both. His "Acadieman Diaries" blog entries state at the top that they are "Par: Acadieman" (By: Acadieman), but they are signed "Dano." In one, Acadieman/LeBlanc comments on the familiar theme of bilingualism. The language is hard to translate, but in the extract below I provide my best shot (in another blog entry LeBlanc tries his hand at "reverse *chiac*," that is, a form that might be spoken by some imaginary counterpart anglophone community under the thumb of francophones, but I don't have either his talent or his nerve). Here I reverse the usual order of presentation, providing the original first. I italicize some of the forms that index *chiac*, which, the attentive reader will notice, do not in fact occur with astonishing frequency. Some are lexical items from English, including discourse markers (anyway, whatever, *ouèlle*/well, fudge, CU), nouns (job, nerve) and verbs assimilated into the conjugation system of French (drive, dare, stuck, pissed off), as well as an intensifier (right), morphosyntactic forms (*ramener* back), and calques (*tourne 40*) from English. Some are nonstandard French syntactic forms (*l'avoir eu écouté*, a rare past tense form; *-tu*, an interrogative particle; *de quoi*, a relativizer), phonetic variations (*tchèque, djeule, aouère*), fixed expressions (*oubédon/ou bien donc, de même, il n'faisait pas beau dans la cabane*). A lot of the nonstandardness comes simply from the adoption of writing conventions for rendering orality (*chépa—je ne sais pas; c't'année—cette année; j'pense—je pense*), plus the inclusion of the text message script form C-U (see you).

Bonne fête bilinguisme!

C'est *tu* juste moi *oubédon* personne parle du fait que le bilinguisme *tourne 40* c't'année? Ce matin j'*drivais* en ville pis j'écoutais la radio, oui j'admets que c'était CBC et non Radio-Canada, *whatever*, c'arrive. J'écoutais une vieille mémère qui, si j'me trompe pas, travaille à l'hôtel de ville de Moncton. Elle défendait l'idée que les *jobs* à l'hôtel de ville ne devraient pas être des postes bilingues. En autre mots, unilingue anglophone, surement pas unilingue francophone. Pis, je pense qu'un journaliste de *tcheque* part, j'pense que c'était le Times-Transcript (surprenant!) qui disait que cette idée nous *ramenait back* au temps de Leonard Jones, et ses idées anti-francophones. Cette vieille dame, avait le *nerve* de dire que parler de même à propos du vieux L.J. était de la calomnie, de suggérer *de quoi d'même*. En outre, dire ses choses là était une insulte à toutes les personnes qui avaient voté pour lui. Ok, whoa! Elle *darait* d'parler d'même *sur* la 40ième anniversaire du biligu-isme? *Fudge. J'étais right pissé off* après de *l'aouère eu écouté*. J'parlais à ma radio, j'jurais . . . *anyway, il n'faisait pas beau dans la cabane*. C'était vraiment une tape dans la *djeule*. Chépa, être un français du sud-est là, *ouèlle*, t'es vrai-ment *stuck* entre les anglais racistes et les français puristes . . . j'ai pas décidé si j'ai plusse peur des loyalistes ou de l'Académie française!?

Chiac word du jour . . .

Picasse: Personne désagréable, déplaisante, cranky.

Ex: Après aouère écouté la vieille plotte à la radio, j'étais pas mal picasse.

C–U.

Dano

[Happy birthday bilingualism!

Is it just me, or is nobody talking about the fact that bilingualism is turning 40 this year? This morning I was driving in town, listening to the radio, yes I admit it was CBC and not Radio-Canada, whatever, it happens. I was listening to an old lady who, if I'm not mistaken, works at Moncton City Hall. She was defending the idea that jobs at City Hall shouldn't be bilingual positions. In other words, unilingual anglophone, surely not unilingual francophone. And I think some journalist from someplace, I think it was the Times-Transcript (surprising!), was saying that that idea takes us back to the days of Leonard Jones and his anti-francophone ideas. The old lady had the nerve to say that talking like that about old L.J. was calumny, to suggest something like that. On top of that, saying those things was an insult to all the people who voted for him. Ok, whoa! She dared to talk like that on the 40th anniversary of biligualism? [*sic*; Acadieman doesn't pay too much attention to the problem of typographical errors, or to the niceties of spelling for that matter.] Fudge. I was really pissed off after having listened to her. I was talking to my radio, I was swearing . . . anyway, things were hot in the kitchen. It was really a punch in the face. Dunno, to be French from the southeast, well, you're stuck between English racists and French purists . . . and I haven't decided if I'm more scared of Loyalists or the Académie française!?

Chiac word of the day:

Picasse: unpleasant, disagreeable, cranky person.

Ex.: After listening to the old dame on the radio, I was pretty picasse.

C-U

Dano] ("Acadieman Diaries," February 17, 2009)

In his entry of February 10, 2009, LeBlanc worries that his *chiac* has been "corrupted" by French: "J'm'aperçois que à la place de dire 'j'peux tu aouère un café?' j'dis 'puis-je avoir un café?' (I notice that instead of saying "C'n I have some joe?" I say "May I please have a cup of coffee?"). He continues, mulling over the problem of authenticity and modernity. (Note the reference to *la Sagouine*, whom we met in chapter 7.)
Extract 8.3

> J'pense que ma génération est stuck dans tcheque weird limbo d'hybridité entre la langue archaïque et la langue contemporaine. Chépa, j'espère que les jeunes buck d'aujourd'hui ne perdent pas les archaïsmes de notre langue, même si l'utilisation est ironique. J'expect pas l'monde de walker around pis parler comme la Sagouine, ça sa arrive seulement à Disneyland . . . euh, j'veux dire le pays de la Sagouine.
> Ouèlle, le soleil se lève, l'aurore? l'aube? Crépuscule? . . . chépu.
> Chiac word du jour. Estropier: Priver d'un membre, mutiler ou mettre dans l'incapacité de servir.
> Ex.: L'acadien, alors très effronté, estropiât à plaisir la langue française.
> Ciaos,
> Dano.

> [I think my generation is stuck in some weird limbo of hybridity between archaic and contemporary language. Dunno, I hope today's young bucks don't lose our language's archaisms, even if their use is ironic. I don't expect people to walk around talking like la Sagouine, that only happens in Disneyland. . . . Uh, I mean the Pays de la Sagouine.
> Well, the sun's coming up, the aurora, the dawn, the first light . . . dunno anymore.
> Chiac word of the day: Estropier: to deprive of a limb, mutilate or make incapable of functioning.
> Ex.: The Acadian, terribly insolent, took great pleasure in mutilating the French language.
> Ciaos,
> Dano.] ("Acadieman Diaries," February 10, 2009)

Like the SSNAP organizers, LeBlanc has no time for purists but remains wedded to an Acadian identity, however ambivalent his stance toward that identity may be. He wants today's "young bucks" to keep using "our language's archaisms, even if their use is ironic." He wants to take "great pleasure in mutilating the French language," but he's still going to insist on using it and on having it recognized as a job requirement at Moncton City Hall. He wants his French to be recognized as including the verbs *expecter*, *driver*, and *walker*, but isn't sure about the right way to say "dawn." He "doesn't know anymore." But by then it's time for a video game, or maybe a cup of coffee, or else a nap, especially if his mother would just stop nagging him.

My second post-national poster boy is a bit younger, but just as ambivalent, and perhaps even more ironic, if such a thing is possible. Damien Robitaille comes from the same area I described in chapter 3 and was born in 1982. He studied first at an English-language university in southern Ontario, where he formed a band called "Mezameeze," which, if you say it out loud, sounds like *mes amis* (my friends) pronounced with a heavy Anglo-Canadian accent. He then attended a music program in Quebec and now, like many francophone performers, lives in Montreal and is active on the francophone music circuit in eastern Canada and in France. He calls himself a "grunge crooner," and onstage he affects (or maybe really has) a slightly awkward, timid, albeit slightly wild-eyed, persona, who nonetheless (or more likely therefore) occasionally comes out with outrageous statements, which he then laughs off a bit maniacally as he breaks into song.

While his French is more standard than LeBlanc's, he shows the same tendency to make fun of the serious militancy of an earlier generation, all the while maintaining a Franco-Ontarian identity. He returns home most summers for the Festival du Village (see chapter 6) and participates in francophone music festivals in Montreal and in France, yet he is still capable of producing a song called "Sexy Séparatiste" (Robitaille 2006). This is shocking not only because you are not supposed to treat the independence movement as a sex object but also because the term "separatist" is usually associated with federalists: those within the movement prefer the terms *indépendantiste* or *souverainiste*.

The lyrics compare a woman's genitals to a fleur-de-lis (the symbol of Quebec), offer to explore her body like Champlain and Cartier, claim that her seductive powers attract immigrants (like Robitaille), and urge her: "Présente ton discours, femme du pays, c'est à ton tour, de venir me parler d'amour" (Present your discourse, woman of the land/country, it's your turn to come speak to me of love). This is a play on the lyrics of Gilles Vigneault's nationalist anthem "Gens du pays," whose refrain, "Gens du pays, c'est à notre tour, de se laisser parler d'amour"—People of the land/country, it's our turn to let ourselves speak of love—has spread widely in Quebec and is used, among other things, to replace the French translation of "Happy Birthday" formerly sung at birthday parties.

Not content to make fun of Québécois nationalism, Robitaille also mocks the image Québécois have of francophones from other provinces. They are convinced by the logic of their ideology that only Quebec is truly modern; everyone else must be stuck in the traditional, if backwoodsy, image of the lumberjack or *voyageur*, with their *chemise à carreaux* and *ceinture fléchée*. They also believe that it is their majority status which guarantees the preservation of French language and culture, and that if you live in places like Ontario and have to learn English, you have to deal with all the complexities of bilingualism, like not being able to say the same thing in both languages.

The following is a set of extracts from an article based on an interview with Robitaille published in the Montreal free weekly alternative newspaper *Voir* (see www.voir.ca). Robitaille sends up his interviewer's expectations (and the interviewer plays it up): he shows up dressed in a Hawaiian

shirt instead of the lumberjack shirt his interviewer thought he would
find; he answers a Romantic question about his heroes with a reflection
on tractors and how you really can't drive them in town, sending up the
interviewer's expectations about country boys always being country boys;
he uses only features of the vernacular you also find in Quebec (*astheur—
à cette heure* / now—at this hour; *au boutte—au bout* / totally—to the end;
ben—bien / well); and he completely resists any notion that being bilingual is in any way a problem, or even remarkable.
Extract 8.4

[. . .]
   He's serious. Or maybe not. Welcome inside the head of Damien
Robitaille.
   Damien Robitaille; mid-twenties, shape of a werewolf in pounds and in
body hair; an author-composer-performer from the country, he could come
from Louisiana, but he comes from [. . .] Ontario; one imagines him in a
lumberjack shirt and he shows up in a Hawaiian one.
   [. . .]
   Whom do you admire the most?
   "I used to admire my grandfather and his tractor. I loved them to bits,
tractors! I wanted to drive one! But not anymore. Not in town."
   [. . .]
   When Damien Robitaille talks to you, he searches for the right word by
stuttering another word. His rhythm is choppy, diffuse. One explains that
by virtue of his Frenglish, and you forgive a guy whose life would have been
easier in the language of Johnny Cash. Daddy a Franco, Mummy an Anglo,
a village where French has to really try hard, you get the picture.
   [. . .]
   Damien, what does the French language allow you to sing that you can't
sing in English?
   "In French, let's say, I'll talk about a *chien* (dog). In English, well, I say dog."

[[. . .]
   Il est sérieux. Peut-être pas. Bienvenue dans la tête de Damien Robitaille.
   Damien Robitaille: mi-vingtaine, shape de loup-garou en poids comme
en poils; auteur-compositeur-interprète de campagne, il pourrait venir de la
Louisiane, mais vient de (l') Ontario; on l'imagine en chemise carreautée et
il nous arrive en chemise hawaïenne.
   [. . .]
   Qui est-ce que tu admires le plus?
   "Dans le temps, j'admirais mon grand-père et son tracteur. J'aimais ça au
boutte, les tracteurs! J'voulais en conduire un! Mais plus asteure. Pas en
ville."
   [. . .]
   Damien Robitaille, quand il vous parle, cherche le mot juste en bégayant
un autre mot. Son rythme est saccadé, éparpillé. On met ça sur le dos de son
franglais et on pardonne tout à un gars qui l'aurait eu plus facile dans la
langue de Johnny Cash. Papa franco, maman anglo, village où le français en
arrache, vous voyez le genre.

[...]
Damien, qu'est-ce que la langue française te permet de chanter que tu
ne peux pas chanter en anglais?
"En français, mettons, je parle d'un chien. En anglais, ben, je dis dog.]"
(David Thibodeau, article in *Voir*, October 20, 2005)

Dano LeBlanc and Damien Robitaille can no longer make revolutionary, consciousness-raising music, literature, or theater. The time for that
has passed. Nor, apparently, are they comfortable selling traditional music
on the tourist circuit. They are still tied to the identity categories with
which they were raised, and they value the linguistic and cultural forms
they were taught to associate with them, but they also recognize their
historical situatedness. They reject the purist dimensions of older forms of
nationalism, while retaining an affection for the authenticating practices
that ended up being marginalized when francophone nationalism became
institutionalized and an educated francophone bourgeoisie (themselves,
really) got created and then commodified its authenticating practices.
They are prepared to resist anglophone domination, but they are also
willing to not only speak English, but to master it (LeBlanc not only studied English literature; he also throws Chaucer around his blog entries).
The lines and directions are no longer clear. So the best thing, maybe, is to
laugh.

8.3 COOL IRONY, HIGH ANXIETY?

Or perhaps not. While among the students at Champlain, the inhabitants
of Lelac, the environmentalists of Planète Juste, and the artists of *Ceci
n'est pas un Acadien* we find social actors coming to grips with, and even
embracing, the idea that it is time to reinvent francophone Canada in
ways that blur boundaries and open up doors, others are concerned about
what may be lost in the process.

In January 2007, the small Quebec town of Hérouxville published a
three-page text on the *normes de vie* (life standards) that newcomers to
the town should expect to encounter, and to accept, if not actively con-
form to. Hérouxville, a fairly typical heartland town, actually has no newcomers, but it was widely understood to represent anxiety about social
change projected onto the outsider as a kind of condensation symbol of all
the ways in which dominant imaginings of Quebec society may be difficult to sustain under current conditions.

The incident served as a trigger to a public debate that had been sim-
mering for a long time, which took the form of a Quebec-government-
instituted process that unfolded between September 2007 and May
2008. Under the title of the Commission de consultation sur les pratiques d'accommodements reliés aux différences culturelles (Consultative
commission on practices of accommodation related to cultural differences), Quebec engaged in an airing of those anxieties and of arguments

countering them. Not surprisingly, most of the anxiety came from places like Hérouxville, while most reports from metropolitan areas were about the small, everyday, and frankly undramatic ways in which life turns out to change or, as often as not, remain much the same.

I read similar kinds of anxieties in a current debate that, as it happens (and again, probably not very surprisingly), involves me and my colleagues. A recent publication (Thériault et al. 2008) aims at a coverage of the issues facing francophone Canada in areas where francophones are a minority. The introduction frames the question this way:

> So these new issues graft themselves onto old ones which remain meaningful. [. . .] No one wants to talk about it directly, but the still major loss of mother-tongue francophones remains disquieting. It undermines the possibility of a francophone space. It renders fragile francophone institutions like the school and threatens the development of new bases of power in other domains [. . .] What of the link among these communities provided by memory? [. . .] How to reconcile pluralist identity with the permanence of claims based on the idea of one of the founding peoples? (Cardinal et al. 2008: 15–16)

> [Ainsi, ces nouvelles problématiques se greffent à d'anciens enjeux toujours chargés de significations. [. . .] Personne ne veut en parler directement mais la perte toujours importante de francophones de langue maternelle en milieu minoritaire demeure inquiétante. Elle mine la possibilité d'un espace francophone. Elle fragilise les institutions francophones comme l'école et hypothèque le développement de nouveaux lieux de pouvoir dans les autres domaines [. . .] Qu'en est-il encore du lien mémoriel de ces communautés? [. . .] Comment concilier le pluralisme identitaire avec la permanence d'une revendication qui s'appuie sur l'idée d'un des peuples fondateurs?] (Cardinal et al. 2008: 15–16)

Here, I think, is the key. For many of the key producers of discourse on *la francité canadienne*, francophone Canada cannot be understood as a discourse produced under certain historical conditions and serving certain interests, a discourse that relies on those conditions for its reproduction and that requires a tremendous amount of work, on a daily basis, to reproduce. It must be understood as a permanent political project, one in which the nation is a value unto itself.

Indeed, this is where I come into it. In a contribution to this volume, Thériault and Meunier (2008) argue that social science has a duty to uphold that project. They take as a counterexample the work of the "école de Toronto" (the Toronto School, whose members, I can assure you, had no idea the school existed), in which apparently I have played a particularly harmful role, since our work, according to them, ignores the "intention vitale du Canada français" (this is hard to translate; something like the "life force," or the "will to live," of French Canada). By ignoring this intention, our efforts *dénationalise* and *ethnicise* francophone Canada: that is, we demote the concept from a nation's political project (defined as making a francophone *civilisation* in North America) to the petty concerns of an ethnic elite.

We have, then, two ontologically distinct views. The one I have tried to advance here is that nations are historically situated constructs that have helped legitimate particular relations between the state and capitalism. In this view, the state is not an actor disconnected from concrete conditions, but one among the many ways we organize ourselves to produce, distribute, and give value to resources.

The francophone "nation" helps us understand this precisely because of its marginality. We see the struggles to position collective interest in a world system without much room for marginals. Indeed, we see how collective interest is formed in the first place by the exploitation of difference by first the British state, then the Canadian, and by the country's economic institutions, to serve their own interests: the creation of a labor pool, and the making of political distinctions on the North American continent. And we see just how much work goes into shaping that interest, keeping it alive, and creating the conditions for its reproduction. Finally, we see clearly through this particular lens the tension common to all nations: making uniformity out of diversity, and stability and timelessness out of change.

This is not (yet?) the dominant view. But I see in Thériault and Meunier's frontal attack a recognition that I and my colleagues may be naming something that is indeed destructive to the political project that we have grown up with and that has provided a significant amelioration of what were not terrific life conditions. That "something" ("on ne sait pas où on va mais on y va") exchanges a power base that has the perverse effect of reproducing exactly the same structural kinds of exclusions against which francophone nationalism rebelled, for something else, as yet unformed, which by its fluidity and mobility may, perhaps, be more inclusive. It will certainly have its own perverse consequences, and we will have to keep an eye on what they turn out to be.

In that sense, ironically, the so-called *milieux minoritaires* now find themselves freer than does Quebec. In the 1970s and 1980s (and, for some people, even today), not having the political apparatus of a territorial state was a huge problem, and I have spent a great deal of time in this book showing how elites dealt with that by creating an institutional nationalism that is alive and kicking today. Under current conditions, however, not having that apparatus may allow greater freedom to plug into the trajectories of resources and people and ideas that are the hallmark of our time. Acadie provides a particularly propitious set of conditions; the deportation, which has been its tragedy, also laid the foundations of a bilingual Atlantic network. If this means that an Acadian can only be defined in the negative (*Ceci n'est pas un Acadien*), well, maybe that's enough for now.

But it is important to point out that this is not an exercise in political philosophy; I am not here writing a manifesto (although I am sorely tempted to do just that). I report here not what I would like to see, but what I see happening, and what sense I can make of it, through the problems of social justice that have been at the heart of this story from the beginning. Those problems, I argue, are tractable not in the abstract but, rather, in the context of how things turn out to work out for people in daily life, and hence my affection for ethnography.

What ethnography shows me is that for every Albert there is a monolingual francophone foreman; for every Lise there is a working-class smoker who is about to drop out of school; for every Gilles there is someone not sure about where being Métis puts them; and for all of them there are Aïshas and Manuels looking for their place in francophone space. (I will add, though, that while I'm a bit worried about Mike, I think Bob will be just fine.) What ethnography shows me is that even for the Alberts and Lises and Gilles, things are not so straightforward. Lise wants to keep those smokers in school, Albert's own family history is not so far from those of his foremen, and Gilles thinks it's high time to open the village up.

Against the clarity of the *intention vitale*, what I have to hold up is complexity. Perhaps that is my manifesto.

8.4 ETHNOGRAPHIES OF DISCURSIVE SHIFTS

Just as it has proven difficult to hang on to the idea of the nation as natural object, so has it proven difficult to hang on to the tools we developed for constructing and reproducing it, the tools of social science. To figure out what goes on around me, I have to work back and forth between the details of the here and now, and the structural relations of difference and inequality that sediment over time, emerging as vested interests and giving some kinds of people access to types of resources that others cannot share.

I have ended up with an (endlessly ongoing) ethnography of a discursive shift. That shift turns out not to happen in linear sequential time, nor to diffuse from centers to peripheries (or, at least, the center of today may be the periphery of tomorrow). This ethnography requires arduous and often tedious discursive work in spaces that often need to be constructed out of leftover interstices, taking form over here while everyone else is looking over there, or that represent innovative uses of spaces originally meant for something else (such as church basements, parking lots, or talent shows). Only occasionally are they overtly oppositional.

Once created, they produce criteria of inclusion and exclusion, which have to be instantiated over and over again for every case, since nothing ever comes in standard sizes. The construction of dominant discourse within them is not simple matter. It requires creative exploitation of existing resources, and sometimes the appropriation of resources circulating elsewhere (indigeneity, for example). It certainly requires a huge investment in the management of contradictions and the marginalization of interests and discourses that threaten the possibility of discursive reproduction.

What a close sociolinguistic look can do is to show just how much daily work is involved. There is no obvious reason why people at a brewery in Montreal in the 1970s, at a school in Toronto in the 1990s, on a festival organizing committee in the early 2000s, or on a blog toward the end of the decade should spend so much time worrying about the right way to say something. For that much effort to go on in so many different spaces over that long a period says something about the social significance not just of sociolinguistic norms, but about how they really get created, challenged, and reproduced.

The same can be said about the effort involved in gaining access to discursive space, in getting a turn at talk and in getting attention. These are major investments into gaining access to spaces where something important is happening, something that can make a difference to your life, or at least to your children's lives. But close inspection shows us that even in the most hierarchical of spaces, different perspectives can clash, and new things come up for which discursive frames are not yet ready and must be fashioned. Nonetheless, we can only bring to those occasions the discursive elements at our disposal; the question is which ones we select and how we use them. Here, the contradictions inherent in every discursive space I've ever come across provide a source of agency and change.

A critical ethnographic sociolinguistics of post-nationalism can locate the discursive spaces and identify what resources are circulating, who has access to them, and what they make of them. It can track simultaneity and circulation to observe what discursive elements are taken up by whom, how, under what circumstances, and to what effect. In that respect, sociolinguistics has a lot to offer to social theory, as a means of empirically engaging with the kinds of work different kinds of actors seem to feel it is critical to engage in, even if that work involves ironically amusing or sarcastically mocking ruminations on the death throes of nationalism.

A critical sociolinguistic ethnography breaks downs the false dichotomy of structure and agency to reveal agents involved in the construction of social order, using the resources they find at hand. The sense-making of post-nationalism is a sociolinguistic activity par excellence, tailor-made for a discipline devoted to the idea that social reality is constructed, that diversity is just a fact of life, and that we can say many different things at the same time. Indeed, we may be partly responsible for it.

8.5 EPILOGUE

The movie described in the following extract is based on a 1998 novel by Tony Burgess, *Pontypool Changes Everything*.

> *Pontypool*
> Shock jock Grant Mazzy has, once again, been kicked-off the Big City airwaves and now the only job he can get is the early morning show at

CLSY Radio in Pontypool Ontario, which broadcasts from the basement of the small town's only church.

What begins as another boring day of school bus cancellations, due to yet another massive snow storm, quickly turns deadly when reports start piling in of people developing strange speech patterns and evoking horrendous acts of violence.

But there's nothing coming in on the news wires. Is this really happening?

Before long, Grant and the small staff at CLSY find themselves trapped in the radio station as they discover that this insane behaviour taking over the town is actually a deadly virus being spread through the English language itself.

Do they stay on the air in the hopes of being rescued or, are they in fact providing the virus with its ultimate leap over the airwaves and into the world?

Website: www.pontypoolmovie.com
Genre: Horror
Cast: Stephen McHattie
Lisa Houle
Georgina Reilly
Director: Bruce McDonald
Opening Date: 2009-03-06 (From the Web site of Maple Pictures Corporation, www.maplepictures.com, accessed March 23, 2009)

I've seen the movie. Mazzy and his producer find a way to fight the virus, using a secret weapon they discover they share. By this time, you should be able to figure out what that weapon is. If not, well, becoming a zombie is probably a fate I deserve.

Notes

Chapter 1

1. The term literally means "pure wool" and is what you see on tags that tell you what garments are made of. The reference is to the expression *Québécois pure laine* or "pure wool Québécois"—that is, someone who is ethnically "pure," or, in this case, descended from the French settlers of the seventeenth- and eighteenth-century colonies of New France. It is usually translated into English in a more politically correct way, as "old stock Québécois." The show is produced by TéléQuébec and began in 2004. I am grateful to Mela Sarkar and Juan Abril for drawing it to my attention.

2. The data that I draw on in this book come from a series of research projects conducted in various parts of Canada, as well as in France, between 1978 and 2007. In each chapter I will provide the details of the funding sources, colleagues, and students who made this work possible.

Chapter 2

1. Sociological accounts include Hughes 1943 and Lieberson 1970; literary accounts include MacLennan 1957 and Richler 1959.

2. The material in this section was first published in Heller 1982.

3. A slightly different version of much of the material in this section was first published in Heller 2008a.

Chapter 3

1. Secondary sources include the memoirs of Gilbert Finn, an Acadian insurance broker who rose to become one of the four members of the Ottawa-based Grande Chancellerie (the highest-ranking group in the order), as well as lieutenant-governor of New Brunswick (Finn 2000); exposés written in the early 1960s by former members (Dubé 1963; Cyr 1964); graduate theses (Laliberté 1983; Trépanier 2007; Belliveau 2008); two scholarly articles (Bertrand 1998; Allaire 2004); and some media accounts, mainly from the early

1990s (Jaillard 1993; Paquin 1993; Vennin 1993–1994), but including a documentary made by Radio-Canada (the French-language Canadian state television company) and aired in May 2001 (Verge 2001) on the occasion of the release of OJC archives, which had been kept closed in order to protect former members who were still alive, and in many cases still in public political life (the last of the closed archives opened in 2010). In the period 2001–2003 and 2005–2006, I worked with Josée Makropoulos and Mireille McLaughlin through the newly opened archives in the Centre de recherche en civilisation canadienne-française (CRCCF) at the Université d'Ottawa and at the Centre de recherche Lionel-Groulx (CRLG) in Montreal, and in 2008 in the National Archives (NA) in Ottawa. I am extremely grateful to the archivists Bernadette Routhier of the CRCCF and François Dumas of the CRLG for their help. Finally, also in 2008, Alexandre Duchêne and I visited an Ottawa-area municipal museum exhibit containing information about the origins of the OJC. See also Heller 2003 and McLaughlin and Heller in press.

2. Minutes of a Grande Chancellerie meeting, 1964: "In 1953, we had 9,822 members. In 1963, we had 10,049 members. In the course of that decade, we recruited 14,965 new initiates, of whom 5,000 remained in our ranks. Why have we lost 5,000 former and 10,000 new [members]?" (En 1953, nous comptions 9822 membres. En 1963, nous comptions 10,049 membres. Au cours de ces dix ans, nous avons recruté 14,965 nouveaux initiés, dont 5000 sont demeurés dans nos rangs. Pourquoi avons-nous perdu 5000 anciens et 10,000 nouveaux [membres]?) All translations mine.

3. For example, Gilbert Finn used his job as insurance agent to carry out OJC work, described in this way (note the use of the impersonal *on* [they] and of the acronym *VR*, both means of obscuring the institution and its agents):

Since my job took me more or less all over the Maritime provinces, over the years they gave me a variety of functions in the Order. As regional visitor (VR), I sometimes represented the Chancellerie, the supreme authority, I visited the commanderies in the territory of the Maritimes, I recruited members and I participated in the development of new groups.

[Comme mon emploi m'amenait à voyager un peu partout dans les provinces Maritimes, on me confia au cours des années diverses fonctions au sein de l'Ordre. À titre de visiteur régional (VR), je représentais parfois la Chancellerie, l'autorité suprême, je visitais les commanderies dans le territoire des Maritimes, je recrutais des membres et je participais à la formation de nouveaux groupes.] (Finn 2000: 72)

Canada's head of state is the governor general, not the prime minister; at the provincial level, the equivalent position is that of lieutenant governor, the position held by Finn for the province of New Brunswick.

4. These and all other names in this text are pseudonyms, unless otherwise indicated.

5. According to the archival material, their cell had twenty members, fairly typical for cells across the country.

Chapter 4

1. This chapter is based on research conducted in 1978–1980 and funded by the Office de la langue française (Québec). I am grateful for the support I received from Denise Daoust, Pierre-Étienne Laporte, and André Martin, and for assistance in fieldwork and the early stages of analysis to Jean-Paul Bartholomot, Laurette Lévy, and Luc Ostiguy. See also the following publications: Heller et al. 1982; Heller 1982, 1985, 1989, 2002.

2. They drew notably on the work of William Mackey and Joshua Fishman (Fishman 1968; Mackey 1968), themselves inspired by that of Heinz Kloss (the most frequently cited work is Kloss 1969). Indeed, Mackey was at the time director of the Centre international de recherche sur le bilinguisme (CIRB) at l'Université Laval in Quebec City, which had been founded in the 1960s with money from the Ford Foundation. The CIRB maintained a long tradition of work on language planning well into the 1990s (Boudreau et al. 2002), and had an important influence on state discourse on language in Quebec. Through the 1960s and 1970s the CIRB also regularly hosted scholars such as Kloss (whose past involvement in Nazi language policy was apparently unknown to his CIRB collaborators, according to conversations I have had with two of them; see Hutton 1999).

In addition, language planning scholars like Joan Rubin, Paul Garvin, and Bjorn Jernudd were frequently brought to Montreal to consult (see texts collected in Martin 1981, which contain frequent citations of Rubin and Jernudd 1971 and Rubin et al. 1977, along with references to Fishman and Mackey).

3. It is worth noting that Catalan sociolinguists were on much the same path around that time, providing a framework based on ideas of "normalization" (*normalització*) and "normativization" (*normativització*) as the two main axes for pursuing linguistic minority emancipation through state-led action: normalization means extending the use of the minorized language to all domains of use (that is, homogeneity is normal), and normativization refers to the idea that getting the language in shape to perform those functions across all domains requires the development of standardized forms (see Ninyoles 1972a,b, 1989; Aracil 1982). It is also

worth noting that the language of "normality" was reinforced in Quebec by the central involvement in Bill 101 of a psychiatrist, Camille Laurin, who explicitly equated the health of a nation with the health of an organism.

4. By "people like Linda" I mean mainly secretaries, for whom francization became part of their generally unrecognized work of linguistic mediation. At the same time, the focus on technical terminology was quite widely shared (among employees, as well of course as with the OLF), showing a general discourse about the salience of that field in the francization process. As the example shows, it was the kind of thing people like Simon and Marc worried about (see also the chapter's first interview extract, in which a francophone foreman discusses franciza-tion). It often showed up in the course of everyday interaction in ways less explicit than the previous extract shows (where Simon and Marc took the time to go to Linda and have it out). In the dispatchers' ex-changes I often found two equivalent technical terms used (for example, "soaker" and *laveuse*; "palletizer" and *empileuse*), sometimes sequentially by turn (one in one turn, the other from the other language by the next speaker in the next turn), and sometimes one after the other in one utterance.

Chapter 5

1. The first school to be founded in a jurisdiction was considered the public school, whether it was Catholic or not. The first one belonging to the other category became the "separate" school. In practice, it is almost always the case that the separate schools were Catholic, and in common parlance "separate" and "Catholic" are usually conflated. However, there are a few localities where the reverse is the case.

2. Much of this work has been reported in Heller 1994a and Heller 2006.

Chapter 6

1. The account in this section draws heavily from Heller 2001b.

Chapter 7

1. See, for example, the following from a Quebec government Web site (www.invest-quebec.com/en/int/secteur; accessed 2005): "In Mon-treal, there are 2.9 million bilingual people in 2002, or nearly 41% of Québec's population. The widespread use of French and English affords client contact centres considerable flexibility, thus facilitating access to major markets. Québec's bilingual labour pool, the biggest in Canada, is a key advantage for businesses that wish to gain access to 7 million

French-speaking Canadians without paying bilingualism bonuses. Over 80 languages in addition to French and English are spoken in Québec." This refers, of course, to exactly the kinds of people who make it difficult to construct Montreal as a francophone public space, in ways that worry the implementers of Bill 101.

2. This section is drawn partly from Heller 2005b.

Bibliography

Alim, H. Samy, Awad Ibrahim, and Alastair Pennycook (Eds.) (2009). *Global linguistic flows: Hip hop cultures, youth identities, and the politics of language.* New York: Routledge.

Allaire, Gratien (2004). "Le Triangle canadien-français au tournant des années 60. Le Conseil de la vie française en Amérique, la Société Saint-Jean-Baptiste de Montréal et l'Ordre de Jacques Cartier." *Francophonies d'Amérique* 17: 108–117.

Alonso, José Antonio (2006). *Naturaleza económica de la lengua.* Madrid: Instituto Complutense de Estudios Internacionales and Fundación Telefónica.

Anctil, Pierre (1991). "Brokers of ethnic identity: The Franco-American petty bourgeoisie of Woonsocket, R.I., 1865–1945." *Quebec Studies* 12: 33–48.

Anderson, Benedict (1983). *Imagined communities.* London: Verso.

Appadurai, Arjun (1996). *Modernity at large: Cultural dimensions of globalization.* Minneapolis: University of Minnesota Press.

Aracil, Lluis (1982). *Papers de sociolingüistica.* Barcelona: Edicions de la Magrana.

Bakhtin, Mikhail (1981). *The dialogic imagination.* Trans. C. Emerson and M. Holquist. Austin: University of Texas Press.

Barth, Fredrik (Ed.) (1969). *Ethnic groups and boundaries.* Boston: Little, Brown.

Basch, Linda, Nina Glick Schiller, and Cristina Szanton Blanc (Eds.) (1994). *Nations unbound: Transnational projects, postcolonial predicaments and deterritorialized nation-states.* London: Routledge.

Baugh, John (2000). *Beyond Ebonics: Linguistic pride and racial prejudice.* Oxford: Oxford University Press.

Bauman, Richard, and Charles Briggs (2003). *Voices of modernity: Language ideologies and the politics of inequality.* Cambridge: Cambridge University Press.

Beaudin, Maurice (2005). "Les francophones des Maritimes: Prospectives et perspectives." In: Jean-Pierre Wallot (Ed.), *La gouvernance linguistique: Le Canada en perspective.* Ottawa: Les Presses de l'Université c 'Ottawa, pp. 77–98.

Beaudin, Maurice (2006). "Sphères économiques et minorité acadienne: Bilan de la recherches et axes prioritaires d'intervention." In: Marie-Linda Lord (Ed.), *L'émergence et la reconnaissance des études acadiennes: À la rencontre de Soi et de l'Autre*. Moncton: Association internationale d'études acadiennes, pp. 137–158.

Beaudin, Maurice, and Donald Savoie (1992). *Le défi de l'industrie des pêches au Nouveau-Brunswick*. Moncton: Les Éditions d'Acadie.

Beck, Ulrich, and Natan Sznaider (2006). "Unpacking cosmopolitanism for the social sciences: A research agenda." *British Journal of Sociology* 57(1): 1–23.

Belliveau, Joël (2008). *Tradition, libéralisme et communautarisme durant les "Trente glorieuses": Les étudiants de Moncton et l'entrée dans la modernité avancée des francophones du Nouveau-Brunswick, 1957–1969*. Ph.D. thesis. Département d'histoire, Université de Montréal.

Bertrand, Gabriel (1998). "L'Ordre de Jacques Cartier et les minorités francophones." In: Gratien Allaire and Anne Gilbert (Eds.), *Francophonies plurielles*. Sudbury: Institut franco-ontarien, pp. 13–58.

Bestor, Ted (2001). "Supply-side sushi: Commodity, market, and the global city." *American Anthropologist* 103(1): 76–95.

Billig, Michael (1995). *Banal nationalism*. London: Sage.

Blackledge, Adrian (2005). *Discourse and power in a multilingual world*. Amsterdam: John Benjamins.

Boudreau, Annette, Lise Dubois, Jacques Maurais, and Grant McConnell (Eds.) (2002). *L'écologie et la sociologie du langage*. Montréal: L'Harmattan.

Bourdieu, Pierre (1972). *Esquisse d'une théorie de la pratique*. Genève: Droz.

Bourdieu, Pierre (1977). "The economics of linguistic exchanges." *Social Science Information* 16(6): 645–668.

Bourdieu, Pierre (1979). *La distinction: Critique sociale du jugement*. Paris: Éditions de Minuit.

Bourdieu, Pierre (1982). *Ce que parler veut dire*. Paris: Fayard.

Bourdieu, Pierre, and Jean-Claude Passeron (1977). *Reproduction in education, society and culture*. London: Sage.

Boutet, Josiane (2001). "Le travail devient-il intellectuel?" *Travailler: Revue internationale de psychopathologie et de psychodynamique du travail* 6: 55–70.

Boutet, Josiane (2008). *La vie verbale au travail: Des manufactures aux centres d'appels*. Toulouse: Octares.

Bouthillier, Guy, and Jean Meynaud (1972). *Le choc des langues au Québec, 1760–1970*. Montréal: Les Presses de l'Université du Québec.

Bowles, Samuel, and Herbert Gintis (1977). *Schooling in capitalist America: Educational reform and the contradictions of economic life*. New York: Basic Books.

Braudel, Fernand (1958). *Écrits sur l'histoire*. Paris: Flammarion.

Breton, André (Ed.) (1998). *Economic approaches to language and bilingualism*. Ottawa: Canadian Heritage and Department of Public Works and Government Services, Government of Canada.

Breton, Raymond (1964). "Institutional completeness of ethnic communities and the personal relations of immigrants." *American Journal of Sociology* 70: 193–205.

Breton, Raymond (1984). "The production and allocation of symbolic resources: An analysis of the linguistic and ethnocultural fields in Canada." *Canadian Journal of Sociology and Anthropology* 21(2): 123–144.

Briggs, Charles (1986). *Learning how to ask: A sociolinguistic reappraisal of the social science interview*. Cambridge: Cambridge University Press.

Briggs, Charles (2005). "Genealogies of race and culture and the failure of vernacular cosmopolitanisms: Rereading Franz Boas and W. E. B. Du Bois." *Public Culture* 17(1): 75–100.

Bucholtz, Mary (2007). "Variation in transcription." *Discourse Studies* 9(6): 784–808.

Burawoy, Michael, Joseph A. Blum, Sheba George, Zsuszsa Gille, Teresa Gowan, Lynne Haney, Maren Klawiter, Steven H. Lopez, Sean O Riain, and Millie Thayer (2000). *Global ethnography: Forces, connections, and imaginations in a postmodern world*. Berkeley: University of California Press.

Burgess, Tony (1998). *Pontypool changes everything*. Toronto: ECW Press.

Cameron, Deborah (2001). *Good to talk?* London: Sage.

Cameron, Deborah (2004). "Talking up skill and skilling up talk: Observations on work in the 'knowledge economy.'" *new formations* 53: 54–64.

Canada, Government of (1994). *Rapport du Vérificateur général du Canada*. Ottawa: Government of Canada.

Canada, Government of (2003). *Le prochain acte: Un nouvel élan pour la dualité linguistique canadienne. Le plan d'action pour les langues officielles*. Ottawa: Privy Council, Government of Canada.

Cardinal, Linda, Anne Gilbert, and Joseph-Yvon Thériault (2008). "Introduction." In: Joseph-Yvon Thériault, Anne Gilbert, and Linda Cardinal (Eds.), *L'espace francophone en milieu minoritaire au Canada*. Montréal: Fides, pp. 9–26.

Caron, Caroline-Isabelle (2007). "Se souvenir de l'Acadie d'antan: Représentations du passé historique dans le cadre de célébrations commémoratives locales en Nouvelle-Écosse au milieu du 20e siècle." *Acadiensis* 36(1): 55–71.

Castells, Manuel (2000). *The information age: Economy, society and culture*. 3 vols. Oxford: Blackwell.

Cholette, Gaston (1993). *L'Office de la langue française de 1961 à 1974: Regard et témoignage*. Québec: Institut québécois de recherche sur la culture.

Choquette, Robert (1977). *Langue et religion: Histoire des conflits anglo-français en Ontario*. Ottawa: Les Éditions de l'Université d'Ottawa.

Choquette, Robert (1987). *La foi gardienne de la langue en Ontario 1900–1950*. Montréal: Bellarmin.

Churchill, Stacy, Normand Frenette, and Saeed Quazi (1985). *Éducation et besoins des Franco-Ontariens: Le diagnostic d'un système d'éducation*. Toronto: Conseil de l'éducation franco-ontarienne.

Cicourel, Aaron (1988). Elicitation as a problem of discourse. In: U. Ammon, N. Dittmar, and K. Matthier (Eds.), *Sociolinguistics: An international handbook of the science of language and society*. Berlin: Walter de Gruyter, pp. 903–910.

Citoyenneté et Immigration Canada (CIC) (2003). *Cadre stratégique pour favoriser l'immigration au sein des communautés francophones en situation minoritaire*. Ottawa: Citoyenneté et immigration Canada.

Citoyenneté et Immigration Canada (CIC) (2005). *Vers la francophonie canadienne de demain: Sommaire des initiatives 2002–2006 pour favoriser l'immigration au sein des communautés francophones en situation minoritaire*. Ottawa: Citoyenneté et immigration Canada.

Clifford, James, and George Marcus (Eds.) (1986). *Writing cultures: The poetics and politics of ethnography*. Berkeley: University of California Press.

Clift, Dominique, and Sheila Arnopoulos (1979). *Le fait français au Québec*. Montréal: Libre Expression.

Coulthard, Malcolm, and Alison Johnson (2007). *An introduction to forensic linguistics: Language in evidence*. London: Routledge.

Crowley, Tony (1996). *Language in history: Theory and texts*. London: Routledge.

Cummins, Jim (2000). *Language, power, and pedagogy*. Clevedon, UK: Multilingual Matters.

Cyr, Raymond (1964). *La Patente: Tous les secrets de la "maçonnerie" canadienne-française. L'Ordre de Jacques Cartier*. Montréal: Éditions du Jour.

Dallaire, Louise, and Réjean Lachapelle (1990). *Demolinguistic profiles: A national synopsis*. Ottawa: Department of the Secretary of State.

Daoust-Blais, Denise, and André Martin (1981). "La planification linguistique au Québec: Aménagement du corpus linguistique et promotion du statut du français." In: André Martin (Ed.), *L'État et la planification linguistique*. Québec: Office de la langue française, pp. 43–69.

Djerrahian, Gabriella, and Normand Labrie (2009). "La reconfiguration linguistique dans une entreprise canadienne à l'ère de la mondialisation." *Francophonies d'Amérique* 25: 105–130.

Dubé, Charles-Henri (1963). "La vérité sur l'Ordre de Jacques-Cartier." *Le Magazine Maclean* 3: 23–26 and 65–74.

Dubois, Lise, Mélanie LeBlanc, and Maurice Beaudin (2006). "La langue comme ressource productive et les rapports de pouvoir entre communautés linguistiques." *Langage et société* 118: 17–42.

Duchêne, Alexandre (2008). *Ideologies across nations: The construction of linguistic minorities at the United Nations*. Berlin: Mouton de Gruyter.

Duchêne, Alexandre (2009). "Marketing, management, and performance: Multilingualism as a commodity in a tourism call center." *Language Policy* 8(1): 27–50.

Duchêne, Alexandre (in press). *Plurilinguisme, mobilité et nouvelle économie globalisée: Pratiques et idéologies langagières dans l'industrie aéroportuaire*. Bern: Peter Lang.

Englund, Harri (2002). "Ethnography after globalism: Migration and emplacement in Malawi." *American Ethnologist* 29(2): 261–286.

Errington, Joseph (2008). *Linguistics in a colonial world: A story of language, meaning, and power*. Oxford: Blackwell.

Fabian, Johannes (1986). *Language and colonial power*. Cambridge: Cambridge University Press.

Fairclough, Norman (2006). *Language and globalization*. London: Routledge.

Farmer, Diane (1996). *Les artisans de la modernité*. Ottawa: Les Presses de l'Université d'Ottawa.

Farmer, Diane, Adrienne Chambon, Normand Labrie, Amal Madibbo, and John Maury (2003). "Urbanité et immigration: Étude de la dynamique communautaire franco-torontoise et des rapports d'inclusion et d'exclusion." *Francophonies d'Amérique* 16: 97–106.

Finn, Gilbert (2000). *Fais quelque chose! Mémoires*. Moncton: Gilbert Finn.

Fishman, Joshua (Ed.) (1968). *Readings in the sociology of language*. The Hague: Mouton.

Foddy, William (1996). "The in-depth testing of survey questions: A critical appraisal of methods." *Quality and Quantity* 30(4): 361–370.

Foley, Douglas (1990). *Learning capitalist culture: Deep in the heart of Tejas*. Philadelphia: University of Pennsylvania Press.

Forgues, Éric (2007). "The Canadian state and the empowerment of the francophone minority communities regarding their economic development." *International Journal of the Sociology of Language* 185: 163–186.

Formatel Consultants, Ltd. (1995). *Plan directeur d'adaptation de la main d'œuvre de la francophonie canadienne*. Ottawa: Comité d'adaptation des ressources humaines de la francophonie canadienne and Formatel.

Foucault, Michel (1975). *Surveiller et punir*. Paris: Gallimard.

Foucault, Michel (1984). "Truth and power." In: Paul Rabinow (Ed.), *The Foucault reader*. New York: Pantheon, pp. 51–75.

Fraser, Matthew (1987). *Québec, Inc.* Toronto: Key Porter Books.

Friedman, Jonathan (2002). "Globalization and localization." In: Jonathan Inda and Renato Rosaldo (Eds.), *Anthropology of globalization: A reader*. Oxford: Blackwell, pp. 233–246.

Gaffield, Chad (1987). *Language, schooling and cultural conflict: The origins of the French-language controversy in Ontario*. Montréal, Kingston: McGill-Queen's University Press.

Gal, Susan (1995). "Lost in a Slavic sea: Linguistic theories and expert knowledge in 19th century Hungary." *Pragmatics* 5(2): 155–166.

Gal, Susan (2007). "Communication as transnational process: 'Translating' in NGOs." Paper presented at the Annual Meeting of the American Anthropological Association, Washington, DC.

Gallant, Nicole, and Chedly Belkhodja (2005). "Production d'un discours sur l'immigration et la diversité par les organismes francophones et acadiens du Canada." *Études ethniques au Canada* 37(3): 35–58.

Gee, James, Glynda Hull, and Colin Lankshear (1996). *The new work order: Behind the language of the new capitalism*. Boulder, CO: Westview Press.

Giddens, Anthony (1984). *The constitution of society*. Berkeley: University of California Press.

Giddens, Anthony (1990). *The consequences of modernity*. Berkeley: University of California Press.

Goldstein, Tara (1997). *Two languages at work: Bilingual life on the production floor*. Berlin: Mouton de Gruyter.

Gramsci, Antonio (1971). *Selections from the prison notebooks of Antonio Gramsci*. New York: International Publishers.

Grillo, Ralph (1989). *Dominant languages*. Cambridge: Cambridge University Press.

Grin, François (1996). "The economics of language: Survey, assessment and prospects." *International Journal of the Sociology of Language* 121: 17–44.

Grin, François (2003). "Language planning and economics." *Current Issues in Language Planning* 4(1): 1–66.

Grisé, Yolande (1982). "Ontarois: Prise de parole." *Revue du Nouvel-Ontario* 4: 81–88.

Gumperz, John (1982). *Discourse strategies*. Cambridge: Cambridge University Press.

Gumperz, John, and Stephen Levinson (Eds.) (1996). *Rethinking linguistic relativity*. Cambridge: Cambridge University Press.

Handler, Richard (1988). *Language and the politics of culture in Quebec*. Madison: University of Wisconsin Press.

Hannerz, Ulf (1996). *Transnational connections: Culture, people, places*. London: Routledge.

Hannerz, Ulf (2003). "On being there . . . and there . . . and there! Reflections on multi-site ethnography." *Ethnography* 4(2): 201–216.

Harvey, David (1989). *The condition of postmodernity*. Oxford: Blackwell.

Hegarty, Peter (2007). "Getting dirty: Psychology's history of power." *History of Psychology* 10(2): 75–91.

Heller, Monica (1982). "Negotiations of language choice in Montréal." In: John Gumperz (Ed.), *Language and social identity*. Cambridge: Cambridge University Press, pp. 108–118.

Heller, Monica (1985). "Ethnic relations and language use in Montréal." In: Nessa Wolfson and Joan Manes (Eds.), *Language of inequality*. Berlin: Mouton de Gruyter, pp. 75–90.

Heller, Monica (1989). "Aspects sociolinguistiques de la francisation d'une entreprise privée." *Sociologie et sociétés* 21(2): 115–128.

Heller, Monica (1990). "French immersion in Canada: A model for Switzerland?" *Multilingua* 9(1): 67–86.

Heller, Monica (1994a). *Crosswords: Language, education and ethnicity in French Ontario*. Berlin: Mouton de Gruyter.

Heller, Monica (1994b). "La sociolinguistique et l'éducation franco-ontarienne." *Sociologie et sociétés* 26(1): 155–168.

Heller, Monica (1996). "Langue et identité: L'analyse anthropologique du français canadien." In: Jürgen Erfurt (Ed.), *De la polyphonie à la symphonie: Méthodes, théories et faits de la recherche pluridisciplinaire sur le français au Canada*. Leipzig: Leipziger Universitätsverlag, pp. 19–36.

Heller, Monica (1999). "Heated language in a cold climate." In: Jan Blommaert (Ed.), *Language ideological debates*. Berlin: Mouton de Gruyter, pp. 143–170.

Heller, Monica (2001a). "Undoing the macro-micro dichotomy: Ideology and categorisation in a linguistic minority school." In: Nik Coupland, Srikant Sarangi, and Christopher Candlin (Eds.), *Sociolinguistics and social theory*. London: Longman, pp. 212–234.

Heller, Monica (2001b). "Critique and sociolinguistic analysis of discourse." *Critique of Anthropology* 21(2): 117–142.

Heller, Monica (2002). *Éléments d'une sociolinguistique critique*. Paris: Didier.

Heller, Monica (2003). "La Patente: L'embryon de la modernisation." In: Monica Heller and Normand Labrie (Eds.), *Discours et identités: La francité canadienne entre modernité et mondialisation*. Fernelmont (Belgique): Éditions modulaires européennes, pp. 147–176.

Heller, Monica (2005a). "Une approche sociolinguistique à l'urbanité." *Revue de l'Université de Moncton* 36(1): 321–346.

Heller, Monica (2005b). "Paradoxes of language in the new economy." *Babylonia*, pp. 32–34.

Heller, Monica, in collaboration with Mark Campbell, Phyllis Dalley, and Donna Patrick (2006). *Linguistic minorities and modernity: A sociolinguistic ethnography*. 2d ed. London: Continuum.

Heller, Monica (2007a). "Gender and bilingualism in the new economy." In: Bonnie McElhinny (Ed.), *Words, worlds and material girls: Language, gender, globalization*. Berlin: Mouton de Gruyter, pp. 287–304.

Heller, Monica (Ed.) (2007b). *Bilingualism: A social approach*. London: Palgrave Macmillan.

Heller, Monica (2007c). "'Langue,' 'communauté' et 'identité': Le discours expert et la question du français au Canada." Special issue,

"Dynamiques et pratiques langagières" (M. Daveluy, Ed.), *Anthropologie et sociétés* 31(1): 39–54.

Heller, Monica (2008a). "Doing ethnography." In: Li Wei and Melissa Moyer (Eds.), *The Blackwell guide to research methods in bilingualism and multilingualism.* Oxford: Blackwell, pp. 249–262.

Heller, Monica (2008b). "Repenser le plurilinguisme: Langue, postnationalisme et la nouvelle économie mondialisée." *Diversité urbaine: Cahiers du Groupe de recherche ethnicité et société,* Hors série (Fall 2008): 163–176.

Heller, Monica (2010). "Language as resource in the globalised new economy." In: Nik Coupland (Ed.), *Handbook of language and globalization.* Oxford: Blackwell, pp 349–365.

Heller, Monica, Jean-Paul Bartholomot, Laurette Lévy, and Luc Ostiguy. (1982). *La francisation d'une entreprise montréalaise: Une analyse sociolinguistique.* Montréal: Office de la langue française, Gouvernement du Québec.

Heller, Monica, and Josiane Boutet (2006). "Vers de nouvelles formes de pouvoir langagier? Langue(s) et économie dans la nouvelle économie." *Langage et société* 118: 5–16.

Heller, Monica, and Normand Labrie (Eds.) (2003). *Discours et identités: La francité canadienne entre modernité et mondialisation.* Fernelmont (Belgique): Éditions modulaires européennes.

Heller, Monica, and Laurette Lévy (1994). "Les contradictions des mariages linguistiquement mixtes: Les stratégies des femmes franco-ontariennes." *Langage et société* 67: 53–88.

Heller, Monica, and Marilyn Martin-Jones (Eds.) (2001). *Voices of authority: Education and linguistic difference.* Westport, CT: Ablex.

Heller, Monica, John Rickford, Marty Laforest, and Danielle Cyr (1999). "Sociolinguistics and public debate." *Journal of Sociolinguistics* 3(2): 260–288.

Hobsbawm, Eric (1990). *Nations and nationalism since 1760.* Cambridge: Cambridge University Press.

Hughes, Everett (1943). *French Canada in transition.* Chicago: University of Chicago Press.

Hutton, Christopher (1999). *Linguistics and the Third Reich: Mother-tongue fascism, race and the science of language.* London: Routledge.

Hutton, Christopher (2005). *Race and the Third Reich.* Cambridge: Polity Press.

Inda, Jonathan, and Renato Rosaldo (Eds.) (2002). *The anthropology of globalization: A reader.* Oxford: Blackwell.

Irvine, Judith (2001). "The family romance of colonial linguistics: Gender and family in nineteenth-century representations of African languages." In: Susan Gal and Kathryn Woolard (Eds.), *Languages and publics: The making of authority.* Manchester: St. Jerome, pp. 13–29.

Irvine, Judith, and Susan Gal (2000). "Language ideology and linguistic differentiation." In: Paul Kroskrity (Ed.), *Regimes of language: Ideologies, polities, and identities*. Santa Fe, NM: School of American Research Press, pp. 35–81.

Jacquet, Marianne, Cécile Sabatier, and Danièle Moore (2008). "Médiateurs culturels et insertion de nouveaux arrivants francophones: Parcours de migration et perception des rôles." *Glottopol* 11: 81–94.

Jaillard, Nicolas (1993). "L'Ordre de Jacques-Cartier: L'armée des ombres." *Ven'd'est* March–April: 32–36.

Jaworski, Adam, and Alison Pritchard (Eds.) (2005). *Discourse, communication and tourism*. Clevedon, UK: Channel View Publications.

Jedwab, Jack (2002). *L'immigration et l'épanouissement des communautés de langue officielle au Canada: Politiques, démographie et identité*. Ottawa: Commissariat aux langues officielles.

Johnson, Derek (1999). "Merchants, the State, and the household: Continuity and change in a 20th century Acadian fishing village." *Acadiensis* 39(1): 57–75.

Johnson, Sally (2001). "Who's misunderstanding whom? Sociolinguistics, public debate, and the media." *Journal of Sociolinguistics* 5(4): 591–610.

Juteau-Lee, Danielle (1980). "Français d'Amérique, Canadiens, Canadiens français, Franco-Ontariens, Ontarois: Qui sommes-nous?" *Pluriel-Débat* 24: 21–42.

Kahn, Emmanuel, and Monica Heller (2006). "Idéologies et pratiques du multilinguisme au Québec: Luttes et mutations dans un site de la nouvelle économie." *Langage et société* 118: 43–64.

Kearney, Michael (2004). *Changing fields of anthropology: From local to global*. Lanham, MD: Rowman and Littlefield.

Kloss, Heinz (1969). *Research possibilities on group bilingualism*. Quebec: Centre international de recherche sur le bilinguisme.

Korazemo, Charles, and Robert Stebbins (2001). "Les immigrants francophones de Calgary: Leurs problèmes d'insertion dans les communautés francophones et anglophones." *Cahiers franco-canadiens de l'Ouest* 13(1): 37–50.

Labov, William (1972). "The logic of non-standard English." In: William Labov, *Language in the inner city*. Philadelphia: University of Pennsylvania Press, pp. 201–240.

Labov, William (1982). "Objectivity and commitment in linguistic science: The case of the Black English trial in Ann Arbor." *Language in Society* 11(2): 165–202.

Lachapelle, Réjean, and Jacques Henripin (1980). *La situation démolinguistique au Canada: Évolution passée et prospective*. Montréal: Institut de recherches politiques.

Lafont, Robert (1977). "À propos de l'enquête sur la diglossie: L'intercesseur de la norme." *Lengas* 1: 31–39.

Laliberté, G.-Raymond (1983). *Une société secrète: l'Ordre de Jacques Cartier*. Montréal: HMH Hurtubise.

Lamarre, Patricia (2009). "Bilingual winks in Montreal's linguistic land-scape: Signs of humour or resistance?" Paper presented at the 7th International Symposium on Bilingualism, Utrecht, The Netherlands.

Lamarre, Patricia, and Diane Dagenais (2003). "Language practices of trilingual youth in two Canadian cities." In: Charlotte Hoffman and Johannes Ytsma (Eds.), *Trilingualism in family, school and society*. Clevedon, UK: Multilingual Matters Ltd., pp. 55–76.

Lamarre, Patricia, and Stéphanie Lamarre (2006a). "Nouvelle économie et nouvelle technologie à Montréal: Entre protection et ouverture linguistique." *Langage et société* 118: 65–84.

Lamarre, Stéphanie, and Patricia Lamarre (2006b). "Lorsque le marché économique n'est ni ici ni ailleurs. . . . Nouvelle économie et nouvelles technologies à Montréal: Pratiques langagières et discours." *Diversité urbaine: Cahiers du Groupe de recherche ethnicité et société* 6(1): 9–24.

Lambert, Wallace (1972). *Language, psychology, and culture*. Palo Alto, CA: Stanford University Press.

Landry, Rodrigue, and Réal Allard (1989). "Vitalité ethnolinguistique et diglossie." *Revue québécoise de linguistique théorique et appliquée* 8(2): 73–101.

Landry, Rodrigue, and Réal Allard (1996). "Vitalité ethnolinguistique: Une perspective dans l'étude de la francophonie canadienne." In: Jürgen Erfurt (Ed.), *De la polyphonie à la symphonie: Méthodes, théories et faits de la recherche pluridisciplinaire sur le français au Canada*. Leipzig: Leipziger Universitätsverlag, pp. 61–88.

Laperrière, Anne, and Denis Beaulé (2004). "Franco-Québécois et Québécois des minorités ethniques: Lignes de fracture et de suture." In: Lucille Guilbault (Ed.), *Médiations et francophonie interculturelle*. Québec: Presses de l'Université Laval, pp. 55–81.

LeBlanc, Marie-Nathalie, Alexandrine Boudreault-Fournier, and Gabriella Djerrahian (2007). "Les jeunes et la marginalisation à Montréal: La culture hip-hop francophone et les enjeux de l'intégration." *Diversité urbaine: Revue du Groupe de recherche ethnicité et société* 7(1): 9–30.

LeBlanc, Matthieu (2008). *Pratiques langagières et bilinguisme dans la fonction publique fédérale: Le cas d'un milieu de travail bilingue en Acadie du Nouveau-Brunswick*. Ph.D. thesis, Département d'études françaises, Université de Moncton.

LeBlanc, Matthieu (2009). "Bilinguals only need apply: Luttes et tensions dans un lieu de travail bilingue en Acadie du Nouveau-Brunswick." *Francophonies d'Amérique* 25.

Lieberson, Stanley (1970). *Language and ethnic relations in Canada*. New York: Wiley.

Lipset, Seymour Martin (1970). *Revolution and counterrevolution: Change and persistence in social structures*. Garden City, NY: Doubleday.

Mackey, William (1968). "The description of bilingualism." In: Joshua Fishman (Ed.), *Readings in the sociology of language*. The Hague: Mouton, pp. 554–584.

MacLennan, Hugh (1957). *Two solitudes*. Toronto: Macmillan.

Madibbo, Amal, and John Maury (2002). "L'immigration et la communauté franco-torontoise: Le cas des jeunes." *Francophonies d'Amérique* 12: 113–122.

Maillet, Antonine (1974). *La Sagouine: Pièce pour une femme seule*. Montréal: Leméac.

Makoni, Sinfree, and Alastair Pennycook (2005). "Disinventing and (re) constituting languages." *Critical Inquiry in Language Studies* 2(3): 137–156.

Malaborza, Sonya, and Mireille McLaughlin (2008). "Les spectacles à grand déploiement et les représentations du passé et de l'avenir: L'exemple de quatre productions canadiennes-françaises en Ontario et au Nouveau-Brunswick." *Cahiers franco-canadiens de l'Ouest* 18(2): 191–204.

Marcus, George (1995). "Ethnography in/of the world system: The emergence of multi-sited ethnography." *Annual Review of Anthropology* 24: 95–117.

Maroney, Heather J. (1992). "'Who has the baby?' Nationalism, pronatalism, and the construction of a 'demographic crisis' in Quebec 1960–1988." *Studies in Political Economy* 39: 7–36.

Martel, Marcel (1997). *Le deuil d'un pays imaginé: Rêves, luttes et déroutes du Canada français*. Ottawa: Presses de l'Université d'Ottawa.

Martin, André (Ed.) (1981). *L'état et la planification linguistique*. Québec: Office de la langue française.

Mason, Jennifer (2002). *Qualitative researching*. 2nd ed. London: Sage.

McLaughlin, Mireille, and Monica Heller (in press). "'Dieu et patrie': Idéologies du genre, de la langue et de la nation au Canada francophone." In: Alexandre Duchêne and Claudine Moïse (Eds.), *Langage, genre et sexualité*. Québec: Nota Bene.

McLaughlin, Mireille, Mélanie LeBlanc, Monica Heller, and Patricia Lamarre (Eds.) (2009). "Les mots du marché: L'inscription de la francophonie canadienne dans la nouvelle économie." Special issue. *Francophonies d'Amérique* 25.

Mehan, Hugh (1979). *Learning lessons: Social organization in the classroom*. Cambridge, MA: Harvard University Press.

Mirchandani, Kiran (2004). "Practices of global capital: Gaps, cracks, and ironies in transnational call centres in India." *Global Networks* 4(4): 355–373.

Moïse, Claudine, Mireille McLaughlin, Sylvie Roy, and Chantal White (2006). "Le tourisme patrimonial: La commercialisation de l'identité franco-canadienne et ses enjeux langagiers." *Langage et société* 118: 85–108.

Muehlmann, Shaylih, and Alexandre Duchêne (2007). "Beyond the nation-state: International agencies as new sites of discourses of bilingualism." In: Monica Heller (Ed.), *Bilingualism: A social approach*. London: Palgrave, pp. 96–110.

Ninyoles, Rafael (1972a). *Idioma y conflicto*. Barcelona: A. Redondo.

Ninyoles, Rafael (1972b). *Idioma y poder social*. Madrid: Tecnos.

Ninyoles, Rafael (1989). *Estructura social y política lingüística*. Alzira: Germania.

Olsson, John (2004). *Forensic linguistics: An introduction to language, crime and the law*. London: Continuum.

Paquin, Christian (1993). "Une néo-Patente: Impossible?" *Ven'd'est* (March–April): 37–39.

Pennycook, Alastair (1994). *The cultural politics of English as an international language*. London: Longman.

Philips, Susan (1983). *The invisible culture: Communication in classroom and community on the Warm Springs Indian Reservation*. Prospect Heights, IL: Waveland Press.

Phillipson, Robert (1992). *Linguistic imperialism*. Oxford: Oxford University Press.

Porter, John (1965). *The vertical mosaic: An analysis of class and power*. Toronto: University of Toronto Press.

Pries, Ludger (2001). "The approach of transnational social spaces." In: Ludger Pries (Ed.), *New transnational social spaces: International migration and international companies in the early twenty-first century*. New York: Routledge, pp. 3–33.

Pujolar, Joan (2001). *Gender, heteroglossia and power: A sociolinguistic study of youth culture*. Berlin: Mouton de Gruyter.

Quell, Carsten (2002). *L'immigration et les langues officielles: Obstacles et possibilités qui se présentent aux immigrants et aux communautés*. Ottawa: Commissariat aux langues officielles.

Rabinow, Paul, and William Sullivan (Eds.) (1979). *Interpretive social science: A reader*. Berkeley: University of California Press.

Rampton, Ben (1995). *Crossing: Language and ethnicity among adolescents*. London: Longman.

Rampton, Ben (2006). *Language in late modernity: Interaction in an urban school*. Cambridge: Cambridge University Press.

Rampton, Ben, Janet Maybin, and Karin Tusting (2007). "Linguistic ethnography: Links, problems, and possibilities." *Journal of Sociolinguistics* 11(5): 575–695.

Rebuffot, Jacques, and Roy Lyster (1996). "L'immersion en français au Canada: Contextes effets et pédagogie." In: Jürgen Erfurt (Ed.), *De la polyphonie à la symphonie: Méthodes, théories et faits de la recherche pluridisciplinaire sur le français au Canada*. Leipzig: Leipziger Universitätsverlag, pp. 277–294.

Richler, Mordechai (1959). *The apprenticeship of Duddy Kravitz*. Toronto: Penguin Canada.

Rickford, John (1999). *African American vernacular English: Features, evolution, educational implications.* London: Blackwell.

Roy, Sylvie (2001). *Valeurs du bilinguisme et pratiques langagières dans la nouvelle économie: Une étude de cas.* Ph.D. thesis, Department of Curriculum, Teaching and Learning, Ontario Institute for Studies in Education, University of Toronto.

Roy, Sylvie (2003). "Bilingualism and standardization in a Canadian call center: Challenges for a linguistic minority community." In: Robert Bayley and Sandra Schecter (Eds.), *Language socialization in multilingual societies.* Clevedon, UK: Multilingual Matters, pp. 269–287.

Roy, Sylvie, and Chantal Gélinas (2004). "Le tourisme pour les Franco-Albertains: Une porte d'entrée au monde." *Francophonies d'Amérique* 17: 131–140.

Rubin, Joan, and Bjorn Jernudd (Eds.) (1971). *Can language be planned?* Honolulu: University of Hawaii Press.

Rubin, Joan, Bjorn Jernudd, Jyotirindra Das Gupta, Joshua Fishman, and Charles Ferguson (1977). *Language planning processes.* The Hague: Mouton de Gruyter.

Said, Edward (2003 [1978]). *Orientalism.* London: Penguin.

Sarkar, Mela, and Lise Winer (2006). "Multilingual code-switching in Quebec Rap: Poetry, pragmatics, and performativity." *International Journal of Multilingualism* 3(3): 173–192.

Schieffelin, Bambi, Kathryn Woolard, and Paul Kroskrity (Eds.) (1998). *Language ideologies: Practice and theory.* Oxford: Oxford University Press.

Sennett, Richard (1998). *The corrosion of character: The personal consequences of work in the new capitalism.* New York: W. W. Norton.

Sheller, Mimi, and John Urry (2006). "The new mobilities paradigm." *Environment and Planning* 38(2): 207–226.

Silva, Emanuel da, and Monica Heller (2009). "From protector to producer: The role of the State in the discursive shift from minority rights to economic development." *Language Policy* 8(2): 95–116.

Silverstein, Michael, and Greg Urban (Eds.) (1996). *Natural histories of discourse.* Chicago: University of Chicago Press.

Sinclair, John, and Malcolm Coulthard (1975). *Towards an analysis of discourse: The English used by teachers and pupils.* London: Oxford University Press.

Sonntag, Selma (2006). "Appropriating identity or cultivating capital? Global English in offshoring service industries." *Anthropology of Work Review* 26(1): 13–19.

Sylvestre, Paul-François (1980). *Penetang: L'École de la Résistance.* Sudbury: Prise de parole.

Tabouret-Keller, Andrée (1988). "La nocivité mentale du bilinguisme, cent ans d'errance." *Euskara Biltzarra.* Vitoria-Gasteiz, Eusko Jaurlaritzaren Argitalpen-Zerbitzu Nagusia: 155–169.

Tan, Peter, and Rani Rubdy (Eds.) (2008). *Language as commodity: Global structures, local marketplaces*. London: Continuum.

Thériault, Joseph-Yvon, Anne Gilbert, and Linda Cardinal (Eds.) (2008). *L'espace francophone en milieu minoritaire au Canada*. Montréal: Fides.

Thériault, Joseph-Yvon, and E.-Martin Meunier (2008). "Que reste-t-il de l'intention vitale du Canada français?" In: Joseph-Yvon Thériault, Anne Gilbert, and Linda Cardinal (Eds.), *L'espace francophone en milieu minoritaire au Canada*. Montréal: Fides, pp. 205–240.

Trépanier, Jamie (2007). "Battling a Trojan Horse: The Ordre de Jacques Cartier and the Knights of Columbus, 1917–1965." M.A. thesis, Dept. of History, York University, Toronto.

Tsing, Anna (2000). "The global situation." *Cultural Anthropology* 15(3): 327–360.

Tsitsipis, Lukas (2007). "Bilingualism, praxis and linguistic description." In: Monica Heller (Ed.), *Bilingualism: A social approach*. London: Palgrave, pp. 277–296.

Urla, Jacqueline (1993). "Cultural politics in an age of statistics: Numbers, nations, and the making of Basque identity." *American Ethnologist* 20(1): 818–843.

Urry, John (2002). *The Tourist Gaze*. 2nd ed. London: Sage.

Vennin, Loïc (1993–1994). "Dossier: La révolution acadienne." *Ven d'est* 29–37.

Vertovec, Steven (2001). "Transnationalism and identity." *Journal of Ethnic and Migration Studies* 27(4): 573–582.

Williams, Raymond (1973). *The Country and the city*. London: Chatto and Windus.

Wolf, Eric (1982). *Europe and the people without history*. Berkeley: University of California Press.

Yarymowich, Maia (2005). "'Language tourism' in Canada: A mixed discourse." In: Françoise Baider, Marcel Burger, and Dionysis Goutsos (Eds.), *La communication touristique: Approches discursives de l'identité et de l'alterité*. Paris: L'Harmattan, pp. 257–273.

DISCOGRAPHY

Arsenault, Angèle (1977). *Libre*. Éd. Angèle Arsenault.

Richard, Denis (2005). *Les chansons du spectacle "Les Défricheurs d'eau."* Caraquet: Les Amis du Village historique Acadien et Productions KLEF.

Robitaille, Damien (2006). *L'homme qui me ressemble*. Montréal: Disques Audiogram.

FILMOGRAPHY

Arcand, Denys (2003). *Les invasions barbares*. Canada/France: Miramax Films.

Belkhodja, Chedly (2006). *Au bout du fil.* Canada: Office national du film.

Golati, Sulani (2005). *Nalini by day, Nancy by night: A film.* New York: Women Make Movies.

McDonald, Bruce (2009). *Pontypool.* Toronto: Maple Films.

Verge, Robert (2001). *L'Ordre de Jacques Cartier, un mystère dévoilé.* Montréal: Réseau de l'Information/RDI de Radio-Canada and Amérimage-Spectra.

Index

CPSIA information can be obtained at www.ICGtesting.com
Printed in the USA
BVOW020026281111

276999BV00003B/6/P